KEITH RICHARDS
ON KEITH RICHARDS
INTERVIEWS AND ENCOUNTERS

EDITED BY SEAN EGAN

CHICAGO REVIEW PRESS

An A Cappella Book

Copyright © 2013 by Sean Egan
All rights reserved
First edition
Published by Chicago Review Press, Incorporated
814 North Franklin Street
Chicago, Illinois 60610

ISBN 978-1-61374-788-9

Cover and interior design: Jonathan Hahn
Cover photograph: Paul Natkin

Library of Congress Cataloging-in-Publication Data
Keith Richards on Keith Richards : interviews and encounters / edited by Sean
Egan. — First edition.
    pages cm
  Includes index.
  ISBN 978-1-61374-788-9 (trade paper)
  1. Richards, Keith, 1943-—Interviews. 2. Rock musicians—England—Interviews.
3. Rolling Stones. I. Egan, Sean, editor. II. Richards, Keith, 1943-, interviewee.

  ML420.R515A5 2013
  782.42166092—dc23
  [B]

                              2013011878

  Printed in the United States of America
  5 4 3 2 1

CONTENTS

INTRODUCTION

Whether it be "The Human Riff," "Mr. Rock 'n' Roll," "Keith Riff-hard," "The World's Most Elegantly Wasted Human Being," or just "Keef," his nicknames speak volumes about the affection held by the rock fraternity for the man who has been the joint most important member of the Rolling Stones for half a century.

In the Stones' early years, Keith Richards—born December 18, 1943—was professionally known as "Keith Richard" and was unquestionably to the rear of both Stones singer Mick Jagger and fellow guitarist Brian Jones in terms of importance, renown, and prominence. The vocalist was naturally the focal point for both media and fans. Jones not only vied with Jagger for status of fan favorite courtesy of his golden good looks but was in demand from journalists impressed by his eloquence and gravitas-conveying posh tones. Nonetheless, that fan favorite principle—the notion that each member of a pop group possessed his own devotees—meant that Richards's views always received at least a by-rotation exposure in the music press.

Richards's position equidistant between the glamour of Jagger and Jones and the semi-anonymity of "Quiet Ones" Charlie Watts (drums) and Bill Wyman (bass) began to shift in 1965 with the release of the Stones' first self-generated UK single, "The Last Time." Courtesy of the phenomenally successful songwriting partnership he developed with Jagger, Richards was transformed within months from merely one of hundreds of Western musicians purveying versions of other people's songs to half of the second-most important songwriting partnership in the world. That Stones fare like "(I Can't Get No) Satisfaction," "Get Off of My Cloud," and "Let's Spend the Night Together" was not just aesthetically brilliant but the exquisite articulation of the grievances of a fractious young generation made Richards and his opinions sociologically significant. In 1967, Richards acquired a fame beyond the parameters of the pop business when a drug bust at his house Redlands and—in the company of Jagger—subsequent trial and brief imprisonment catapulted him onto the front pages of British national newspapers.

Journalists increasingly began requesting quotes from the guitarist, genuinely keen to get his perspective rather than grumpily settling for it in lieu of Jagger's or Jones's availability. Richards blossomed with his increasing importance, the taciturn, big-eared, acne-scarred ruffian of the early days transformed into a stylish physical symbol of the rebellious spirit of rock music. It wasn't all image either. Kicking an audience member in the face for spitting, punching a journalist in the jaw for suggesting the July 1969 Hyde Park concert was disrespectful to the memory of the just-deceased Jones, and squaring up to Hell's Angels at the December 1969 Altamont festival suggested a man who walked it like he talked it. For all these reasons, by the early 1970s, wannabe rock stars and regional rebels across the world were imitating Richards's big belt buckles, trailing scarves, shark tooth necklace, mirrored shades, and—especially—tangled, shoulder-length mane of black hair.

When Richards made the front cover of *Rolling Stone* in August 1971, it served to confirm that he was now a counter-cultural icon as important as Jagger. As the 1970s wore on, he became more than even that. Jagger's hitherto unassailable position as scourge of the authoritarian establishment whose fusty values his generation sought to overthrow began to look increasingly suspect as he hobnobbed with the type of dignitaries and socialites with whom Richards wouldn't be seen dead. Meanwhile, thrillingly for some, Richards being seen dead became an increasingly likely prospect: knowledge of his heroin addiction was an open secret much discussed in the music papers, as well as in the mainstream press on the occasions of his frequent arrests. The outlaw image engendered by Richards's implicit defiance of the authorities and his tangoing with the Grim Reaper communicated to the rock audience a retention of anti-establishment integrity. Though that logic might have been confused, he at least provided a dramatic counterpoint in his druggie murk to Jagger's glitzy carryings-on. Richards's infamous 1977 Toronto drug bust ended that "wasted" lifestyle where the responsibility of raising two children and the trauma of the death of a third had not. Although the prospect of a life sentence for trafficking brought about his cleanup, Richards dines out on his smack decade to this day. It gave him a myth that Stones fans and journalists are more than happy to indulge and bolster. Richards, in turn, cooperates in the process by turning horror stories of addled irresponsibility into funny anecdotes. He may now be more or less law-abiding, but his outlaw aura will never die.

On one level, Richards's interviews have been what one would expect of a man with his image. His spurning of banality and rejection of euphemism were right in line with that no-nonsense rebel mien. Yet, other aspects of his character revealed by his increasingly frequent audiences with the press were surprising. Few journalists came away from a Richards interview without noting in print how warm and unpretentious was a man who one might more readily assume to be aloof, sinister, and self-regarding. Moreover, he was an unusually articulate and intelligent individual. Witness how the aforesaid 1971 *Rolling Stone* interview is speckled with comments that reveal a man steeped in the hardly rock 'n' roll subject of history. He was also perennially honest, answering questions about sensitive subjects like band interrelations, the death of Brian Jones, and personal drug use with a degree of candor Jagger was too haughty (some would say sensible) to even entertain.

Richards is not always a reliable witness. Checking his versions of events against the known facts reveals that he tends to conflate or telescope incidents for reasons of poetry. This leads to such widely disseminated myths as the story of Stones manager Andrew Loog Oldham locking him and Jagger in a kitchen and not letting them out until they'd written their first song. Though the incident is not a complete fabrication, Jagger and Oldham's separate testimonies suggest that the reality was more mundane and elongated than Richards's recollection would have it. Moreover, as he has gotten older, the Richards persona has become encrusted with a submission to tabloid cliché. From the early 1980s onward, he began playing up to his image of rock outlaw via stylized self-deprecation about his days as a bad boy and menace to society, something that has become embarrassingly pronounced in recent years, although no less so than his verbal usage of Americanisms like "baby." However, his frankness continues to outweigh his posturing. This became an ever more important asset as the decades wore on: whereas Mick Jagger's interviews have become exercises in obfuscation and almost irritatingly sustained politesse, Richards's have remained likeable, open, and scathing about cant.

This collection spans the five decades of the Rolling Stones' career. It contains Richards interviews from such celebrated publications as *Melody Maker*, *Rolling Stone*, *Zigzag*, *Record Collector*, and *GQ* as well as interviews that have never previously appeared in print. It charts the journey of Richards from gauche young pretender to swaggering epitome of the zeitgeist to beloved elder statesman of rock. Some may find the values of the Richards of yore objectionable. Some may be dismayed by the pantomime persona Richards has latterly become. Few would dispute, however, that these pages illustrate that when Keith Richards sits down in front of a microphone, a certain kind of magic occurs.

—SEAN EGAN

1 |

I'D LIKE TO FORGET ABOUT *JUKE BOX JURY* SAYS KEITH RICHARD

KEITH RICHARDS | 1964

This ghostwritten Richards column from Britain's now-defunct music weekly *Melody Maker* is an interesting snapshot of the Stones in mid-July 1964, a year and one month after the release of their debut single. The guitarist uses his turn in the spotlight to praise some fellow "beat" groups, bang the drum for R&B, and comment on the Stones' first number one in any of the four competing British charts. The bulk of the column, though, is understandably dedicated to a very controversial appearance the Stones had made a week before on record review TV show *Juke Box Jury*, where they had the temerity to be sniffy about almost every new release they were played, including the latest by the exalted Elvis Presley. Richards—as straight-talking then as he is now—shrugs his shoulders at the furor. Such exhibitions of sullen indifference to public opinion were then uncommon and only bolstered the group's burgeoning image as champions of the younger generation's rebellious ideals.

All right, so Juke Box Jury wasn't a knockout. Now everybody's had a go at us, I'd like the chance to reply.

I think the whole programme's very limited for a start. We all sat, consciously, knowing there were five of us, and we had a few seconds each after each record.

We weren't great, and that's a fact. But the records they played us! They were NOTHING! Don't misunderstand— they weren't bad records, but there didn't seem anything to say about them.

It wasn't that the singing or guitars were out of tune on any particular record, but they were all records with nothing much about them. We were lost. And I think it came across.

We were all lost, except for Charlie and maybe Mick. I agree we didn't come over well, but it wouldn't be much different if we did it again, quite honestly.

It's the way the show's run that restricts you. Juke Box Jury doesn't suit the Stones.

I'll say one thing for our show on Juke Box, though. I'm sure that's what helped us reach number one. If nothing else, it kept our image up!

People thought the worst of us before they saw us. When they finally looked at Juke Box Jury, it was the confirmation that we were a bunch of idiots.

We don't care that much what people think. But I can tell you this: it's difficult to say anything sensible in a few seconds, especially with unspectacular records. But I could tell things were not going well on the show.

We don't particularly care about whether we go back on the Jury. It was an experience I personally would rather forget.

Having a number one hit's a good feeling, but we're not all mad about it.

I'd hate everybody to think that just because we've made the top spot this time, we'll have to do it every time we have a single out. All the Stones agree that as long as we get in the top ten, we'll be very happy.

As it happens, I think "It's All Over Now" is the best single we've done, and I'm glad to say the group improves every time it makes a single. At least, we think so.

I like the overall sound on this new one more than I did on anything before.

Glad Mick wrote a bit last week about the Paramounts. We all think they're good and deserve to make it.

Wayne Fontana has a very good group, though. Give them the right material and they'll be there.

It's all very well people having a go at the rhythm-and-blues thing and saying it's not authentic.

But there's a lot more good come out of the scene than many people allow.

For instance, the trad boom didn't do much good for the real thing, did it? People only got interested in British copies of the real thing.

Now, in R&B, people are digging British groups—and if you look at the chart you get big names like Howlin' Wolf, Chuck Berry, Bo Diddley and Tommy Tucker.

That's what's really pleased me about it all. If our stuff has got people interested in R&B by some of the great American stars, we'll have done some good.

I personally reckon that this can be built up. The next step for groups like ours could be to do more gospel. Pop music tastes are changing, and I don't see why we can't get people interested in such people as Solomon Burke.

I don't think he's selling very big, but I'd like him to, because he's great.

People who knock the R&B scene don't give it enough credit for interesting people in something they'd never have heard of.

I'm fed up of people calling us non-authentic. Why can't we play what we like?

Who's laying down the rules?

2 |

KEITH TALKS ABOUT SONGWRITING

KEITH RICHARDS | 1964

The Rolling Stones Book was a monthly from Beat Publications released to cash in on the success of the group in the same way that the same stable's *The Beatles Book* had already capitalized on the ascendency of the Fab Four. During its lifetime from June 1964 to November 1966, the fact that *The Rolling Stones Book* had three dozen or so pages to fill on a regular basis with purely Stones material meant that every member received exposure. Though the boast that the "boys" edited it themselves can be taken with a pinch of salt, the monthly often saw the band speaking more frankly and indeed caustically than they did in the music press (although to be fair, the music press in those days would probably have toned down any controversial remarks on the grounds that they might upset their readers).

This feature from the third issue of the magazine, dated August 10, 1964, captures Richards at a point where he, with Jagger, was just dipping his toes into the forbidding pool that was songwriting.

Note: for "Marion Faithful" read "Marianne Faithfull."

Mick and I have been writing songs together for about a year now. We didn't make a lot of fuss about it when we started, we just began working at it, because it was something that we both like doing.

In fact, very few people realised that we did write songs until Gene Pitney recorded "That Girl Belongs to Yesterday." Gene's a big mate of ours and has helped us terrifically by turning that particular number into a big hit.

You never know how things are going to turn out in this business, but being a professional songwriter would suit me fine.

Two other numbers of ours are out now. "As Tears Go By" has been recorded by the new girl singer, Marion Faithful, and our version of "Tell Me" has been released as a single in the States, and I understand it's doing very well over there.

At the moment, we've got about a dozen songs sort of half finished. Most of them are intended for our next L.P. but we've got a lot of work to do on them yet and it gets more and more difficult to find time every week. Sometimes, we can finish a song in ten minutes, but others hang around for months on end.

I usually write the music with a title in mind, then Mick adds the words. I can't write a note of music, of course, but then neither could most of the best songwriters of the last fifty years. I don't find any difficulty as I've got a very good memory and can easily complete a song after I've been keeping the bits in my head for several weeks.

If I suddenly get what I think is a good idea, I do sometimes put it on tape but not very often. Mick's just the same—how he remembers words which he first thought of a month or so back, I just don't know.

Every songwriter has a number of songs which he wished he'd written. All of Dionne Warwick's stuff—in fact, anything by Burt Bacharach and Hal David. Those two are really brilliant. Their ideas are so original.

The great thing about songwriting is that despite the thousands and thousands of songs which have been written there are still so many melodies yet to be discovered. But, one thing I still have not been able to do—that's write a number good enough for the Stones to use as an "A" side in England. Most of the numbers that Mick and I write are pretty complicated whilst the Stones need relatively simple ones with very few chord changes in them. But, it does sound crazy saying that we can't write stuff for the Stones when we're part of them.

Of course, my big ambition is to have lots of hits but, also, I would like to have our songs recorded by lots of different artistes. I'd love to see what someone like Dionne Warwick would do with some of our numbers. No, that's daft, ANYTHING she did with them would please me. I like the music business so much that if I didn't make it with song writing I think

I'd have a bash at being a record producer aiming at selling my discs in both the British and American markets. Trouble in this country is that practically every British artiste is established in his or her own style and it gets more and more difficult to create anything new. In the States, on the other hand, they are forever experimenting and getting new sounds. Often nowadays, the Americans only put a rhythm section on records but it comes out sounding like a full orchestra. It's fantastic!

Being a record producer is a tough job but I think I could handle it. Andrew Oldham takes our sessions now, but all of the Stones have a say in what goes on and it's terrific experience. Really I wouldn't like to do the whole job on my own, I'd rather have someone working with me, like Mick for example. I don't think that any one person can possibly get all the ideas.

In my opinion, many record producers are in a rut. There are so many new sounds floating around just waiting to be discovered, and only people like Phil Spector and Andrew Oldham, are brave enough to experiment with them. I'd like to try and get a variation on the American group sound, with the singers sounding like part of the orchestration. The 4 Seasons, who are very big in the States, are one of the best examples of this.

I don't think that there's any other form of recording I'd like to tackle, simply because you can't express yourself if you have to keep to a style that has been fixed already. Apart from songwriting and record-producing, the only other ambition I've got is to buy a huge house on a small tropical island where it's always about 100°. I'd just sit in the sun all day and have some servants (including Mick Jagger) looking after me! That would be my idea of heaven!

3 |

SUE MAUTNER TAKES YOU ROUND KEITH'S HOUSE

SUE MAUTNER | 1966

Keith Richards's picturesque thatched, moated West Sussex house Redlands looms large in his legend, not least because it was the location of a drug bust in 1967; the trial that resulted underlined the Stones' anti-establishment credentials. A series of mysterious fires at the property that generated nudge-nudge, wink-wink public discussion of their causes is another reason for Redlands's high-profile. Though published only the year before the famous bust, Sue Mautner's article for issue 25 of *The Rolling Stones Book* captures Richards's occupation of Redlands at a far more innocent and carefree time.

A couple of the staff mentioned in passing also play a part in Richards's legend. The chauffer—Patrick—is the man Richards has long suspected tipped off the police about the Redlands drug party they raided. The gardener may well be horticulturist-with-a-large-tread Jack Dyer, inspiration for "Jumpin' Jack Flash."

Fortunately it was a beautiful sunny day when I drove down to Keith's fifteenth century house in Sussex, because "Mr Richard hasn't arrived yet," said the old gardener as I approached the drive.

Fortunate for me because after driving for two-and-a-half hours I had become somewhat stuck to the seat of my car, so it was a good opportunity to stretch my legs and generally nose around the beautiful thatched-roofed house, which is surrounded by a moat on which float some very talkative ducks—obviously they were talking about the weather, what else!

I walked round the back of the house to find a horse grazing in the next field, which later on I found out belonged to Keith—not the horse but the field (he just happened to loan the field to its owner). Lying on the beautifully mowed lawn was a rather old-looking paddle boat—obviously that would also be explained later. As I wandered towards the back of the house there was a dartboard hanging up on the stone wall, and I guessed that someone had been there before—quite a clever piece of detection, because the darts had been left in. Much to my surprise (and only because I was being so nosy) I found the porch door open, so I took the liberty of entering.

The first room I found myself in was the lounge—no furniture, just a massive oak-panelled room with parquet flooring, wooden beams, two enormous stone pillars and a huge stone fireplace with a gigantic flute coming down the chimney. Keith had already moved some of his belongings because there was a white fur rug on the floor, an electric piano, a harpsichord and a guitar plus his record and book collection and of course his hi-fi.

I was very interested and surprised to learn that his books consisted of "The Great War," "Dictionary of Slang," "Guns," "Great Sea Battles," "Drawings of Rembrandt" and books on England, and even more surprised with his record collection. Amongst the Beatles, Otis Redding, Dylan, Simon and Garfunkel, the Everlys, the Temptations and Elvis were albums of "Chopin's Nineteen Waltzes," Rossini and Segovia.

Half an hour had gone by and still no sign of Keith, so I picked up the phone and dialled his office. "Sorry Sue, tried to get you before but you'd left. Keith's been held up at a meeting but he shouldn't be very long," came the reply. So I decided the best thing to do was to look over the rest of the house. But before I ventured upstairs I placed a record on the player.

The upstairs consisted of five bedrooms and a bathroom, I knew which was Keith's room, because the bed was unmade, and there was a pair of shoes and a Dennis Wheatley book lying on the floor. All the rooms were unfurnished and like the downstairs it was all wooden beams and floors. One bedroom had half the floor missing so I could see immediately into the kitchen.

One side of an L.P. later I came downstairs through the large dining room and into the kitchen to find some dirty dishes, a burnt sausage in the frying pan on the cooker, a rifle on the wall, a spur hanging on the other wall and a clock on the door, not to mention a truncheon hanging from the ceiling (Keith pinched it off of a gendarme in Paris). Being a female my immediate reaction was to put the kettle on for a cuppa. Whilst selecting my next record the kettle began to whistle furiously, I remembered spotting a bottle of milk in the passage between the garage and the house, so I left the kettle whistling and went out to fetch the milk which a stray cat had got to before me, nevertheless he wasn't clever enough to open it.

As I was pouring out my tea Keith drove up in his Bentley Continental plus L plates and Patrick.

"Sorry I'm late, how did you get in?" Keith was very annoyed with the builders for leaving the house unlocked, so it was just as well I arrived early.

"Hope you don't mind me making myself at home," I said, "have a cup of tea."

"What do you think of the place?", said Keith, "of course it's not furnished yet, I want to do it bit by bit. I'm going to mix the furniture and have modern and Tudor.

"As you can see," said Keith pointing to some old chests, "I've bought some pieces off of the people who lived here before. I'm going to have mauve paint in the dining room and probably the lounge and spotlights on the walls. I've got this interior decorator who did the *Queen Mary* as it is today.

"Come and take a look outside. I'm having a wall built round the front of the house, which will now be the back if you see what I mean, because I'm extending the path round to the back and making it the front. Anyway I think this should be the front because it's got a porch, and the only reason you think the other side is the front, is because of the drive."

"Who's boat is that?" I enquired. "Oh, that belonged to the owner, I bought it off him, you can paddle round the moat in it, but at the moment it's got a hole in the side!"

"See that cottage over there," said Keith pointing to just outside the grounds. "As it's so cheap I'm going to buy it and have a couple of staff living there. A husband and wife preferably, so she can cook and clean the house, and he can do all the odd jobs. At the moment the gardener comes in everyday except Thursday."

As we went back inside I mentioned to Keith that whilst nosing around I noticed some sound-proof equipment in the garage. "Yes, I'm turning one of the bedrooms into a recording studio. There's so much to be done, I'm knocking down walls and blocking out doors. Downstairs I'm making a small cloakroom for people to hang their coats in, and wait till you see the kitchen finished, I've got this cooker which disappears into the wall.

"You know, it's marvellously situated here. There's a little shopping village where you just ring up and they send your order round, and also I'm only a mile from the sea."

Patrick poked his head round the door to tell Keith that his bacon and eggs were ready. Keith put on a Simon and Garfunkel album and we joined him in the kitchen.

"I'm still going to keep my London flat, because if I've been to a party or something it will be too late to drive all the way down here. I'm also going to get a run-around car, something like a Mustang or even a jeep."

Keith polished-off his bacon and eggs and said he had to be off, as he was catching a plane to Cannes. "I'm going there just for a couple of days," said Keith putting on his fur jacket which one would expect a woman to wear.

"Do you like it, I bought it off this girl for £20 'cos she was broke," said Keith as he stepped into his Bentley plus his L plates!

4 |

THE *ROLLING STONE* INTERVIEW: KEITH RICHARD

ROBERT GREENFIELD | 1971

Robert Greenfield's epic, rambling interview with Richards in the August 19, 1971, issue of *Rolling Stone* was significant on two counts. First, courtesy of the amazingly candid answers of its subject, it provided a permanent treasure trove of research material for Stones scholars. The second was that it served to thrust Richards center stage in the public consciousness with Mick Jagger. Although the show business convention that had led to the Stones' lead singer being granted the most attention had been eroded over recent years, Richards's being featured on the ultra-cool magazine's cover and across twelve of its oversize interior pages confirmed once and for all that the guitarist was no mere sidekick. He was now well on his way to the status of living embodiment of rock 'n' roll.

Most reprints of this interview—even those published by *Rolling Stone*—omit large chunks. This is a rare unexpurgated publication.

Note: for "Marlan" read "Marlon."
for "Alan Klein" read "Allen Klein."

Keith plays in a rock & roll band. Anita is a movie star queen. They currently reside in a large white marble house that everyone describes as "decadent looking." The British Admiral who built it had trees brought from all over the world in ships of the line, pine and cypress and palm. There is an exotic colored bird in a cage in the front garden and a rabbit called Boots that lives in the back. A dog named Oakie sleeps where he wants.

Meals are the only recurring reality and twenty three at a table is not an unusual number. The ceilings are thirty feet from the floor and some nights, pink lightning hangs over the bay and the nearby town of Ville-france, which waits for the fleet to come back so its hotels can turn again into whorehouses.

There is a private beach down a flight of stairs and a water bed on the porch. Good reference points for the whole mise-en-scène are F. Scott Fitzgerald's "Tender Is the Night" and the Shirelles' greatest hits. There is a piano in the living room and guitars in the TV room. Between George Jones, Merle Haggard, Buddy Holly, and Chuck Berry, Keith Richard manages to sneak in a lick now and then like a great acoustic version of "The Jerk" by the Larks one morning at 4 AM.

A recording studio will soon be completed in the basement and the Stones will go to work on some tracks for the new album, Mick Jagger having returned from his honeymoon. They will tour the States soon.

Most of it is in the tapes, in the background. Two cogent statements, both made by Keith may be kept in mind while reading the questions and answers (which were asked and answered over a ten-day period at odd hours).

"It's a pretty good house; we're doing our best to fill it up with kids and rock 'n' roll."

"You know that thing that Blind Willie said? 'I don't like the suits and ties / They don't seem to harmonize.'"

What were you doing right at the beginning?
I was hanging out at art school. Yeah. Suburban art school. I mean in England, if you're lucky you get into art school. It's somewhere they put you if they can't put you anywhere else. If you can't saw wood straight or file metal. It's where they put me to learn graphic design because I happened to be good at drawing apples or something. Fifteen . . . I was there for three years and meanwhile I learned how to play guitar. Lotta guitar players in art school. A lot of terrible artists too. It's funny.

Your parents weren't musical?
Nah. My grandfather was. He used to have a dance band in the Thirties. Played the sax. Was in a country band in the late Fifties, too, playin' the US bases in England. Gus Dupree . . . King of the Country Fiddle. He was

a groove, y'know . . . a good musician . . . He was never professional for more than a few years in the Thirties.

What did your father do?
He had a variety of professions. He was a baker for a while. I know he got shot up in the First World War. Gassed or something.

Were you raised middle class?
Working class. English working class . . . struggling, thinking they were middle class. Moved into a tough neighborhood when I was about ten. I used to be with Mick before that . . . we used to live close together. Then I moved to what they'd call in the States a housing project. Just been built. Thousands and thousands of houses, everyone wondering what the fuck was going on. Everyone was displaced. They were still building it and really there were gangs everywhere. Coming to Teddy Boys. Just before rock and roll hit England. But they were all waiting for it. They were practicing.

Were you one of the boys?
Rock and roll got me into being one of the boys. Before that I just got me ass kicked all over the place. Learned how to ride a punch.

It's strange, 'cause I knew Mick when I was really young . . . five, six, seven. We used to hang out together. Then I moved and didn't see him for a long time. I once met him selling ice creams outside the public library. I bought one. He was tryin' to make extra money.

Rock and roll got to England about '53, '54, you were eleven . . .
Yeah. Presley hit first. Actually, the music from Blackboard Jungle, "Rock Around the Clock," hit first. Not the movie, just the music. People saying, "Ah, did ya hear that music, man." Because in England, we had never heard anything. It's still the same scene: BBC controls it.

Then, everybody stood up for that music. I didn't think of playing it. I just wanted to go and listen to it. It took 'em a year or so before anyone in England could make that music. The first big things that hit were skiffle— simple three chord stuff. It wasn't really rock and roll. It was a lot more folky, a lot more strummy. Tea chest basses. A very crude sort of rock and roll. Lonnie Donegan's the only cat to come out of skiffle.

But we were really listening to what was coming from over the Atlantic. The ones that were hitting hard were Little Richard and Presley and Jerry Lee Lewis. Chuck Berry was never really that big in England. They dug him but . . . all his big big hits made it . . . but maybe because he never came over. Maybe because the movies he made like *Go Johnny Go* never got over because of distribution problems. Fats Domino was big. Freddie Bell and the Bellboys too; all kinds of weird people that never made it in America.

They loved the piano. Looking back on it, all the piano boys really had it together for England. More than just the cat that stood there with the guitar.

Did you start really playing in school then?
Yeah. It's funny going back that far. Things come through but . . . I'll tell you who's really good at pushing memories: Bill. He's got this little mind that remembers everything. I'm sure it's like he rolls a tape.

How things were at the start is something. It's when everybody's got short hair. And everybody thought it was long. That's the thing. I mean, we were really being put down like shit then for having long hair. Really. Now, people go into offices with longer hair.

When I went to art school, people were just startin' to grow their hair and loosen up. You got in there on the favors of the headmaster. You go there and show him your shit, the stuff you've done at ordinary school, during art lessons, and he decides. You don't have to do anything apart from going to see him. He says, "You takin' anything? What are you on?" And you're about 15 or 16 and you don't even know what the fuck they do in art school. You have this vague picture of naked ladies sittin' around. Drawing them . . . well, I'll try that.

So you go there and you get your packet of Five Weights [cigarettes] a day. Everybody's broke . . . and the best thing that's going on is in the bog [toilet] with the guitars. There's always some cat sneaked out going through his latest Woody Guthrie tune or Jack Elliot. Everybody's into that kind of music as well. So when I went to art school I was thrown into that end of it too. Before that I was just into Little Richard. I was rockin' away, avoidin' the bicycle chains and the razors in those dance halls. The English get crazy. They're calm, but they were really violent then, those cats. Those suits cost them $150, which is a lot of money. Jackets down to here. Waistcoats. Leopardskin lapels . . . amazing. It was really "Don't step on mah blue suede shoes." It was down to that.

I really, literally, got myself thrown out of school. I was livin' at home but I had to go everyday. When you think that kids, all they really want to do is learn, watch how it's done and try and figure out why and leave it at that. You're going to school to do something you wanna do and they manage to turn the whole thing around and make you hate 'em. They really manage to do it. I don't know anyone at that school who liked it or anyone my age who liked to be at school. One or two people who went to a decent school had a good teacher, someone who really knew how to teach. The nearest thing I been to it is Wormwood Scrubbs [an English prison] and that's the nick. Really, it's the same feeling.

So you spent three years there and it was coming to degree time . . .
That's when they got me. It was 1958, they chucked me out. It's amazing—Lennon, all those people, were already playing. I hadn't really thought about playing. I was still just jivin' to it. I went straight into this art school, and I heard these cats playing', heard they were layin' down some Broonzy songs. And I suddenly realized it goes back a lot further than just the two years I'd been listenin'. And I picked up the nearest guitar and started learnin' from these cats. I learned from all these amateur art school people. One cat knew how to play "Cocaine Blues" very well, another cat knew how to play something else very well. There were a lot better guitar players at school than me.

But then I started to get into where it had come from. Broonzy first. He and Josh White were considered to be the only living black bluesmen still playing. So let's get that together, I thought, that can't be right. Then I started to discover Robert Johnson and those cats. You could never get their records though. One heard about them. On one hand I was playing all that folk stuff on the guitar. The other half of me was listenin' to all that rock and roll, Chuck Berry, and sayin' yeah, yeah.

And one day, I met Jagger again, man. Of all places, on the fucking train. I was going to the school and he was going up to the London School of Economics. It was about 1960. I never been able to get this one together, it's so strange. I had these two things going and not being able to plug 'em together, playing guitar like all the other cats, folk, a little blues. But you can't get the sounds from the States. Maybe once every six months someone'll come through with an album, an Arhoolie album of Fred McDowell. And you'd say: There's another cat! That's another one. Just blowin' my mind, like one album every six months.

So I get on this train one morning and there's Jagger and under his arm he has four or five albums. I haven't seen him since the time I bought an ice cream off him and we haven't hung around since we were five, six, ten years. We recognized each other straight off. "Hi, man," I say. "Where ya going?" he says. And under his arm, he's got Chuck Berry and Little Walter, Muddy Waters. "You're into Chuck Berry, man, really?" That's a coincidence. He said, "Yeah, I got few more albums. Been writin' away to this, uh, Chess Records in Chicago and got a mailing list thing and . . . got it together, you know?" Wow, man!

So I invited him up to my place for a cup of tea. He started playing me these records and I really turned on to it. We were both still living in Dartford, on the edge of London and I was still in art school.

There was another cat at art school named Dick Taylor, who later got the Pretty Things together. Mick found out—"Oh, you play?" he said to me. That's what amazed him. Mick had been singin' with some rock and roll bands, doin' Buddy Holly. . . Buddy Holly was in England as solid as Elvis. Everything came out was a record smash number one. By about '58, it was either Elvis or Buddy Holly. It was split into two camps. The Elvis fans were the heavy leather boys and the Buddy Holly ones all somehow looked like Buddy Holly.

By that time, the initial wham had gone out of rock and roll. You were getting "By the Light of the Silvery Moon" by Little Richard and "My Blue Heaven" by Fats, "Baby Face." They'd run out of songs in a way, it seemed like. England itself was turning on to its own breed of rock and rollers. Cliff Richard at the time was a big rocker. Adam Faith. Billy Fury, who did one fantastic album that I've lost. He got it together once. One really good album. Songs he'd written, like people do now, he got some people he knew to play together and did it. His other scene was the hits, heavy moody ballads and the lead pipe down the trousers. They were all into that one.

To get back to Mick and I . . . He found out that I could play a little and he could sing a bit. "I dig to sing," he said, and he also knew Dick Taylor from another school they'd gone to and the thing tied up so we try and do something. We'd all go to Dick Taylor's house, in his back room, some other cats would come along and play, and we'd try to lay some of this Little Walter stuff and Chuck Berry stuff. No drummer or anything. Just two guitars and a little amplifier. Usual back room stuff. It fell into place very quickly.

Then we found Slim Harpo, we started to really find people. Mick was just singing, no harp. And suddenly in '62, just when we were getting together, we read this little thing about a rhythm and blues club starting in Ealing. Everybody must have been trying to get one together. "Let's go up to this place and find out what's happening." There was this amazing old cat playing harp . . . Cyril Davies. Where did he come from? He turned out to be a panel beater from North London. He was a great cat, Cyril. He didn't last long. I only knew him for about two years and he died.

Alexis Korner really got this scene together. He'd been playin' in jazz clubs for ages and he knew all the connections for gigs. So we went up there. The first or the second time Mick and I were sittin' there Alexis Korner gets up and says, "We got a guest to play some guitar. He comes from Cheltenham. All the way up from Cheltenham just to play for ya."

Suddenly, it's *Elmore James*, this cat, man. And it's *Brian*, man, he sittin' on his little . . . he's bent over . . . da-da-da, da-da-da . . . I said, what? What the fuck? Playing bar slide guitar.

We get into Brian after he finishes "Dust My Blues." He's really fantastic and a gas. We speak to Brian. He'd been doin' the same as we'd been doin' . . . thinkin' he was the only cat in the world who was doin' it. We started to turn Brian on to some Jimmy Reed things, Chicago blues that he hadn't heard. He was more into T-Bone Walker and jazz-blues stuff. We'd turn him on to Chuck Berry and say, "Look, it's all the same shit, man, and you can do it." But Brian was also much more together. He was in the process of getting a band together and moving up to London with one of his many women and children. God knows how many he had. He sure left his mark, that cat. I know of five kids, at least. All by different chicks, and they all look like Brian.

He was a good guitar player then. He had the touch and was just peaking. He was already out of school, he'd been kicked out of university and had a variety of jobs. He was already into living on his own and trying to find a pad for his old lady. Whereas Mick and I were just kicking around in back rooms, still living at home.

I left art school and I didn't even bother to get a job. We were still kids. Mick was still serious, he thought he was, everyone told him he ought to be serious about a career in economics. He was very much into it.

But Brian, he was already working at it. We said, "We're just amateurs, man, but we dig to play." He invited me up to listen to what he was getting together in some pub in London. It's then it starts getting into back rooms of pubs in Soho and places. That's where I met Stew [Ian Stewart]. He was with Brian. They'd just met. He used to play boogie-woogie piano in jazz clubs, apart from his regular job. He blew my head off too, when he started to play. I never heard a white piano like that before. Real Albert Ammons stuff. This is all '62.

A lot of these old cats had been playin' blues in those clubs for ages, or thought they were playin' blues. Just because they'd met Big Bill Broonzy at a party or played with him once, they thought they were the king's asshole.

Music was their love. They all wanted to be professional but in those days a recording contract was a voice from heaven. It was that rare. Not like now when you get a band together and hustle an advance. It was a closed shop.

Were you and Mick and Brian very strange for them?
That's right. They couldn't figure us out. Especially when I tried to lay Chuck Berry shit on them. "What are ya hangin' with them rock and rollers for?" they'd ask. Brian kicked a lot of them out and I really dug it. He turned around and said, "Fuck off, you bastards, you're a load of shit and I'm going to get it together with these cats." This cat Dick Taylor

shifted to bass by then. We were really looking for drums. Stew drifted with us for some reason. I sort of put him with those other cats because he had a job. But he said no too. "I'll stick around and see what happens with you."

So we got another back room in a different pub. Competition. Not that anybody came. Just rehearsin'.

Stew at that time used to turn up at rehearsals in a pair of shorts, on his bike. His piano used to be by the window and his biggest fear, the only thing that really stopped him at piano, was the thought that his bike might get nicked while he was playin'. So every now and then when someone walked past his bike, he'd stretch up and put his head out the window and keep playin', sit down again and then he'd see someone else lookin' at his bike. Up and up, still playin'.

Were you playing electric then?
Yeah. With homemade amps, old wireless sets. It took a while longer to get the electric bit together. At the time we thought, "Oh, it just makes it louder," but it ain't quite as simple at that.

Brian was the one who kept us all together then. Mick was still going to school. I'd dropped out. So we decided we got to live in London to get it together. Time to break loose. So everybody left home, upped and got this pad in London, Chelsea.

Different Chelsea than now?
Edith Grove. World's End. That place . . . every room got condemned slowly. It was like we slowly moved till we were all in the end room. Every room was shut up and stunk to hell, man. Terrible. Brian's only possession was a radio-record player. That, and a few beds and a little gas fire. We kept on playin', playin', playin'.

Brian kicked his job. He was in a department stare. He got into a very heavy scene for nickin' some bread and just managed to work his way out of it. So he thought, "Fuck it. If I work anymore I'm gonna get in real trouble." Get into jail or something.

He only nicked two pound . . . but he quit his job and his old lady had gone back to Cheltenham so he was on the loose again.

Are you gigging?

We didn't dare, man, we didn't dare. We were rehearsin' drummers. Mick Avory came by, the drummer of the Kinks. He was terrible, then. Couldn't find that off beat. Couldn't pick up on that Jimmy Reed stuff.

Is everybody still straight?

It was very hard to find anything. No one could afford to buy anything anyway. A little bit of grass might turn up occasionally but . . . everybody'd dig it . . . everybody's turn-on was just playing. It didn't matter if you were pissed. That was it. That was the big shot.

Mick was the only one who was still hovering because he was more heavily committed to the London School of Economics and he was being supported by a government grant, and his parents and all that. So he had a heavier scene to break away from than me because they were very pleased to kick me out anyway. And Brian too, they were glad to kick out. From university for making some chick pregnant or something.

Brian and I were the sort of people they were glad to kick out. They'd say, "You're nothing but bums, you're gonna end up on skid row," and that sort of thing. Probably will anyway. But Mick was still doing the two things. Brian and me'd be home in this pad all day tryin' to make one foray a day to either pick up some beer bottles from a party and sell 'em back for thruppence deposit or raid the local supermarket. Try and get some potatoes or some eggs or something.

I went out one morning and came back in the evening and Brian was *blowing harp*, man. He's got it together. He's standin' at the top of the stairs sayin', "Listen to this." *Whooooow. Whooow.* All these blues notes comin' out. "I've learned how to do it. I've figured it out." One day.

So then he started to really work on the harp. He dropped the guitar. He still dug to play it and was still into it and played very well but the harp became his thing. He'd walk around all the time playing his harp.

Is there anything going in London in terms of music then?

Alexis had that club together and we'd go down once a week to see what they were doing and they wanted to know what we were doing. "It's coming," we'd tell 'em. "We'll be gigging soon." We didn't know where the fuck do ya start? Where do ya go to play?

But you were living together, unlike Cyril Davies or the older blues musicians, because you were young and broke . . .

Yeah. Just Mick and myself and Brian. We knew Charlie. He was a friend. He was gigging at the time, playing with Alexis. He was Korner's drummer. We couldn't afford him.

One day we picked up a drummer called Tony Chapman who was our first regular drummer. Terrible. One of the worst . . . cat would start a number and end up either four times as fast as he started it or three times as slow. But never stay the same.

We did say, "Hey Tony, d'y'know any bass players?" He said, "I do know one." "Tell him come to next rehearsal." So we all turned up and in walks . . . Bill Wyman, ladies and gentleman. Huge speaker he's got, and a spare Vox eight-thirty amp which is the biggest amp we've ever seen in our lives. And that's spare. He says, "You can put one of your guitars through there." Whew. Put us up quite a few volts goin' through there.

He had the bass together already. He'd been playin' in rock bands for three or four years. He's older than us. He knows how to play. But he doesn't want to play with these shitty rock bands anymore because they're all terrible. They're all doing that Shadows trip, all those instrumental numbers, Duane Eddy, "Rebel Rouser." There was no one who could sing very good.

Also, they don't know what to play anymore. At that point, nobody wants to hear Buddy Holly anymore. He's an old scene already to the rock and roll hip circuit. It's that very light pop scene they're all into . . . Bobby Vee was a big scene then. You wouldn't dream of going to play in a ballroom. They'd just hurl bricks at you. Still have to stick to this little circuit of clubs, back rooms for one night, a shilling for everyone to get in. For people who didn't want to go to ballrooms. Who wanted to listen to something different.

Most of these clubs at the time are filled with dixieland bands, traditional jazz bands. An alternative to all that Bobby Vee stuff. There was a big boom in that: the stomp, stompin' about, weird dance, just really tryin' to break the ceiling to a two beat. That was the big scene. They had all the clubs under control. That's where Alexis made the breakthrough. He managed to open it up at the Ealing Club. Then he moved on to the Marquee and R&B started to become the thing. And all these traddies, as they were called, started getting worried. So they started this very bitter opposition.

Which is one reason I swung my guitar at Harold Pendleton's head at the Marquee thing, because he was the kingpin behind all that. He owned all these trad clubs and he got a cut from these trad bands, he couldn't bear to see them die. He couldn't afford it.

But Alexis was packin' em in man. Jus' playing blues. Very similar to Chicago stuff. Heavy atmosphere. Workers and art students, kids who couldn't make the ballrooms with supposedly long hair then, forget it, you couldn't go into those places. You gravitated to places where you wouldn't get hassled. The Marquee's a West End club, where we stood in for Alexis a couple of times.

With Charlie drumming?
No. Our first gig was down at the Ealing Club, a stand-in gig. That's the band without Charlie as drummer. We played everything. Muddy Waters. A lot of Jimmy Reed.

Still living in Chelsea?
Yeah. We had the middle floor. The top floor was sort of two school teachers tryin' to keep a straight life. God knows how they managed it. Two guys trainin' to be school teachers, they used to throw these bottle parties. All these weirdos, we used to think they were weirdos, they were as straight as . . . havin' their little parties up there, all dancing around to Duke Ellington. Then when they'd all zonked out, we'd go up there and nick all the bottles. Get a big bag, Brian and I, get all the beer bottles and the next day we'd take 'em to the pub to get the money on 'em.

Downstairs was livin' four old whores from Liverpool. Isn't that a coincidence. "'Allo dahlin', 'ow are ya? All right?" Real old boots they were. I don't know how they made their bread, working . . . They used to sort of nurse people and keep us together when we really got out of it.

The cat that supported Brian, this is a long story. He came from Brian's hometown. He got 80 quid a year for being in the Territorial Army in England, which is where you go for two weeks on a camp with the rest of these guys. Sort of a civil defense thing. They all live in tents and get soakin' wet and get a cold and at the end they learn how to shoot a rifle and they get 80 quid cash depending on what rank you've managed to wangle yourself.

This cat arrived in London with his 80 quid, fresh out of the hills, from his tent. And he wants to have a good time with Brian. And Brian took him for every penny, man. Got a new guitar. The whole lot.

This weird thing with this cat. He was one of those weird people who would do anything you say. Things like, Brian would say, "Give me your overcoat." Freezing cold, it's the worst winter and he gave Brian this Army overcoat. "Give Keith the sweater." So I put the sweater on.

"Now, you walk twenty yards behind us, man." And off we'd walk to the local hamburger place. "Ah, stay there. No, you can't come in. Give us two quid." Used to treat him like really weird. This cat would stand outside the hamburger joint freezing cold giving Brian the money to pay for our hamburgers. Never saw him again after that.

No, no, it ended up with us tryin' to electrocute him. It ended up with us gettin' out of our heads one night. That was the night he disappeared. It was snowing outside. We came back to our pad and he was in Brian's bed. Brian for some reason got very annoyed that he was in his bed asleep. We had all these cables lyin' around and he pulled out this wire. "This end is plugged in, baby, and I'm comin' after ya."

This cat went screaming out of the pad and into the snow in his underpants. "They're electrocuting me, they're electrocuting me." Somebody brought him in an hour later and he was blue. He was afraid to come in because he was so scared of Brian.

Brian used to pull these weird things. The next day the cat split. Brian had a new guitar, and his amp re-fixed, a whole new set of harmonicas.

I guess the craziness comes from the chemistry of the people. The craziness sort of kept us together. When the gigs become a little more plentiful and the kids started picking up on us was when we got picked up by Giorgio Gomelsky. Before he was into producing records. He was on the jazz club scene. I don't know exactly what he did, promoting a couple of clubs a week. He cottoned on to us and sort of organized us a bit.

We still didn't have Charlie as a drummer. We were really lacking a good drummer. We were really feeling it.

All I wanted to do is keep the band together. How we were going to do it and get gigs and people to listen to us? How to get a record together? We couldn't even afford to make a dub. Anyway we didn't have a drummer to make a dub with.

By this time we had it so together musically. We were really pleased with the way we were sounding. We were missing a drummer. We were missing good equipment. By this time the stuff we had was completely beaten to shit.

And the three of you get on? Are you the closest people for each other?
We were really a team. But there was always something between Brian, Mick and myself that didn't quite make it somewhere. Always something. I've often thought, tried to figure it out. It was in Brian, somewhere; there was something . . . he still felt alone somewhere . . . he was either completely into Mick at the expense of me, like nickin' my bread to go and have a drink. Like when I was zonked out, takin' the only pound I had in me pocket. He'd do something like that. Or he'd be completely in with me tryin' to work something against Mick. Brian was a very weird cat. He was a little insecure. He wouldn't be able to make it with two other guys at one time and really get along well.

I don't think it was a sexual thing. He was always so open with his chicks . . . It was something else I've never been able to figure out. You can read Jung. I still can't figure it out. Maybe it was in the stars. He was a Pisces. I don't know. I'm Sag and Mick's a Leo. Maybe those three can't ever connect completely all together at the same time for very long. There were periods when we had a ball together.

As we became more and more well-known and eventually grew into that giant sort of thing, that in Brian also became blown up until it became very difficult to work with and very difficult for him to be with us. Mick and I were more and more put together because we wrote together and Brian would become uptight about that because he couldn't write. He couldn't even ask if he could come and try to write something with us. Where earlier on Brian and I would sit for hours trying to write songs and say, "Aw fuck it, we can't write songs."

It worked both ways. When we played, it gave Brian ... man, when he wanted to play, he could play his ass off, that cat. To get him to do it, especially later on, was another thing. In the studio, for instance, to try and get Brian to play was such a hassle that eventually on a lot of those records that people think are the Stones, it's me overdubbing three guitars and Brian zonked out on the floor.

It became very difficult because we were working non-stop ... I'm skipping a lot of time now ... when we were doing those American tours in '64, '65, '66. When things were getting really difficult. Brian would go out and meet a lot of people, before we did, because Mick and I spent most of our time writing. He'd go out and get high somewhere, get smashed. We'd say, "Look, we got a session tomorrow, man, got to keep it together." He'd come, completely out of his head, and zonk out on the floor with his guitar over him. So we started overdubbing, which was a drag cause it meant the whole band wasn't playing.

Can you tell me about Oldham?
Andrew had the opportunity. He didn't have the talent, really. He didn't have the talent for what he wanted to be. He could hustle people and there's nothing wrong with hustling ... it still has to be done to get through. You need someone who can talk for you. But he's got to be straight with you too.

Was he in the business before the Stones?
Yeah, he was with the Beatles. He helped kick them off in London. Epstein hired him and he did a very good job for them. One doesn't know how much of a job was needed but he managed to get them a lot of space in the press when "Love Me Do" came out and was like number nine in the charts and the kids were turning on to them and it was obvious they were going to be big, big, because they were only third on the bill and yet they were tearing the house down every night. A lot of it was down to Andrew. He got them known. And he did the same gig for us. He did it. Except he was more involved with us. He was working for us.

He had a genius for getting things through the media. Before people really knew what media was, to get messages through without people knowing.

Anita: But Brian, he never got on with Andrew.

Keith: Never. I've seen Brian and Andrew really pissed hanging all over each other but really basically there was no chemistry between them. They just didn't get on. There was a time when Mick and I got on really well with Andrew. We went through the whole *Clockwork Orange* thing. We went through that whole trip together. Very sort of butch number. Ridin' around with that mad criminal chauffeur of his.

Epstein and Oldham did a thing on the media in England that's made it easier for millions of people since and for lots of musicians. It's down to people like those that you can get on a record now. They blew that scene wide open, that EMI-Decca stranglehold. EMI is still the biggest record company in the whole fucking world despite being an English company. They can distribute in Hong Kong. They have it sewn up in the Philippines and Australia and everywhere. No matter who you go through, somewhere in the world, EMI is dealing your records. It's a network left over from the colonial days and they've kept hold of it.

Oldham made money for the Stones.

Yeah. I mean, God knows how much money has been made on the Stones name and how much of it has got through to us and how much got through to people along the way. Without mentioning any names but there is one guy I'm still going to get.

It's not money. It's like, what do you want? And how do you want to get it? And do you want to keep it cool? It's not simple, cut and dried. By the time it goes through all those peoples' hands they're pretty soiled those dollar bills. To work it out any other way, you have to end up like them to do it.

How long was Andrew involved?

From '63 to the end of '67. It still goes on though. I got a letter the other day about some litigation, Oldham versus Eric Easton, who was our first manager proper. Oldham was only half of the team, the other was Eric Easton, who was just a bumbly old Northern agent. Handled a couple semi-successful chick singers and could get you gigs in ball rooms in the North of England. Once it got to America, this cat Easton dissolved. He went into a puddle. He couldn't handle that scene.

Was Charlie drumming with you when Andrew first saw you work?
I'll tell you how we picked Charlie up. I told you about the people Brian was getting a band together with and then he turned on to us and he told those other people to fuck off, et cetera. Our common ground with Brian back then was Elmore James and Muddy Waters. We laid Slim Harpo on him, and Fred McDowell.

Because Brian was from Cheltenham, a very genteel town full of old ladies, where it used to be fashionable to go and take the baths once a year at Cheltenham Spa. The water is very good because it comes out of the hills, it's spring water. It's a Regency thing, you know Beau Brummel, around that time. Turn of the 19th century. Now it's a seedy sort of place full of aspirations to be an aristocratic town. It rubs off on anyone who comes from there.

The R&B thing started to blossom and we found playing on the bill with us in a club, there were two bands on, Charlie was in the other band. He'd left Korner, and was with the same cats Brian had said fuck off to about six months before. We did our set and Charlie was knocked out by it. "You're great, man," he says, "but you need a fucking good drummer." So we said, "Charlie, we can't afford you, man." Because Charlie had a job and just wanted to do weekend gigs. Charlie used to play anything then—he'd play pubs, anything, just to play, cause he loves to play with good people. But he always had to do it for economic reasons. By this time we're getting three, four gigs a week. "Well, we can't pay you as much as that band but . . ." we said. So he said, OK and told the other band to fuck off, "I'm gonna play with these guys."

That was it. When we got Charlie, that really made it for us. We started getting a lot of gigs. Then we got that Richmond gig with Giorgio and that built up to an enormous scene. In London, that was *the* place to be every

Sunday night. At the Richmond Station Hotel. It's on the river Richmond, a fairly well-to-do neighborhood but kids from all over London would come down there on a Sunday night.

There's only so far you can go on that London scene; if you stay in that club circuit eventually you get constipated. You go round and round so many times and then suddenly, you're not the hip band anymore, someone else is. Like the High Numbers, they took over from us in a lot of clubs. The High Numbers turned out to become the Who. The Yardbirds took over from us in Richmond and on Sunday nights we'd find we were booked into a place in Manchester.

Where are you recording now, with Giorgio?
Not with Giorgio. Eric and Andrew fucked Giorgio because he had nothing on paper with us. They screwed him to get us a recording contract. We were saying to Giorgio, "What about records?" and he didn't have it together for the record thing. Not for a long time afterwards either. He was still very much a club man. We knew that to go any further and reach out a bit, we wanted to get off the club thing and get into the ballrooms where the kids were. It turned out to be right.

It was difficult the first few months though. We were known in the big cities but when you get outside into the sticks, they don't know who the fuck you are and they're still preferring the local band. That makes you play your ass off every night so that at the end of two hour-long sets, you've got 'em. You've gotta do it. That's the testing ground, in those ballrooms where it's really hard to play.

Stew is driving you around now?
Yeah, there was this whole thing, because for us Stew is one of the band up until Andrew. "Well, he just doesn't look the part," Andrew said, "and six is too many for them to remember the faces in the picture." But piano is important for us. Brian at that time is the leader of the band. He pulled us all together, he's playing good guitar, but his love is the harmonica. On top of that, he's got the pop star hangup—he wants to sing, with Mick, like "Walking the Dog."

Are you singing?

Naw, I was getting into writing then though. Andrew was getting on to me to write because he sussed that maybe I could do it if I put my mind to it.

What are some of the first things you wrote?

They're on the first album. "Tell Me," which was pulled out as a single in America, which was a dub. Half those records were dubs on that first album, that Mick and I and Charlie and I'd put a bass on or maybe Bill was there and he'd put a bass on. "Let's put it down while we remember it" and the next thing we know is, "Oh look, track eight is that dub we did a couple months ago." That's how little control we had, we were driving around the country every fucking night, playing a different gig, sleeping in the van, hotels if we were lucky.

A lot of it was Andrew's choice. He selected what was to be released. He was executive record producer, so-called. While we were gigging, he'd get that scene together. But remember then, it was important to put out a single every three months. You had to put out a 45, a red-hot single, every three months. An album was something like Motown—you put the hit single on the album and ten tracks of shit and then rush it out. Now, the album is the thing. Marshall has laid the figures on me and *Sticky Fingers* album has done more than the single. They're both number one in the charts but the album's done more than the single.

The concept's changed so completely. Back then it was down to turning on 13-year-old chicks and putting out singles every three months. That was the basic force of the whole business. That was how it was done.

That's another thing. Both the Beatles and us had been through buying albums that were filled with ten tracks of rubbish. We said, "No, we want to make each track good. Work almost as hard on it as you would work on a single." So maybe we changed that concept.

Still, we were on the road every night so there are probably a couple of tracks in there that are probably bummers because Andrew said, "Well, put that on." Because up until the Beatles and ourselves got into records, the cat who was singing had absolutely no control, man. None at all. He had no say in the studio. The backing track was laid down by session men, under the A and R man, artists and repertoire, whatever the fuck that means. He controlled the artist and the material. Bobby Vee or Billy Fury just laid down the vocal. They weren't allowed to go into the booth and say, "I want my voice to sound like this or I want the guitar to sound like this." The man from the record company decided what went where.

That's why there became longer and longer gaps between albums coming out because we got into trying to make everything good.

The first three albums are pretty close though.
The first one was done all in England. In a little demo studio in "Tin Pan Alley" as it used to be called. Denmark Street in Soho. It was all done on a two-track Revox that he had on the wall. We used to think, "Oh, this is a recording studio, huh? This is what they're like?" A tiny little backroom.

When we got into RCA in Hollywood, fuckin' huge Studio A, with Dave Hassinger engineering we said, "We can really do it here. It's all laid out. All you have to do is not let them take you over." Engineers never even used to work, man. They'd flick a few switches and that was it. The machinery was unsophisticated in those days, four track was the biggest there was.

Suddenly a whole new breed of engineers appears, like Glyn Johns, people who are willing to work with you, and not with someone from the record company. There are all those weird things which have broken up in the record industry, which haven't happened for movies yet. There are no more in between men between you and the engineer and you can lay it down. If you want a producer or feel you need one, which most people do, it's a close friend, someone you dig to work with, that translates for you. Eventually we found Jimmy Miller, after all those years.

Slowly and slowly, we've been finding the right people to do the right thing like Marshall Chess, like Jo Bergman. All those people are as important as we are. Especially now that we've got Rolling Stones records, with the Kali tongue . . . nobody's gotten into that yet, but that's Kali, the Hindu female goddess. Five arms, a row of heads around her, a sabre in one hand, flames coming out the other, she stands there, with her tongue out. But that's gonna change. That symbol's not going to stay as it is. Sometimes it'll take up the whole label, maybe slowly it'll turn to a cock, I don't know yet.

You going to put two pills on the tongue?
We're going to do everything with it, slowly. Don't want to let it grow stale. It's growing change. Got to keep it growing.

What was the first time Oldham saw the band?
It was in March, 1963. The next week he took us right into a big studio and we cut "Come On." We were always doing other people's material but we thought we'd have a go at that—"Oh, it sounds catchy." And it worked out. At the time it was done just to get a record out. We never wanted to hear it. The idea was Andrew's—to get a strong single so they'd let us make an album which back then was a privilege.

Were you still a London band then?
Completely. We'd never been out of the city. I'd never been further north than the north of London.

Was Andrew a change in the kind of people you had to deal with?
He faced us with the real problems. That we had to find the hole to get out of the circle of London clubs and into the next circle. Lot of hustle, a lot of blague.

Did you have an image thing already?
It's funny. He tried . . . people think Oldham made the image, but he tried to tidy us up. He fought it. Absolutely. There are photographs of us in suits he put us in, those dog-tooth checked suits with the black velvet collars. Everybody's got black pants, and a tie and a shirt. For a month on the first tour, we said, "All right. We'll do it. You know the game. We'll try it out." But then the Stones thing started taking over. Charlie'd leave his jacket in some dressing room and I'd pull mine out and there'd be whiskey stains all over it or chocolate pudding. The thing just took over and by the end of the tour we were playing in our own gear again because that's all we had left. Which was the usual reason.

You weren't the socially "smart" band yet?
No. The Beatles went through it, and they put us through it. They have to

know you. They've changed a lot too you know. A lot of them have gone through some funny trips. Some titled gentlemen of some stature are now roaming around England like gypsies and they've acquired this fantastic country Cockney accent. "Ai sole a fe 'orses down 'ere. Got a new caravan like and we're thinking of tripping up to see . . ." But it's great.

It must have been amazing early on, when some young lord or some young titled lady would come to see you play?
Brian and I were really fascinated by them. They used to make us really laugh, from a real working class thing. It was so silly to us. It happened so fast that one never had time to really get into that thing, "Wow, I'm a Rolling Stone." We were still sleeping in the back of this truck every night because of the most hard-hearted and callous roadie I've ever encountered, Stew. From one end of England to another in Stew's Volkswagen bus. With just an engine and a rear window and all the equipment and then you fit in. The gear first though.

But to even get out of London then was such a weird trip for Mick and me. The North. Like we went back this year right, on the English tour, and it hasn't changed a bit, man. In the Thirties, it used to look exactly the same, in the middle of the depression. It's never ended for those people.

You're travelling alone?
Sure. Never carry chicks. Pick it up there or drop it. No room, man. Stew wouldn't allow it. Crafty Bill Wyman. For years we believed that he couldn't travel in the back of the bus or he'd spew all over us so he was always allowed to sit in the passenger seat. Years later, we find out he never gets travel sick at all.

Is the first album out?
No, we released two singles before the album. The first single was "Come On" with Muddy Waters' "I Wanna Be Loved" on the other side. We were learning to record. Andrew too. He'd never made a record in his life, and he was producing. Just to walk in and start telling people, it took guts. Andrew had his own ideas on what we were supposed to sound like. It's only been in the last few years with Jimmy that it's changed. The music went through Andrew then. He was in the booth.

*Was there a period when it was all the same, just working, but you knew
something was building?*
It's weird. I can remember. You know it in front. Being on the road every
night you can tell by the way the gigs are going, there's something enormous coming. You can feel this energy building up as you go around the
country. You feel it winding tighter and tighter, until one day you get
out there halfway through the first number and the whole stage is full of
chicks screaming "Nyeehhh." There was a period of six months in England we couldn't play ballrooms anymore because we never got through
more than three or four songs every night, man. Chaos. Police and too
many people in the places, fainting.

We'd walk into some of those places and it was like they had the Battle
of the Crimea going on, people gasping, tits hanging out, chicks choking,
nurses running around with ambulances.

I know it was the same for the Beatles. One had been reading about
that, "Beatlemania." "Scream power" was the thing everything was judged
by, as far as gigs were concerned. If Gerry and the Pacemakers were the
top of the bill, incredible, man. You know that weird sound that thousands of chicks make when they're really lettin' it go. They couldn't hear
the music. We couldn't hear ourselves, for years. Monitors were unheard
of. It was impossible to play as a band on stage, and we forgot all about it.

Did you develop a stage act?
Not really. Mick did his thing and I tried to keep the band together. That's
always what it's been, basically. If I'm leapin' about, it's only because something's goin' drastically wrong or it's going drastically right.

Mick had always dug visual artists himself. He always loved Diddley
and Chuck Berry and Little Richard for the thing they laid on people on
stage. He really dug James Brown the first time he saw him. All that organization . . . ten dollar fine for the drummer if he missed the off beat.

What was Brian like onstage?
He'd worked out these movements. In those days, little chicks would all
have their favorites. Yeah, when you think the Rolling Stones magazine, the
Beatles magazine came out once a month. Big sort of fan thing. It was a very
old thing that one had the feeling had to change. All those teenyboppers.

It might have been a great last gasp.
Yeah, I think so. Chicks now maybe they feel more equal. I think chicks and guys have gotten more into each other, realized there's the same in each. Instead of them having to go through that completely hysterical, completely female trip to let it out that way. Probably now they just screw it out.

Was it innocent hysteria?
They used to tell us, "There's not a dry seat in the cinema." It was like that.

Were you being approached by the kids?
Yeah, I got strangled twice. That's why I never wear anything around my neck any more. Going out of theatres was the dodgiest. One chick grabs one side of the chain and another chick grabs the other side . . . Another time I found myself lying in the gutter with shirt on and half a pair of pants and the car roaring away down the street. Oh shit, man. They leap on you. "What do you want? What?"

You have to get a little crazy from that.
You get completely crazy. And the bigger it got, America and Australia and everywhere it's exactly the same number. Oh, we were so glad when that finished. We stopped. We couldn't go on anymore. And when we decided to get it together again, everybody had changed.

Was it the same kind of madness in the States before it changed?
Completely different kind of madness. Before, America was a real fantasy land. It was still Walt Disney and hamburger dates, and when you came back in 1969 it wasn't anymore. Kids were really into what was going on in their country. I remember watching Goldwater-Johnson in '64 and it was a complete little show. But by the time it came to Nixon's turn two years ago, people were concerned in a really different way.

Rock music as politics?
Who knows, man? I mean they used to try and put it down so heavy, rock 'n' roll. I wonder if they knew there was some rhythm in there that

was gonna shake their house down. I used to pick up those posters down South that say, "Don't let your kid buy Negro records. Savage music. It will twist their minds." Real heavy stuff against a black radio station or black records.

Was it a big thing to finally see the black lifestyle in America for the first time?
It was a real joy. It was like I imagined but even better. Always a gas to see Etta James or B.B. King work for the first time. Some of those old blues cats. Wherever I go I still try and see whoever I can, I've heard is good or is still alive. I saw Arthur Crudup and Bukka White last time. Incredible.

We all went to the Apollo Theatre the first time over. Joe Tex and Wilson Pickett and the complete James Brown Review. Could never get over the fact that they were into that soul bag in '64. Those suits, those movements, the vocal groups. It became obvious then the spades were going to change their music. They were into that formal, professional thing, which is not half as exciting as when they just let it go. And music ties in with all the rest. Like a real rebellion against that soul thing. Like "Papa's Got a Brand New Bag." You were always told it was going to be heavy going up there, but it never was.

Actually, the first gig was in San Bernardino. It was a straight gas, man. They all knew the songs and they were all bopping. It was like being back home. "Ah, love these American gigs" and "Route 66" mentioned San Bernardino, so everybody was into it. The next gig was Omaha with the motorcycles and 600 kids. Then you get deflated. That's what stopped us from turning into pop stars then, we were always having those continual complete somebody hittin' you in the face, "Don't forget, boy." Then we really had to work America and it really got the band together. We'd fallen off in playing in England 'cause nobody was listening, we'd do four numbers and be gone. Don't blink, you'll miss us.

There was one ballroom number in Blackpool during Scots week when all the Scots come down and get really drunk and let it rip. A whole gang of 'em came to this ballroom and they didn't like us and they punched their way to the front, right through the whole 7000 people, straight to the stage and started spitting at us. This guy in front spitting. His head was just football size, just right. In those days for me, I had a temper, and

"You spit on me?" and I kicked his face in. It was down to the pressure of the road too. America to Australia to Canada to Europe, then recording.

You did some recording the first time over?
Yeah, at Chess "Michigan Avenue" and "It's All Over Now" and "Confessing the Blues." Oldham was never a blues man, which was one reason he couldn't connect with us. But a lot of things like "Spider and the Fly" were cut at the end of a session, while some guy was sweeping up. "Play with Fire" is like that, with Phil Spector on tuned-down electric guitar, me on acoustic, Jack Nitzsche on harpsichord, and Mick on tambourine with echo chamber. It was about seven o'clock in the morning. Everybody fell asleep.

Did you meet Spector that first time over?
I think we met him in England before we even went to the States. We were still into the blues. Phil Spector was a big American record producer, kind of just another person that Andrew wanted you to meet. Although I really dug his sound, those records. Always wanted to know how he got such a big sound, and when I found out it was a 170-piece orchestra, OK. Jack Nitzsche was Phil's arranger and a very important part of that whole sound. It was Jack's idea of harmonies and spacing. But it's nice he's singing with Crazy Horse now. He couldn't stand to . . . even get him to play the piano you used to have to do a whole Jack number. It's great he's doing it.

Brian had some kind of genius for finding people, didn't he?
He did. He got us together . . . Charlie, Mick and me.

He brought Nico to the Velvet Underground.
He was into Dylan too, very early on. He was the only one of us who hung out with Dylan for a bit. A lot of people know Brian that I don't know, that I didn't know knew him who come up and say, "Yeah, I knew Brian."

He was great. It was only when you had to work with him that he got very hung up. Anita could tell you a lot about Brian, obviously, because she was Brian's chick for a long time. Brian did have that thing for pulling people together, for meeting people, didn't he?

Anita: Mixing. Mix it. Mix it, Charlie. Fix it, Charlie.

Keith: We're just trying to figure out why Brian couldn't be with Mick and me at the same time. "Why can't Mick come in?" "No, no" he'd say . . . he was a big whisperer too, Brian. Little giggles . . . you don't meet people like that. Since everybody got stoned, people just say what they want to say.

Brian got very fragile. As he went along, he got more and more fragile and delicate. His personality and physically. I think all that touring did a lot to break him. We worked our asses off from '63 to '66, right through those three years, non-stop. I believe we had two weeks off. That's nothing, I mean I tell that to B.B. King and he'll say, "I been doing it for years." But for cats like Brian . . . He was tough but one thing and another he slowly became more fragile. When I first met Brian he was like a little Welsh bull. He was broad, and he seemed to be very tough.

For a start, people were always laying stuff on him because he was a Stone. And he'd try it. He'd take anything. Any other sort of trip too, head trips. He never had time to work it out 'cause we were on the road all the time, always on the plane the next day. Eventually, it caught up.

Right until the last, Brian was trying to get it together. Just before he died, he was rehearsing with more people. Because it happened so quickly people think . . .

Anita: They think he was really down. But he was really up.

Keith: And they also think that he was one of the Stones when he died. But in actual fact, he'd left. We went down to see him and he said, "I can't do it again. I can't start again and go on the road again like that again." And we said, "We understand. We'll come and see you in a couple weeks and see how you feel. Meantime, how do you want to say. Do you want to say that you've left?" And he said, "Yeah, let's do it. Let's say I've left and if I want to I can come back." "Because we've got to know. We've got to get someone to take your place because we're starting to think about getting it together for another tour. We've got itchy feet and we've got Mick Taylor lined up." We didn't really, we didn't have Mick waiting in the wings to bring on. But we wanted to know if we should get someone else or if Brian wanted to get back into it again. "I don't think I can," he said, "I don't think I can go to America and do those one-nighters any more. I just can't." Two weeks later, they found him in the pool, man.

In those two weeks, he'd had musicians down there every day. He was rehearsing. I'd talk to him every day and he'd say, "It's coming along fine. Gonna get a really funky little band together and work and make a record."

Do you think his death was an accident?
Well, I don't want to say. Some very weird things happened that night, that's all I can say. It could have as well been an accident. There were people there that suddenly disappeared . . . the whole thing with Brian is . . .

Anita: They opened the inquiry again six months after his death.

Keith: But nothing happened. None of us were trying to hush it up. We wanted to know what was going on. We were at a session that night and we weren't expecting Brian to come along. He'd officially left the band. We were doing the first gig with Mick Taylor that night. No, I wouldn't say that was true. Maybe Mick had been with us for a week or so but it was very close to when Mick had joined. And someone called us up at midnight and said, "Brian's dead."

Well, what the fuck's going on? We had these chauffeurs working for us and we tried to find out . . . some of them had a weird hold over Brian. There were a lot of chicks there and there was a whole thing going on, they were having a party. I don't know, man, I just don't know what happened to Brian that night.

Do you think he was murdered?
There was no one there that'd want to murder him. Somebody didn't take care of him. And they should have done because he had somebody there who was supposed to take care of him. Everyone knew what Brian was like, especially at a party. Maybe he did just go in for a swim and have an asthma attack. I'd never seen Brian have an attack. I know that he was asthmatic. I know that he was hung up with his spray but I've never seen him have an attack. He was a good swimmer. He was a better swimmer than anybody else around me. He could dive off those rocks straight into the sea.

He was really easing back from the whole drug thing. He wasn't hitting 'em like he had been, he wasn't hitting anything like he had. Maybe the combination of things. It's one of those things I just can't find out. You know, who do you ask?

Such a beautiful cat, man. He was one of those people who are so beautiful in one way, and such an asshole in another. "Brian, how could you do that to me, man?" It was like that.

How did you feel about his death?

We were completely shocked. I got straight into it and wanted to know who was there and couldn't find out. The only cat I could ask was the one I think who got rid of everybody and did the whole disappearing trick so when the cops arrived, it was just an accident. Maybe it was. Maybe the cat just wanted to get everyone out of the way so it wasn't all names involved, et cetera. Maybe he did the right thing, but I don't know. I don't even know who was there that night and trying to find out is impossible.

Maybe he tried to pull one of his deep diving stunts and was too loaded and hit his chest and that was it. But I've seen Brian swim in terrible conditions, in the sea with breakers up to here. I've been underwater with Brian in Fiji. He was all right, then. He was a goddamn good swimmer and it's very hard to believe he could have died in a swimming pool.

But goddammit, to find out is impossible. And especially with him not being officially one of the Stones then, none of our people were in direct contact so it was trying to find out who was around Brian at that moment, who he had there. It's the same feeling with who killed Kennedy. You can't get to the bottom of it.

Anita: He was surrounded by the wrong kind of people.

Keith: Like Jimi Hendrix. He just couldn't suss the assholes from the good people. He wouldn't kick out somebody that was a shit. He'd let them sit there and maybe they'd be thinking how to sell off his possessions. He'd give 'em booze and he'd feed 'em and they'd be thinking, "Oh, that's worth 250 quid and I can roll that up and take it away." I don't know.

Anita: Brian was a leader. With the Stones, he was the first one that had a car. He was the first into flash clothes. And smoke. And acid. It was back when it seemed anything was possible. Everybody was turning on to acid, young and beautiful and then a friend of Brian's died and it affected him very much. It made it seem as if the whole thing was a lie.

Did he stop taking acid then?

Anita: No. He got further into it. And STP. DMT, which I think is the worst, no? Too chemical. The first time Brian and I took acid we thought it was like smoking a joint. We went to bed. Suddenly we looked around and all these Hieronymus Bosch things were flashing around. That was in 1965. Musically he would have got it together. I'm sure of it. He and Keith couldn't play together any more. I don't know what causes those things but they couldn't.

Was there a gap between Brian and the rest of the Stones because he had taken acid and they hadn't?

Anita: Yes, as far as I know, Mick took his first trip the day he got busted, in '67. Keith had started to suss, he saw us flying around all over the place. He started to live with us. Every time Brian was taking trips, he was working, making tapes. Fantastic.

He didn't dig the music the Stones were making and he really got a block in his head that he couldn't play with them. Now, he would dig it. He never really stopped playing. It was just so different from what they were playing, he couldn't play in sessions. I'm positive he could have gotten it together. Positive. He was just a musician. Pure, so pure a musician.

Keith: I remember once in Philadelphia some kids had picked up on an interview Brian had done with somebody, he'd used one of those intellectual words like "esoteric." And so, right in the front, these kids had big signs that said, "Brian, you're so esoteric." It had that aura. It was down to *Sixteen* magazine. Everything you did in America then, it could all be in *Sixteen* magazine.

It was a thing when the Beatles and the Stones came over on that first wave . . . in New York, they were on the radio all the time with Murray the K . . .

Ah, Murray. The fifth Beatle and the sixth Rolling Stone. Nobody realizes how America blew our minds and the Beatles too. Can't even describe what America meant to us. We first started listenin' to Otis when we got to the States, and picked up our first Stax singles. And Wilson Pickett. That's what's so amazing about Bobby Keys, that cat, man, he was there from the beginnin'.

*If you come from the city, somehow you're aware of black music but if say,
you're from Nebraska . . .*

Nebraska. We really felt like a sore pimple in Omaha. On top of that, the
first time we arrived there, the only people to meet us off the plane were
twelve motorcycle cops who insisted on doing this motorcade thing right
through town. And nobody in Omaha had ever heard of us. We thought,
"Wow, we've made it. We must be heavy." And we get to the auditorium
and there's 600 people there in a 15,000 seat hall. But we had a good time.

The only thing that went down heavy there was a cop scene. It was
then I realized what Lenny Bruce was talking about. We were sitting
back in the dressing room. First time in Omaha in '64. Drinkin' whiskey
and coke out of cups, paper cups, just waiting to go on. Cops walked in.
"What's that?" "Whiskey." "You can't drink whiskey in a public place." I
happened to be drinking just Coke actually. "Tip it down the bog." I said,
"No man, I've just got Coca-Cola in here."

I look up and I got a .44 lookin' at me, right between the eyes.
Here's a cop, tellin' me to tip Coca-Cola down the bog. Wouldn't be
there if it wasn't for Coca-Cola. But that's when I realized what it could
get into.

Lenny Bruce gave his life . . .

They really got him strung up. He must have read every lawbook. His
last gigs were all Constitution and Federal law. In England, that's where
they did him way back. They left him alone in America until the English
bothered about him and when he went back, they threw the shit at him.

The same thing happened to Jerry Lee Lewis, man. He was ridin' on
the crest of a wave until he came to England with his 13-year-old wife. The
English busted him for it and said, y'know, "Get out of the country. This
is scandalous." When he got back to the States he suddenly found out he
couldn't gig anymore, straight from being number one.

*England's so strange. The way they've taken over the Stones, as "our" Stones
and "good on ya, boys," for making it.*

The English are very strange. They're tolerant up to a point where they're
told not to be. You get to a point up there where somebody turns around

and swings a little finger. They've had it in their hands so long, the power. They haven't been fucked since Cromwell, man.

Three weeks before I left, I was just goin' out my front door. Up screams a squad car. "Hello, Keith. How are ya, boy? All right? Let's roll up your sleeve, eh? Let us have a look at your veins. Not on the heavy stuff, are ya?" Just like that. "How's Anita and the baby? What's this? This smell like hash to you, Fred?"

In the States, you know the cops are bent and if you want to get into it, OK, you can go to them and say, "How much do you want?" and they'll drop it. In England, you can drop fifty grand and the next week they'll still bust you and say, "Oh, it went to the wrong hands. I'm sorry. It didn't get to the right man." It's insane.

This whole Western Civilization would be fine if everybody works, if they did it right but they don't. They're all trying to fuck each other, behind each other's backs. The people in England think their police are the finest police force in the world. They don't even know, man . . . what goes on. If they were told, they wouldn't wanna believe it. What goes on in London. They'd turn the other way and pretend they hadn't heard.

The 1967 bust was arranged, wasn't it?
The News of the World got hold of someone who was working for us. I think it was the cat who was driving me, at the time. They knew we were going to be down there at a party. Really, just something I'd done a million times before and I've done a million times since. I simply said, "Let's go down to my place for a weekend." It just so happened we all took acid and were in a completely freaked out state when they arrived. They weren't ready for that.

There's a big knock at the door. 8 o'clock. Everybody is just sort of gliding down slowly from the whole day of sort of freaking about. Everyone has managed to find their way back to the house. TV is on with the sound off and the record player is on. Strobe lights are flickering. Marianne Faithfull has just decided that she wanted a bath and has wrapped herself up in a rug and is watching the box.

"Bang, bang, bang," this big knock at the door and I go to answer it. "Oh look, there's lots of little ladies and gentlemen outside." He says, "Read this," and I'm goin' whaa, whaa." All right.

There was this other pusher there who I really didn't know. He'd come with some other people and was sittin' there with a big bag of stash. They even let him go, out of the country. He wasn't what they were looking for.

When it came down to it, they couldn't pin anything at all on us. All they could pin on me was allowing people to smoke on my premises. It wasn't my shit. All they could pin on Mick was these four amphetamine tablets that he'd bought in Italy across the counter. It really backfired on them because they didn't get enough on us. They had more on the people who were with us who they weren't interested in. There were lots of people there they didn't even bring up on charges.

Because you were young kids with a lot of money or because they saw you as leaders of some kind of movement?
Both. First, they don't like young kids with a lot of money. But as long as you don't bother them, that's cool. But we bothered them. We bothered 'em because of the way we looked, the way we'd act. Because we never showed any reverence for them whatsoever. Whereas the Beatles had. They'd gone along with it so far, with the MBEs and shaking hands. Whenever we were asked about things like that we'd say, "Fuck it. Don't want to know about things like that. Ballocks. Don't need it." That riled 'em somewhere.

It came from quite a way up, that thing. It was CID.

Was the bust physically heavy?
No. It might have been. But we were just gliding off from a 12-hour trip. You know how that freaks people out when they walk in on you. The vibes were so funny for them. I told one of the women with them they'd brought to search the ladies, "Would you mind stepping off that Moroccan cushion. Because you're ruining the tapestries." We were playin' it like that. They tried to get us to turn the record player off and we said, "No. We won't turn it off but we'll turn it down." As they went, as they started going out the door, somebody put on "Rainy Day Women" really loud. Everybody must get stoned. And that was it.

What usually happens is that someone gets busted, the papers have it the next day. For a week they held it back to see how much bread they could get off us. Nothing was said for a week. They wanted to see. Unfortunately none of us knew what to do, who to bum the bread to and so went via slightly the wrong people and it didn't get up all the way.

Mick can tell you how much. It was his bread. Quite a bit of bread.

Eventually after a couple of weeks the papers said the Rolling Stones have been raided for possession. The first court thing didn't come up for three months. Just a straight hearing. That was cool. The heavy trial came in June, about five months after. It was really startin' to wear us out by then. The lawyers were saying "It seems really weird, they want to really do it to you."

I didn't play it that way anyway. When the prosecuting counsel asked me about chicks in nothing but fur rugs, I said, "I'm not concerned with your petty morals which are illegitimate." They couldn't take that one.

The rumor that there was an orgy going on was part of the thing too, wasn't it? Nobody was in the state for an orgy, man. They should have come some other times, they would have really . . . They tried to make it seem as bad as they could. So OK, here come the sentences. Mick and Robert Fraser, who was another cat who got done, already been in the local jail for two days, waiting. They'd already been found guilty. They were waiting for their sentence until they'd gone through with my one. Mick gets three months for those four amphetamine pills. They give me a year, for allowing people to smoke in my house.

Now Wormwood Scrubs is a 150 years old, man. I wouldn't even want to play there, much less live there. They take me inside. They don't give you a knife and fork, they given you a spoon with very blunt edges so you can't do yourself in. They don't give you a belt, in case you hang yourself. It's that bad in there.

They give you a little piece of paper and a pencil. Both Robert and I, the first thing we did is sit down and write. "Dear Mum, don't worry . . . I'm in here and someone's workin' to get me out, da-da-da." Then you're given your cell. And they start knockin' on the bars at six in the morning to wake you up.

All the other prisoners started droppin' bits of tobacco through for me, 'cause in any jail tobacco is the currency. Some of them were really great. Some of them were in for life. Shovin' papers under the door to roll it up with. The first thing you do automatically when you wake up is drag the chair to the window and look up to see what you can see out the window. It's an automatic reaction. That one little square of sky, tryin' to reach it.

It's amazing. I was going to have to make those little Christmas trees that go on cakes. And sewing up mailbags. Then there's the hour walk when you have to keep moving, round in a courtyard. Cats comin' up behind me, it's amazing, they can talk without moving their mouths, "Want some hash? Want some acid?" Take acid? In here?

Most of the prisoners were really great. "What you doin' in here? Bastards. They just wanted to get you." They filled me in. "They been waiting for you in here for ages," they said. So I said, "I ain't gonna be in here very long, baby, don't worry about that."

And that afternoon, they had the radio playing, this fucking Stones record comes on. And the whole prison started, "Rayyyyy!" Goin' like mad. Bangin' on the bars. They knew I was in and they wanted to let me know.

They took all the new prisoners to have their photographs taken sitting on a swivel stool, looked like an execution chamber. Really hard. Face and profile. Those are the sort of things they'll do automatically if they pick you up in America, you get fingerdabs and photographs. In England, it's a much heavier scene. You don't get photographed and fingerprinted until you've been convicted.

Then they take you to the padre and the chapel and the library, you're allowed one book and they show you where you're going to work and that's it. That afternoon, I'm lyin' in my cell, wondering what the fuck was going on and suddenly someone yelled, "You're out, man, you're out. It's just been on the news." So I started kickin' the shit out of the door, I said, "You let me out you bastards, I got bail."

So they took me to the governor's office and signed me out. And when it got up to the appeal court, they just threw it out in ten minutes. This judge had just blown it. I mean, he said things to me while I was up there that if I'd caught him by himself I'd have wrung his neck. When he gave me the year sentence, he called me "scum" and "filth," and "People like this shouldn't be . . ."

Was the bust some kind of confirmation of things you already knew?
Yeah. It kind of said, "OK, from now on it's heavy." Up till then, it had been show biz, entertainment, play it how you want to, teenyboppers. At that point you knew, they considered you to be outside . . . they're the ones who put you outside the law. Like Dylan says, "To live outside the law, you must be honest."

They're the ones that decide who lives outside the law. I mean, you don't decide, right? You're just livin'. I mean your laws don't apply to me, nobody says that, because you can't. But they say it. And then you have to decide what you're going to do from then on.

It was the summer too. You had just started to turn on to acid.
Yeah, we had picked it up in America in '66, on that last tour in the summer and we came home and just laid back and started to get it on. We had been working for a long time without stopping, without thinking for a long time. For three years. The bust ended it. We knew it was going to be heavy. We split England about a week after the bust.

Keith: We just carried on down in Morocco for a while. Soon after then it's "You have to come back to England to speak to the lawyers." Slowly you start to straighten out again.

Anita: Mick was on his first trip at the bust.

Keith: I'm not sure. I know he took a lot more after that.

Was "Between the Buttons" cut after the bust?
No, that was done after the American tour. The album that was done while we were waiting to go in and on trial was *Satanic Majesties*. It was made in between court sessions and lawyers with everyone sort of falling apart. I ended up with chicken pox. At the appeal, when I got up, I was covered with spots, man. It was too much. It was the last thing, they couldn't take it. They couldn't even get me into court because I was diseased.

Flowers was put together in America by Andrew Oldham, just to put something out because they were begging for product. In fact, all that stuff had been cut a year or so before and rejected by us as not making it. I was really surprised when people dug it, when it even came out. Andrew was kind of getting pissed off with us by then because we were getting stoned and been busted. It hung him up that he couldn't carry on hustling because he didn't know if we were going to jail or what. And we kept saying, "Andrew, Andrew . . ."

I remember "Dandelion" as a single in the States in flower power summer. With the other side, "We Love You" with the sound of the jail door. We didn't have a chance to go through too much flower power because of the bust. We're outlaws.

But there's a time in everybody's life when they come out, when they bloom and it was just about then for the Stones.
Keith: Brian was like that at Monterey.
    Anita: He was on STP at Monterey.

Did he come back from there with a lot of things in his head?
Keith: Yeah, he did.
    Anita: With a lot of STP.
    Keith: He changed . . . because we changed around Brian, Anita, and I. We had that whole thing in Morocco and that kind of blew Brian too, on top of everything else. The thing I've forgotten about was when we were in court waiting to hear if there was to be bail before the real trial, that's when they busted Brian, man. They had it timed down to the minute. When we were actually in the fucking courtroom up in London, an hour and a half drive away, they were going into Brian's house to do him so that the papers would come out with "Rolling Stones Keith Richard and Mick Jagger on trial for this, meanwhile Brian Jones just been found with this"—so they could lay that on. "Well, they must be guilty."
    Anita: They were going to come down and see us . . . and we called from Brian's house and said, "Don't bother. The cops are here."
    Keith: "Don't come down. We'll come up." Unbelievable. It's really weird because people think of England as far more tolerant and genteel than America but when they laid that one on us, when they want to lay it down, they can be just as heavy. They just don't carry guns, that's all.

But some good came out of it. There was a rally and Release grew up around it.
Sure. The thing that shocked the cops was the *Times* coming out in our
favor. The *Times*! The tabloid of the Establishment came out and said,
"Why are you trying to break a butterfly on a wheel? What is this? What
have they done?" The *Times* people, they're the ones that can absorb, see?
They're the ones who can say, "You're just a butterfly. Let's just keep you a
butterfly and leave it at that."

*To talk about the music then, with Brian into acid before anyone and hav-
ing been to the West Coast, was there a reluctance to play just rock and roll?*
There was a point where it was difficult to do that. People would say.
"What you playin' that old shit for?" Which really screwed me up 'cause
that's all I can play. We just sort of laid back and listened to what they were
doing in Frisco whereas Brian was making great tapes, overdubbing. He
was much more into it than we were. And we were digging what we were
hearing, for what it was but that other thing in you is saying, "Yeah. But
where's Chuck Berry? What's he doing?" It's got to follow through. It's got
to connect.

*The feeling that a lot of people had first in '69, that they didn't want to work
for other people, do you think that might have rubbed off on the Stones?*
With the Stones though, you're always involved in that other scene, that
financial scene. Another heavy trip. But it's more under control now. I
mean ask John Lennon and Paul McCartney if we aren't more together
than they are with it. They're not. Because it's a very hard thing. You can
get it any way you want it, but it's who gets it for you, and how much do
you want? For doing what?

I don't want to go to America and be called a capitalist bastard because
of what the tickets cost. In '69, I didn't know what the tickets were costing.
You just go and play some music and when you get there you find out and
you're in the deep end already.

What were you paying in '66 to see us? Because I don't want to make
the prices so high that there is a whole stratum of kids that can't afford
to see us. They're probably the funkiest kids, you know? They're the ones
that would come and dig to see it and have a good time at doin' it too.

Like in Poland, in Warsaw in '67. Nearest thing to that Long Beach riot I ever saw.

You did a concert in Warsaw?
Man, fantastic. We get there, behind the Iron Curtain, do the whole bit, all very uptight. There's Army at the airport. Get to the hotel which is very jail-like. Lots of security people about, a lot like America. And it gets even more like America as it goes along. We're invited by the Minister of Culture, on a cultural visit, and we're playing in the Palace of Culture. We get there to do our gig. We go on "Honksi-de-boyski, boysk. Zee Rolling Stones-ki."

And who's got the best seats in the house right down front? The sons and daughters of the hierarchy of the Communist Party. They're sitting there with their diamonds and their pearls . . . and their fingers in their ears. About three numbers, and I say, "Fuckin' stop playin' Charlie. You fuckin' lot, get out and let those bahstads in the back down front." So they went. About four rows just walked out. All the mumma and daddy's boys.

Outside, they've got water cannons . . . the only scene I ever seen near it was when we tried to get out of the Long Beach Auditorium in 1965 when a motorcycle cop got run over and crushed. Exactly the same equipment, man. Deployed in the same way. All the cops had white helmets and the big long batons. Exactly the same uniforms.

There were 2000 kids that couldn't get in because of the sons and daughters. They wouldn't have had a riot there if they'd let the kids in. Only later I found out Poland is one of the most corrupt countries in the world.

There can't be many bands that have been played behind the Iron Curtain.
I always figured the Beatles were perfect for doing that. They were perfect for opening doors. But somewhere along the line, they got heavy. They wanted to be the ones to actually do it. They copped all the goodies for doing it. Sure enough.

When they went to America they made it wide open for us. We could never have gone there without them. They're so fucking good at what they did. If they'd kept it together and realized what they were doing, instead of now doing "Power to the People" and disintegrating like that in such a tatty way. It's a shame.

The Stones seem to have done much better in just handling success.
Anita: As far as I can see, it has always been a question of the Stones being from London and the Beatles being from Liverpool.

Keith: Maybe, because you're not English you can see it that way. It's true enough that the Beatles' first obstacle was to get out of Liverpool and get into London. We kicked off in London so it was no hang-up. Brian knew about those problems because he came from a provincial town in England. He had to conquer London first, that was his thing. He felt very happy when he made it in London, when we were the hip band in London.

For Mick and me, it didn't mean a thing, because it was just our place. We thought "Well, at least we've got a foothold in our own fucking town."

Do you and Mick still write now the way you used to then?
Well, I haven't seen him for a couple weeks because he went and got married, but basically yes. We do bits that we hear and then we throw them all together on a cassette or something, and listen to it. Mick writes more melodies now than he used to.

The first things, usually I wrote the melody and Mick wrote the words. It's not gotten like the Lennon-McCartney thing got where they wrote completely by themselves. Every song we've got have pieces of each other in it. The only thing in *Sticky Fingers* I don't have anything to do with is "Moonlight Mile," 'cause I wasn't there when they did it. It was great to hear that because I was very out of it by the end of the album and it was like listening, really listening. It was really nice. We were all surprised at the way that album fell together. *Sticky Fingers*—it pulled itself together.

How about "Satisfaction"?
I wrote that. I woke up one night in a hotel room. Hotel rooms are great. You can do some of your best writing in hotel rooms, I woke up with a riff in my head and the basic refrain and wrote it down. The record still sounded like a dub to me. I wanted to do . . . I couldn't see getting excited

about. I'd really dug it that night in the hotel but I'd gone past it. No, I didn't want it out, I said. I wanted to cut it again. It sounded all right but I didn't really like that fuzz guitar. I wanted to make that thing different. But I don't think we could have done, you needed either horns or something that could really knock that riff out.

With "Satisfaction," people start to wonder what certain phrases mean like "smoke another kind of cigarette."
A lot of them are completely innocent. I don't think that one is. It might have been. I don't know if it was a sly reference to drugs or not. After a while, one realizes that whatever one writes, it goes through other people, and it's what gets to them. Like the way people used to go through Dylan songs. It don't matter. They're just words. Words is words.

There was a time when for the Beatles and us . . . Dylan was another punch in the face. Someone said, "You've got to look outside what you're doing." He was someone else who was working hard but . . . good musicians too, that cat always picked 'em. Robbie Robertson . . . Kooper.

Al Kooper's a gas to play with. We cut a version of "Brown Sugar" with Al Kooper, it was a good track. He's playing piano on it at Bobby Keys', and my birthday party which was held at Olympic Studios. A lot of people came; Eric's on guitar. We wanted to use it cause it's a new version but there's something about the Muscle Shoals feel of the album one, that we got into at the end of the last American tour. Charlie really fills the sound and it was so easy to cut down there. We do a track a day there which is amazing. If you've been playing every night you can record quickly.

That's why we all moved . . . people say, "Why the south of France?" It's just the closest place where we can relax a bit and then record. That's why we're all living in the same . . . to transfer all that equipment, I hope it's worthwhile.

After you came back to England from the first or second American tour, did you have some kind of acceptance, were you starting to get respectable?
Still came across some opposition. It wasn't that complete acceptance

that the Beatles had. Always being kicked out of our hotel for not being dressed properly or something.

How is it that the Stones are banned from essentially every hotel in Manchester?
It's from years ago. They're so ridiculous with their little rules. For us to arrive at a place at 3 o'clock in the morning and be told we couldn't have anything to eat or that the drink cupboard is locked, immediately it's "Wadda you mean?" You're off a gig and you've been traveling for five hours and you've been doing it every day for a year. Eventually, they just ban you and night porters put up their bars when they hear you coming.

The funniest thing that happened like that was the court case for peeing in the gas station. That was just in that period, when the Rolling Stones were real big biggies. One night coming back from a gig in North London, Bill Wyman, who has this prodigious bladder, decided he wanted to have a pee. So we told the driver to stop. The car is full up with people and a few other people say, "Yeah, I could get into that. Let's take a pee." So we leap out and we had chosen a gas station that looked closed but it wasn't. There they are, up against the wall, spraying away.

And suddenly this guy steps out. And a cop flashes his torch on Bill's cock and says "All right. What you up to then?" And that was it. The next day it was all in the papers. Bill was accused and Brian was accused of insulting language. Because what they did them for was not peeing but for trespassing.

All these witnesses come up. "There he was, your Honor, he was facing the wall, and well, he was, uh, urinating."

How about the wall of the toilet for the corner of "Beggars Banquet"?
Anita, Mick and I found this wall. Barry Feinstein photographed it. It was a great picture. A real funky cover. The fight they gave us—we dug in our heels. They really wouldn't budge. It stopped the album from coming out. Eventually it got to be too much of a drag. It went on for nine months or so.

It was like them saying, "We don't give a shit if your album never goes out." After that, we knew it was impossible and started looking around to do it differently. The main thing about having your own label is that you're not solely confined to putting out Rolling Stones material. If we come across anyone else we like or any other thing we dig that people are saying, we can put it on record. It doesn't all have to be our product. Somebody said they got hold of some tapes of Artaud explaining a few things. That would be great to put out.

Did the Stones sign a film deal for five films when Oldham was handling things?
I think there was definitely a film clause. We were part of Andrew's hangup. One of the first things he put out in the English press were that talks were going on for the Stones to appear in their own full-length feature movie. Just to make people keep their ears open a little more. It never got together.

Later on we paid for *Only Lovers Left Alive*, which is a book. I haven't read it for years. It seemed corny then but . . . it was quite a heavy book, some nice things in it. We saw some very straight English film directors about it and they really put us off. Their concept of how it should be. Them trying to turn us on to it really turned us off it.

Would you want to make a movie?
It would just have to happen. I couldn't think about going into it. Mick wanted to do something and nobody was together enough, he didn't have a band together enough to do anything and he felt he'd like to learn about films. There was only one way he could do that. And after, we understood more about the movies because he went through a whole movie.

What do you think of "Performance"?
I thought it was a great movie. There were a lot of things in there. It was heavy, I mean Donald Cammell is heavy, he wrote it. We've known him since '65 or '66. Anita and I went back to England for that, we hadn't been living there. I mean they did that movie in '68. In the fall.

Donald had so many hassles getting it out. They kept making him re-edit it, I don't know how many times. It was the last film Anita did before Marlan.

Did you go to Rome to write that album?

No, to Positano, south of Naples. We'd been there before. We knew the place vaguely and someone offered us their house there. It was empty, barren, very cold. Huge fires and we just sat and wrote. Did "Midnight Rambler" there, "Monkey Man" and some others.

Do you think "Let It Bleed" is the Stones' best album?

I haven't heard it for a long time and I believe things like "Midnight Rambler" come through better live, because we've extended it more. Sometimes when you record something you go off half-cocked because maybe you haven't ever played it live. You've just written it and you record it. From then on you take it and keep on playing it and it gets different. I remember I was into 12-string bottlenecks then.

That song is Mick way out on his persona, isn't it?

Usually when you write you just kick Mick off on something and let him fly on it, just let it roll out and listen to it and start to pick up on certain words that are coming through and it's built up on that. A lot of people still complain they can't hear the voice properly. If the words come through it's fine, if they don't, that's all right too because anyway they can mean a thousand different things to anybody.

But the song's almost psychotic isn't it?

It's just something that's there, that's always been there. Some kind of chemistry. Mick and I can really get it on together. It's one way to channel it out. I'd rather play it out than shoot it out.

People come to Stones concerts to work it out.

Yeah, which in turn has been interpreted as violence or "a goddamn riot" when it's just people letting it out. Not against anybody but with each other. That rock and roll thing, even when it was young, those songs created a domestic revolution. When the parents were out, there were all those parties. Eddie Cochran and all those people, they created some kind of thing which has followed through now and is being built on.

Like "Streetfighting Man"?

The timing of those things is funny because you're really following what's going on. That's been interpreted thousands of different ways because it really is ambiguous as a song. Trying to be revolutionary in London in Grosvenor Square. Mick went to all those demonstrations and got charged by the cops.

The basic track of that was done on a mono cassette with very distorted overrecording, on a Phillips with no limiters. Brian is playing sitar, it twangs away. He's holding notes that wouldn't come through if you had a board; you wouldn't be able to fit it in. But on a cassette if you just move the people, it does. Cut in the studio and then put on a tape. Started puttin' percussion and bass on it. That was really an electronic track, up in the realms.

Some songs, with a 16-track, I don't really need all that. It's nice to make it simpler sometimes. "Parachute Woman" is a cassette track.

"Salt of the Earth"?

No, that's studio. Mick's words, but I think I was there for a bit of them too. I'd forgotten about that actually. Nearly all Mick, that one. Funny year, '68, it's got a hole in it somewhere. Coming out of the bust and other stuff . . . I was in L.A. for a couple months.

When did you start to meet with Alan Klein?

Andrew got Klein to meet us, to get us out of the original English scene. There was a new deal with Decca to be made and no one really knew, everyone wanted to know about it, in a business we'd never thought of. Who's actually making the money. He was managing financial advisor for Donovan and the Dave Clark Five, Herman's Hermits, who were all enormous then.

The first time we met was in London. The only thing that impressed me about him was that he said he could do it. Nobody else had said that. The thing that he really wanted was the Beatles and the Stones together, to have them both. He did it. But as he picked one up, he dropped the other. A juggling act. Then he didn't get Paul either, which was a real fuckup, coming at such a time that it really did them in. In a way, he was probably the last straw in the whole thing for the Beatles. To be set against each other in things like that is such a downer. To have to go through that court thing that they did in London.

Did the Stones decide together to go with Klein?
I really pushed them. I was saying, "Let's turn things around. Let's do something." Either we go down to Decca and tell them to do it with us . . . which is what we did that very day with Klein, just went down there and scared the shit out of them.

You originally signed a two-year contract with them?
Yeah, in '63. He did a good job, man. Andrew told us that Klein was a fantastic cat for dealing with those people, which we couldn't do. Andrew knew he didn't know enough about the legal side of it to be able to do it. So we had to get someone who knew how to do it or someone who'd fuck it up once and for all. Then it would be up to us to deal with him.

Andrew had gotten together his own label and we had the feeling that he had what we wanted and could go ahead and do his own stuff. He was no longer that into what we were doing and we weren't sure what we wanted to do, because of the busts. He didn't want to get involved in all of that, so it seemed the right time. It just fell apart.

Did it feel like an end to anybody?
It did to Brian, thinking about it. Not to me. I just sort of picked it up again. I think Brian felt that was it. He was really a sensitive cat, too sensitive, the thought of going back on the road really horrified him, in '66 when we last saw America it was 45's and teenyboppers and in three years it established a completely different order. What a change in America, just amazing.

And he was OK on that last tour?
Yeah, we were all very stoned. The last gig was in L.A. We came back to England with pockets full of acid. In '65 you hardly saw any grass. By '66, it was becoming common. It was still a spade trip before that, a spade laid it on you and it was a pleasure to get a joint. It was one of those turn-ons,

like when we get to America, we'll get joints laid on us if we get a spade act with us.

Apart from a visit to New York in '67 to do the cover for *Satanic Majesties*, which we constructed in a day, and a couple months in '68, I was there just before the Convention . . . the only contact I had was the underground press and whatever came through.

Were the Springfield going in L.A. then?
Jack Nitzsche had told me about Neil Young and I had seen the Springfield in a club in New York in '66. Hendrix too, at Ondines. He was fantastic. Doing Dylan songs and "Wild Thing" in a club with a pickup band. Fantastic. One of those cats you just knew you were going to see again. He was like Brian too. We were on the European tour when both Jimi and Janis died, so I didn't really get into it till I got back, a few months later.

Did it scare you?
Not really, because I don't feel as fragile as those people.

You live in the same world.
Yeah, but they were very vulnerable. Like Brian was. He really got it all off on stage and he didn't want to fuck with anybody after. I didn't know Jimi that well, but he had a lot of people hangin' 'round that he didn't need and that's what screwed Brian. We're talking about people I really didn't know that well, so I can only relate it to Brian.

Did you do a lot of traveling in the years when the Stones didn't work as a band?
Went to Morocco for quite a while. I drove down through Spain. It's incredible. It's like getting stoned for the first time to go through the Casbah. Mick and everybody ended up there because it was after the bust. Everybody sort of ran. Met Achmed down there, Anita had known him from before, when she went with Brian, but then in '67 he was just getting his thing together . . . he had this beautiful little shop and he'd tell all these incredible stories, and he made this incredible stuff. I haven't been there for two or three years and I keep meaning to go back.

It was quiet in Tangier then. Just a few American kids. Brion Gysin was there too. That cat who wrote *The Process*. Weird. I'm expecting him down here, with Burroughs, they're talking about *Naked Lunch* and trying to get it together for a movie.

How did that picture of the band in drag come about?
There was a big rush for "Have You Seen Your Mother Baby?" Jerry Schatzberg took the picture and Andrew ordered a truckload of costumes and Brian just laid on me this incredible stuff. He just said, "Take this." We walked down from Park Lane in that gear and we did the pictures. It was very quiet, Saturday afternoon, all the businesses are shut but there's traffic . . .

Wearing high heels?
Yeah, and the whole bit. Bill in a wheel chair. It took a while to get this picture and going back, what do you do? Do you take half the stuff off and walk back . . . or do you keep it on? Anyway, I'm thirsty, let's go and have a beer. We all zip down to this bar. Hey, what voice do you do? We sat there and had a beer and watched TV and no one said anything. But it was just so outrageous because Bill stayed in his wheelchair and Brian was pushing him about.

Do you like that record?
I loved the track of it. I never did like the record. It was cut badly. It was mastered badly. It was mixed badly. The only reason we were so hot on it was that the track blew our heads off, everything else was rushed too quickly. Tapes were being flown . . . and lost. It needed another couple weeks. The rhythm section thing is almost lost completely.

Along with "Stupid Girl" and "Under My Thumb" and other songs of that time, there's a real down-on-chicks feeling in it.
It was all a spinoff from our environment . . . hotels, and too many dumb chicks. Not all dumb, not by any means but that's how one got. When you're canned up—half the time it's impossible to go out, it's a real hassle to go out—it was to go through a whole sort of football match. One just

didn't. You got all you needed from room service, you sent out for it. Limousines sent tearing across cities to pick up a little bag of this or that. You're getting really cut off.

Of course, there was still "Lady Jane."
Brian was getting into dulcimer then. Because he dug Richard Farina. It has to do with what you listen to. Like I'll just listen to old blues cats for months and not want to hear anything else and then I just want to hear what's happening and collect it all and listen to it. We were also listening to a lot of Appalachian music then too. To me, "Lady Jane" is very Elizabethan. There are a few places in England where people still speak that way, Chaucer English.

Brian played flute on "Ruby Tuesday."
Yeah, he was a gas. He was a cat who could play any instrument. It was like, "there it is, music comes out of it, if I work at it for a bit, I can do it." It's him on marimbas on "Under My Thumb" and mellotron on a quite a few things on *Satanic Majesties*. He was the strings on "Two Thousand Light Years from Home," Brian on mellotron, and the brass on "We Love You," all that Arabic riff.

How about "Goin' Home"? It was one of the earlier jams to be put on a pop album.
It was the first long rock and roll cut. It broke that two minute barrier. We tried to make singles as long as we could do then because we just like to let things roll on. Dylan was used to building a song for 20 minutes because of the folk thing he came from.

That was another thing. No one sat down to make an 11 minute track. I mean "Goin' Home," the song was written just the first two and a half minutes. We just happened to keep the tape rolling, me on guitar, Brian on harp, Bill and Charlie and Mick. If there's a piano, it's Stew.

Did you record during those years you didn't gig?
A lot of recording, and getting together with Jimmy Miller in '68 or late '67 when we started *Beggars Banquet*. It's really a gas to work with

Jimmy. We'd tried to do it ourselves but it's a drag not to have someone to bounce off of. Someone who knows what you want and what he wants. I wouldn't like to produce, there's too much running up and down, too much legwork.

John Lennon said that the Stones did things two months after the Beatles. A lot of people say "Satanic Majesties" is just "Sergeant Pepper" upside down. But then I don't know. I never listened any more to the Beatles than to anyone else in those days when we were working. It's probably more down to the fact that we were going through the same things. Maybe we were doing it a little bit after them. Anyway, we were following them through so many scenes. We're only just mirrors ourselves of that whole thing. It took us much longer to get a record out for us, our stuff was always coming out later anyway.

I moved around a lot. And then Anita and I got together and I lay back for a long time. We just decided what we wanted to do. There was a time three, four years ago, in '67, when everybody just stopped, everything just stopped dead. Everybody was tryin' to work it out, what was going to go on. So many weird things happened to so many weird people at one time. America really turned itself round, the kids . . . coming together. Pushed together so hard that they sort of dug each other.

For us too, we had always been pushed together . . . not bein' able to get hotel rooms. Even now, it's one of the last things I say, you never pull that thing . . . that you're a Rolling Stone. I like to be anonymous, which is sort of difficult.

How long did "Satanic Majesties" take to cut?
It wasn't meant to be that ambitious, it just got that way. It must have taken nearly all of '67 to get it together. Started in February and March and it came out in November.

The design was yours?
Michael Cooper was in charge of the whole thing, under his leadership. It was handicrafts day . . . you make Saturn, and I'll make the rings. I forget the name of those people, those 3D postcards. Thing is, everyone

looks round on that one. They take pictures at slightly different times and distances and they're put together and the heads move but after it gets scratched you don't really see it anymore.

People always ask, "Are John and George in there?" I don't even know, I'd forgotten if they're all in there. They are all in there. And Paul and Ringo.

And who else?
Lyndon Johnson and Mao . . . We just started . . . we had to put a stop to it. We were getting the whole of Sergeant Pepper in there, just for the hell of it. It was gettin' late and Michael finally got Saturn suspended . . . It was really funny . . . we should have done a gig that night.

Hidden things like that . . . like Paul is dead.
Ohhhhh. We were in L.A. when that came down. Just playing before the tour started. It's incredible. I've never heard the things they say are on the albums. I've read about it but I've never gotten into it enough to sort of try and slow down a track. Somebody should make a tape of the whole thing and lay it down. All those connections and pictures. But the thing is, he's alive.

It's a weird kind of paranoia. To think that people are working on you that way.

"Two Thousand Lightyears from Home." Were you into reading science fiction then?
Not so much. We got into a lot of those English eccentrics. People finding out all about these magnetic lines. We hung around a lot with John Michelle, wandered around England a few weekends, and he showed us obvious things. I mean, bloody obvious. He's into the pyramids in Egypt. There are an awful lot of straight professors who are aiding in that thing. Michelle's incredible. I haven't seen him for ages. He's the sort you never see for years . . . and then he pops up.

And all those flying saucers kept appearing. A whole rash of them in England. There was one right near my place that two cops had seen. We all rushed out to a village about fourteen miles from my place. They'd seen it and chased it and lost it. The whole story got lost and you never heard any more about it, but two cops around our way, man, were really spaced out.

Is that where "God ride the music" comes from?
There was a cat in America, Charles Foot, who collected useless information, about levitating plates with violin notes. I don't know where he is now either.

Where did the title "Beggars Banquet" come from?
It comes from a cat called Christopher Gibbs. Mick laid it on me but it was Christopher who arrived at that mixture. Although we had all been throwing around "Tramps' Mushup" or something. On the same idea. We wanted to do the picture, that idea came first, the beggars thing came first. "Sticky Fingers" was never meant to be the title. It's just what we called it while we were working on it. Usually though, the working titles stick. Mick was very into that tattered minstrel bit then.

Did "Let It Bleed" have anything to do with "Let It Be"?
Not a thing. Just a coincidence because you're working along the same lines at the same time at the same age as a lot of other cats. All trying to do the same thing basically, turn themselves and other people on. "Let It Bleed" was just one line in that song Mick wrote. It became the title . . . we just kicked a line out. We didn't know what to call that song. We'd gone through "Take my arm, take my leg" and we'd done the track. We dug that song so . . . maybe there was some influence because Let It Be had been kicked around for years for their movie, for that album. Let it . . . be something. Let it out. Let it loose.

Do you sing for the first time alone on that album?
Please. My voice first appeared solo on the first verse of "Salt of the Earth." We did the chorus together, me and Mick. If I write a song, I usually write it all but it's difficult. Somebody's always got their finger in there. I thought I wasn't on "Moonlight Mile" but the last riff everybody gets into play-

ing is a riff I'd been playing on earlier tapes before I dropped out. "Wild Horses," we wrote the chorus in the john of the Muscle Shoals recording studio 'cause it didn't finish off right.

Does it have to do with Marlan's birth?
Yeah, cause I knew we were going to have to go to America and start work again, to get me off me ass, and not really wanting to go away. It was a very delicate moment, the kid's only two months old, and you're goin' away. Millions of people do it all the time but still . . .

How about earlier stuff like "Paint It Black"?
Mick wrote it. I wrote the music, he did the words. Get a single together.

What's amazing about that one for me is the sitar. Also, the fact that we cut it as a comedy track. Bill was playing an organ, doing a takeoff of our first manager who started his career in show business as an organist in a cinema pit. We'd been doing it with funky rhythms and it hadn't worked and he started playing it like this and everybody got behind it. It's a two-beat, very strange. Brian playing the sitar makes it a whole other thing.

There were some weird letters, racial letters. "Was there a comma in the title? Was it an order to the world?"

How about "Get Off My Cloud"?
That was the follow-up to "Satisfaction." I never dug it as a record. The chorus was a nice idea but we rushed it as the follow-up. We were in L.A. and it was time for another single. But how do you follow "Satisfaction"? Actually, what I wanted was to do it slow like a Lee Dorsey thing. We rocked it up. I thought it was one of Andrew's worse productions.

"Mother's Little Helper"?
In those days, Mick and I were into a solid word-music bag unless I thought of something outstanding, which could be used in the title or something. I would spend the first two weeks of the tour, because it was done on the road, all of it was worked out . . . an American tour meant you started writing another album. After three, four weeks you had enough

and then you went to L.A. and recorded it. We worked very fast that way and when you came off a tour you were shit hot playing, as hot as the band is gonna be.

"Nineteenth Nervous Breakdown," "Have You Seen Your Mother Baby," "Mother's Little Helper," they're all putting down another generation.
Mick's always written a lot about it. A lot of the stuff Chuck Berry and early rock writers did was putting down that other generation. That feeling then, like in '67. We used to laugh at those people but they must have gotten the message right away because they tried to put rock 'n' roll down, trying to get it off the radio, off records. Obviously they saw some destruction stemming from . . . they felt it right away.

The Mayor of Denver once sent us a letter asking us to come in quietly, do the show as quietly as possible, and split the same night, if possible. "Thank you very much, we'll be very pleased to see you in the near future." I've got that letter with the seal of Denver on it. That's what the mayors wanted to do with us. They might entertain the Beatles, but they wanted to kick us out of town.

Part of the Stones image is sex trips.
Yeah, on our first expedition to the United States we noticed a distinct lack of crumpet, as we put it in those days. It was very difficult, man. For cats who had done Europe and England, scoring chicks right, left, and center, to come to a country where apparently no one believed in it. We really got down to the lowest and worked our way up again. Because it was difficult.

In New York or L.A., you can always find something in a city that big if that's what you want. But when you're in Omaha in 1964 and you suddenly feel horny, you might as well forget it. In three years, in two years, every time you went back it was . . . the next time back it was like, it only took someone from outside to come in and hit the switch somewhere.

Did you have guys trying to hustle you?
Yeah, in America we went through a lot of that. In France and England too, not groupies as such, they have some concrete reason for being around. They work for a radio station, they contribute to some obscure

magazine. It's hard to suss if they want to know what's going on or if they just want to be around for a second-hand thrill. Out of just being around.

Unlike the Beatles, the Stones, and Mick in particular, have always had the uni-sexual thing going.
Oh, you should have seen Mick really . . . I'll put it like this, there was a period when Mick was extremely camp. When Mick went through his camp period, in 1964, Brian and I immediately went enormously butch and sort of laughin' at him. That terrible thing . . . that switching around confusion of roles that still goes on.

Anita is something very special for the Stones.
It's because she's an amazing lady. She's worked with Mick, Mick and I work together . . . she's an incredible chick. She found us, through Brian. A long time ago. She's been involved in it all . . . Anita . . . yeah . . . there are some people you just know are gonna end up all right. It's really nice. That's why we had Marlan . . . because . . . we just knew it was the right time . . . we're very instinctive people. He's traveled around, though, even before he was born, to Peru. We found out in South America she was pregnant.

What was South America like?
I really like to go to places I know nothing about. Brazil is an amazing place, aside from the amazing hangovers from the Spanish thing that run it. North of Rio it gets really primitive, and Mick's been there a couple times.

But even Rio, man, on New Years, on the beach practicing macumba. Whole place turns into . . . thousands of thousands of people living in shacks on hills and every time they knock one down, three or four new ones pop up . . . an even more incredible city is Sao Paulo. Which is, in the south, as fast as New York, as speedy as that in tropical conditions, it pours down rain for ten minutes then the sun comes out and it's a hundred and twenty, and the place starts to steam. Millions of people rushing about . . . all for Coca Cola. It's just like New York.

Lot of good guitar players down there. All over South America, it must be the most widely played instrument.

Did you get the earring in South America?
The one that's hanging there? Yeah. Not the hole. I bought the earring in Peru. I re-bent this one after I got into a fight . . . I mean that's why I say I never mention the Rolling Stones when I'm just going about my business. We had a car crash down there and settled it all and some little bureaucrat from the local harbor has to butt in so someone mentioned, "Oh, that's one of the Rolling Stones." Is it? Bang. Someone leaps in. Telephones flying. And when someone hits them back, it's pistols. "They've got a gun. Call the police." Mention the Rolling Stones and get a smack in the face.

I know what we did do in South America. Went to a ranch and wrote "Honky Tonk Women" because it was into a cowboy thing. All these spades are fantastic cowboys. Beautiful ponies and quarter horses. Miles from anywhere. Just like being in Arizona or something.

"Honky-Tonk" is always the song that brings people up to dance, isn't it?
We've never known why. There's always been a few songs that do that. If they weren't dancing by then, you'd know you weren't getting it on. The guitar is in open tuning on that, I learned that particular tuning off Ry Cooder.

It's been said that the Stones brought him over for "Let It Bleed" and ripped him off.
He came over with Jack Nitzsche, and we said, "Do you want to come along and play?" The first thing Mick wanted was to re-cut "Sister Morphine" with the Stones, which is what we got together. He's also playing mandolin on "Love in Vain" or . . . he's on another track too. He played beautifully, man. I heard those things he said, I was amazed. I learned a lot of things off a lot of people. I learned a lot watching Bukka White play. He taught me the tuning and I got behind it.

He says you kept him in the studio with the tapes going and then just used some of his stuff and stole the rest.
If the cat . . . first of all, he was never brought over for the album, which is the main thing. He came over with Jack Nitzsche to get the music for some movie. He came by and we played together a lot, sure. I mean, he's a gas to play with. He's amazing. I wasn't there for a lot of it, but Bill and

Charlie still talk about it. They really dug to play with him. I mean, he's so good.

I had already been into open tuning on *Beggars Banquet*, "Street Fighting Man." Just a different tuning. Those old cats are always turning a few machineheads. I learned a lot of things from watching Chuck Berry's hands on *Jazz on a Summer's Day*. It got shown a lot in Europe.

I remember Brian, Mick and I on the way to one of our first gigs stopped into a cinema because we had a few hours to kill to see this movie. I had a guitar with me in just a soft case. We had just gotten in on Chuck Berry's bit, which is what everybody wanted to turn on to, particularly. We were watching and walking and I tripped over this fucking guitar and smashed it to pieces. "Dyonnng" . . . it made this huge noise, strings going and wood splintering.

But you learned from his hands.
It was the only way to watch someone play then.

Tell us the interesting story of how you got your ear pierced.
Well, the cat who was doing it—a jeweler or he studied it—was on about 15 Mandrax. Very stoned. Doing it the good old-fashioned way. None of your anaesthetics and machinery. With a sewing needle and ice. Me next. Rubs the ice on and he's dodging back and forth. God knows how he managed to do it. And he just made it. It's right at the lobe.

I've always wanted a pierced ear. I made me first bottleneck and had me ear pierced the same night, with about fifteen of the Living Theatre and I was about the fourth ear. He did Anita's, too, at a special angle. By then he had another ten Mandrax and was completely out of it. Try it from the front. No, let's go at it from the back.

But a lot of people got their ear pierced that night, it was around the time of the Hyde Park concert.

That was June, 1969. You hadn't worked for two years but had you become better musicians?
No, you always get worse laying off, in one way. You get rusty. Which you can put right if you start playing together. None of us were worried about it. I learned a lot though. I played a lot of acoustic guitar. I did a lot of writ-

ing; I didn't use to but I dug to do it. I was writing in a different way, not for a hit single or to keep that riff going.

Everybody let their hair grow.
The thing is we were already getting so hassled with our hair like it was. You really weren't safe in some places. I've chopped it off now for the sun. It's usually long in the winter. You couldn't go into Omaha, you'd get the shit beat out of you.

We did a lot of things in those years, traveled, I hung around a lot with the Living Theatre when they were in Rome and London. They were still working on stage doing things which made the audience no longer an audience, which got them involved.

Did the Stones get more theatrical? "Midnight Rambler" is a piece of theatre.
It's all experiments. I know there are certain things you can do up there when the lights are on you. But the gas of it is when the whole place looks the same, when the house lights are up, when the stage then looks just as tatty as the rest of the auditorium and everybody's standing up. That's the real turn on. Not the theater, although that song's a gas, and I dig to play it. It's when the audience decides to join, that's when it really knocks you out.

You've only got to see a few people dancing, and I turn and watch, and play for them to dance to. It's like you can play for a body that moves. It's always them turning you on so that you can turn them on some more.

Was the Hyde Park concert scheduled before Brian's death?
It was. Don't forget, it was our first thing with Mick Taylor. We wanted to get Mick Taylor up on stage to be seen. We wanted to do something in London. And we wanted it to be free. Which is also a bastard. Because the two free things we've done have been that and Altamont. Both so totally different. People trying to pull that old riff on us, going there in armor. Maybe it was the wisest thing. So we went in an armored ambulance. Took about two hours to drive through the crowd. And we played pretty bad. Until near the end, 'cause we hadn't played for years. And nobody minded 'cause they just wanted to hear us play again. It was nice they

were glad to see us because we were glad to see them. Coming after Brian's death, it was like a thing we had to do. We had that big picture of him on stage and it comes out looking like a ghost in some pictures.

Was his death still unreal?
It didn't hit me for months because I hadn't seen him a lot. The only time we'd see him was down at the courthouse, at one of his trials. They really roughed him up, man. He wasn't a cat that could stand that kind of shit and they really went for him like when hound dogs smell blood. "There's one that'll break if we keep on." And they busted him and busted him. That cat got so paranoid at the end like they did to Lenny Bruce, the same tactics, break him down. Maybe with Mick and me they felt, well, they're just old lads.

Mick read a poem for Brian at the concert.
He read something from Shelley. He wanted to do it for Brian. It's a tough thing . . . the first thing you've done on stage before an audience in two years. To get up and read a Shelley poem. He wanted to do it for Brian. He said it was necessary to make some sort of incantation.

And the butterflies . . . they were really nice. Biggest public gathering in London for over two hundred years. The last time they had a gathering that big in England, it started a people's revolt. Had to be put down with the dragoons.

You did songs from "Beggars Banquet."
Yeah. It had already been out quite a while because we'd had *Let It Bleed* almost finished. We took it with us to the States where we met Bobby and Jim Price.

The whole Satan trip really comes out after "Beggars Banquet."
I think there's always been an acceptance . . . I mean Kenneth Anger told me I was his right-hand man. It's just what you feel. Whether you've gotten that good and evil thing together. Left hand path, right hand path, how far do you want to go down?

How far?
Once you start, there's no going back. Where they lead to is another thing.

The same place?
Yeah. So what the fuck? It's something everybody ought to explore. There are possibilities there. A lot of people have played on it, and it's inside everybody. I mean, Doctor John's whole trip is based on it.

Why do people practice voodoo? All these things bunged under the name of superstition and old wives' tales. I'm no expert in it. I would never pretend to be, I just try to bring it into the open a little. There's only so much you can bring into the open.

There's got to be people around who know it all, man. Nobody ever really finds out what's important with the kinds of government you've got now. Fifty years after, they tell you what really went on. They'll let you know what happened to Kennedy in a few years' time. It's no mystery. An enormous fuckup in the organization, a cog went wrong, and they'll say who did it. But by then it won't matter, they'll all be dead and gone and "Now it's different, and in this more enlightened age . . ."

"I shouted out who killed the Kennedys." Does that thing hold for Mick too, or is it more a show business thing?
Mick and I basically have been through the same things. A lot of it comes anyway from association and press and media people laying it on people. Before, when we were just innocent kids out for a good time, they're saying, "They're evil, they're evil." Oh I'm evil, really? So that makes you start thinking about evil.

What is evil? Half of it, I don't know how much people think of Mick as the devil or as just a good rock performer or what? There are black magicians who think we are acting as unknown agents of Lucifer and others who think we are Lucifer. Everybody's Lucifer.

Does that produce things like Altamont?
As I said, I particularly didn't like the atmosphere there by the time we went on. After a day of letting some uniforms loose, what can you expect? Who do you want to lay it on? Do you want to just blame someone, or do

you want to learn from it? I don't really think anyone is to blame, in laying it on the Angels.

If you put that kind of people in that kind of position . . . but I didn't know what kind of people they were. I'd heard about the Angels but I haven't lived in California and San Jose, I have no contact with those people. I don't know how uncontrolled they are, how basic their drives are.

But when the Dead told us, "It's cool. We've used them for the last two or three years, Kesey cooled them out," I was skeptical about it but I said, "I'll take your word for it. I've taken everybody's word for it up till now that they know what they're doing when they put on a show." You have to accept that for a start, that it's gonna be together when you get there or else you never get to any gigs. Few ripoff promoters in the Midwest though . . .

Who put the Angels in that position? Specifically.
Specifically? . . . we asked the Dead basically if they would help us get a free concert together. First we had this idea we want to do a free concert and we want to do it in Frisco because that's where they do a lot of free concerts. Who do you ask and who's done more free concerts than anybody—the Grateful Dead. It's very nice, man, we hung around, talked about lots of things, played a bit. They said this is how they done it and this is a big one and they think they can get it together.

It comes down to how many people can you put together. In India they're used to that many people turning up for a religious occasion. But this was not a religious occasion and also it was in the middle of the fucking desert, in California with freeways. We were so hassled. We were in Muscle Shoals, trying to make a record. Meanwhile they're going through all these hassles with people saying, yeah, you can set up a stage and put up all your equipment and then saying, "Fuck off." We'd been going through it throughout the whole tour, man. "Golden Gate Park, yes it's on. No no. City officials say no." Then they pack across the Bay.

We're still in Alabama, into making records. And so we have to take people at their word. We have to trust them. And they could do it, and they did. But it wasn't their fault they didn't have enough time to think about the parking or how people are going to get there or the johns or the

... they thought of them to a certain extent but nobody knew exactly how many people were coming any way. Then you get there and what a fucking place, man. Well, let's just make the best of it.

I went out there the night before Mick. Mick went back. I stayed there. I just hung around, met a few nice people. It was really beautiful. That night before, everywhere I went was a gas. People were sitting around their fires, really cool, getting high and I ended up in a trailer and woke up when it was about a hundred and ten degrees inside.

Were you there when Mick got hit?
I was there the whole fucking day in that trailer. Also, it's the last gig. Do this and we go home. So everybody is in sort of that final mad rush. We'd done this incredible flight from New York to West Palm Beach and sat on the tarmac in the plane for nine hours at LaGuardia, in New York while they got it ready. We got to the gig eight hours behind schedule, after a helicopter flight. We got on at four o'clock in the morning. Below zero. And that was the last gig of the tour proper.

Those kids waited all night to see you.
They were great. Such a sight. That place wasn't much better than Altamont. Everyone was frozen stiff. We got it on for a bit but everybody dug it. It was a gas. By the time we finished and got back to the hotel on the beach, dawn was coming up, the sun was warm and we went to Muscle Shoals.

When did you first feel things might turn out badly?
The Airplane's gig. When I heard what they done to Marty Balin, they're gettin' out of hand. It's just gonna get worse, I thought, obviously it's not going to get better. Nothing's gonna cool them out once they start. What a bummer. What can you do? Just sit tight.

Did you consider not going on?
Can you think what that would have caused on top of getting all the people to the place? Talk about one cat getting killed ... on top of that, everybody was very sensitive. America suddenly seems to have developed this hyper-sensitivity to life and death that I'd never seen them concerned with before. I never saw them concerned when a cop got crushed at Long Beach.

I don't care who it is. Some Angel or whatever . . . the underground suddenly leaps up in a horrified shriek when some spade hippie gets done, which is a terrible thing, but they never got uptight if some cop got done. Some cop, he's probably on extra duty, and he gets crushed at a pop concert. That one really brought me down. I could never believe it ended up in the 15th page of the Herald-Tribune or whatever it was called. That sort of thing makes you want to stop. I don't demand sacrifices at this stage of the game.

What information were you getting at Altamont as to what was going on?
Ah, it's obvious, man. Maybe they'll do me the next time I go there, but they were out of control, man. The Angels shouldn't have been asked to do the job. I didn't know if the Angels were still like Marlon Brando had depicted fifteen years before, or whether they'd grown up a little or if they're still into that "don't touch my chromework" bit. All right. Someone else should have known that. If they didn't, then the Angels kept it very well hidden for a long time.

Who should have known? Sam Cutler?
Sam Cutler was with us all the time, man.

Ronnie Schneider? John Jaymes?
They should have known. I think the Dead should have known. Rock Scully should have known, I think. He didn't. I spoke to him, we all spoke to him and he trusted those cats, man, to do just a good job of keeping the stage clear of people so no plugs'll get pulled out and no chaos would ensue. Somewhere along they flipped.

The people look very very stoned in "Gimme Shelter."
People were just asking for it. All those nude fat people, just asking for it. They had those victims' faces. That guy was pathetic. Most of this I've seen from the movie, same as anyone else. Most of the people who've seen what went down at Altamont have caught it from the movie. When I was there, I just heard a bit, I never actually saw anything flying till we went on.

What did you see when you went on?
The usual sort of chaotic scene.

Did you wait purposely until it was dark to go to heighten the effect?
Oh man, I'd been there 24 hours, I couldn't wait to get out of that place. It was fuckups, the beatups, the chaos, our people telling us not to go on yet, let the people cool down a bit. Those campfire sessions, they always go on longer than expected anyway.

What happens when you come out on stage?
Perfectly normal. Go into "Jumpin' Jack Flash." It felt great and sounded great. I'm not used to bein' upstaged by Hell's Angels—goddammit, man, somebody's motorbike. I can't believe it. For a stunt. What is the bike doin' there anyway, in the fourth row of the fucking . . . it would have looked better up on stage and it would have been safer too.

So the cat left his bike there and it got knocked over so that was the first one. "Oh dear, a bike's got knocked over." Yes, I perfectly understand that your bike's got knocked over, can we carry on with the concert? But they're not like that. They have a whole thing going with their bikes, as we all know now. It's like Sonny Barger. "If you've spent $1700 . . ."

Well, if that's what you want to get together, that's fine but I really don't think if you leave it in front of half a million people, you can't expect it to not to get knocked over.

What if someone tried to do your guitar? They'd get punched out very quickly, wouldn't they?
I don't kill him, man. And I don't get five hundred buddies of mine to come down and put their boot in too. I don't have it organized to that extent. If someone tries to do my guitar, and I don't want it to be done, it's between him and me. I don't call in Bill Wyman to come in and do him over for me, with one of his vicious ankle-twisters or chinese burns.

I didn't see any killings. If I see any killing going on, I shout "Murder." You dig, when you're on stage you can't see much, like just the first four rows. It's blinding, like a pool of light in complete darkness, unless someone out there lights up a cigarette. All you see is lights out there. If someone strikes one or shines one. Since all this went on 10 or 15 rows back, the only time we were aware of trouble was when suddenly a hundred cats would leap in front of us and everybody would start yelling.

But you stopped playing right after the stabbing and Sam Cutler went to the mike for a doctor.

Someone asked for a doctor, yeah. Half of our concerts in our whole career have been stopped for doctors and stretchers. How much responsibility for the gig are you going to lay on the cat who's playing and how much on the cat that organized it? Rolling Stones' name is linked with Altamont. It wasn't our production particularly. Our people were involved but they were relying on local knowledge.

There were all these rumors flashing around. "There's a bomb gone off and 20 people have been blown to bits, man." You say, "I think you got it wrong, man, I'm sure you got it wrong." 'Cause you've been hearing crazy rumors all day, that you're dead, as ridiculous as that. By the time you're in California and you've gone through a whole tour and you've heard all those rumors that seem to go round and around and around . . . you don't believe anything. I don't believe anything at the end of an American tour ever.

Mick seemed to know something was going on, he tried to cool it out.

The same as Grace Slick tried earlier. "Be cool, be cool." For all the control one can have over an audience, it doesn't mean you can control the murderers. That's a different thing, man, you can't make someone's knife disappear by just looking at him. Somehow in America in '69—I don't know about now, and I never got it before—one got the feeling they really wanted to stick you out.

Like at the Rainbow Room press conference. So ridiculous, cats asking what to do about the Vietnam War. "What are you asking me? You've got your people to get that one together." And they're asking you about everything, about your third eye . . . it's very nice. But you can't be God. You can't ever pretend to play at being God . . . Altamont, it could only happen to the Stones, man. Let's face it. It wouldn't happen to the BeeGees and it wouldn't happen to Crosby, Stills, and Nash.

Except that they were there and it didn't make a difference.

Were they? I heard they were in some airport and didn't come, all those rumors. The wisest people I saw were Jerry Garcia and Phil Lesh in that movie: "Those Angels beatin' the shit out of people? I ain't goin' in there." I don't blame the Dead for not working. I just wish they . . . ah, it's too late. Maybe what saves the whole thing is making a movie about it and showing what went down and maybe a little less belief in uniforms.

Does the money from that film go to Meredith Hunter's family?
I don't know, man. As far as I know, the Maysles, the cats who made it, told me that the premiers in various cities have been to help street clinics . . . I don't know about the Meredith Hunter scene because it's all litigation. It's all lawyers.

I've never met his mother. They should get something from somebody. Because . . . I don't know. I get like Charlie when I get down and think about it. The cat was waving a gun, man, and he looked very spaced out.

But the gun was unloaded.
Tell it to Wild Bill Hickock, man.

How did John Jaymes get to the Stones?
Ronnie Schneider we'd known. He's Klein's nephew but he broke away from him. He's a smart cat. I dig Ronnie. He'd been on a lot of tours with us handling business and hung around with us. He was the only cat we knew in '69 who could handle the Stones tour that everybody knew, that we could leave to get on with it till we got there.

How Jaymes got in, I don't know. First met him in L.A. I don't know the whole riff that goes down there. Just like I don't know the whole riff about America, who organizes it all. Occasionally, they show up. Leave it at that. They laid some good shit on me, those people.

The story is that Jaymes had ex-narcos who did heavy numbers on the Stones.
He was an ex-narco.

And he had bodyguards . . . were you being held prisoner?
Oh no, man. It's nice . . . I get the riff, I get the riff. No, there was some

paranoia among the organizational people about Uncle Alan. It comes down to the . . . uh . . . the Jewish trade unions and the Italian trade unions, y'see. There are these two trade unions. And they just love to fuck with each other. And it was down to family connections, as far as I could see. And I just wanted to get on with the tour.

And Jaymes' people were going to protect you.
No, in the crew, there were street cats, Chip Monck's crew, very together cats. But there were stories of things being dropped on their heads from unusually high places and weird coincidences. Just things I hear. You never know if it's the truth or rumors. Everyone gets paranoid. There's a lot of other peoples' paranoia beside your own, which you can probably cope with. How many strings can you pull at once? Twelve is my maximum . . . six is my speciality.

But no one liked Jaymes, did they?
Ah, on the last American tour we did in '66, you never expected to meet anyone you liked. All you expected to meet were assholes and maybe laugh at them, and that's where the whole cynical thing really was fed. Being left adrift with the editor of *Sixteen* magazine for two days. Or having the prizewinner of some schnooky competition in Iowa to have lunch with. I think once in Harrisburg, Pennsylvania, we did wind up with the Mayor and his daughter in the civic banqueting hall.

She escaped intact?
I think Brian let rip with a few golden oldies. I know we ended up in the supermarket across the road, buying records.

What were the concerts on the tour like before Altamont?
I remember enjoying them. There's always a bummer. It was probably West Palm Beach. You could enjoy the people for hanging around that long but it was too fucking cold to play properly and we tried to do the whole show . . . too fucking cold. A bummer. After Madison Square Garden, came out of three shows there to freeze your balls off in a Florida swamp. We always get 'em.

It was the first time you saw that America.
It was the first time we played it. Mick and I had been to L.A. in '68, the Strip every night, I dug what was going on there. Brian and I popped over a few times in '67 incognito. Went over in December '66 with Brian. Down in Watts a lot. Very stoned. We got so out of it we wanted to go back and do some more. Without having to play a gig every night. It was the only place we knew where to score, man.

And then Mick and I went in '68 to mix down *Beggars Banquet* with Jimmy and stayed for two months. Hung out with Taj and the Burritos. Went to the Palomino a lot. I think England has such a high standard in heavy drugs. Well, the system for junkies was beautiful. It's fucked up now because it's a halfway thing. They really had it under control. It depends how you want to see junk.

It's two years since I've been to America, which is the longest period ever I'm away. I hear stories. You hear how that junk thing is getting heavier and heavier. I been through all that. It depends how you want to see it. There's a lot of Chinese shit around. That's all I can say. That's another one of those rumors.

You get young kids as junkies in the cities.
You know what it does. It's on the wrong end. They should turn on to it when they're 60. All these old ladies down here, learn a lesson from these old chicks. For a start look at its effect on a nine-year-old. Say he kicks when he's 15. More than likely he'll only be 10 or 11 when he's 15. His voice will break suddenly. Puberty is delayed.

But these old ladies, they leave it alone, then start hitting morphine and horse and they don't feel things like lumbago and arthritis and the plague or old age and things like that. They live to 90, 105. It's a particular Europe trip. Old rich people.

If you're going to get into junk, it stands to reason you should . . . for a start, in guys particularly, it takes the place of everything. You don't need a chick, you don't need music, you don't need nothing. It doesn't get you anywhere. It's not called "junk" for nothing. Why did Burroughs kick it, after 25 years? He's thankful he kicked it, believe me.

How about for making music?
People have offered me a lot of things over the years, mainly to keep going. "Work ya bastard. Take one of these." I've tried a lot of shit. I don't even know what it is. I personally think . . . it depends if you're ready. Same with alcohol. You should find out what it does. If you don't know what it does and you're just putting it in, for the sake of it, you're a dummy.

What it does depends on what form you take it in. Some people snort, some people shoot it. You tell me what it does. The Peruvians, they chew it, and that's the trip. You can buy it in any grocery store and you eat it with a hunk of limestone and it just freezes you . . . at 11,000 feet it's hard to breathe anyway. Those cats have 47 percent more red corpuscles than us lowlanders. Huge lungs, and they're chewing it all the time. You buy it along with your eggs and your lemons. It depends how you take it.

People also say the drunker you are, the better you play.
All those things are true. The first time you go out every time roaring drunk, after five years you're a fucking wreck. And you still might think it's a gas, but you're making it for yourself, which is cool, but people are coming and paying and you're not turning them on, you're only turning yourself on. And you don't know.

What works for you?
It used to be booze. It used to be this . . . I try not to get behind anything for too long anymore because . . . I've been hung up on things. I've got to travel on, I've got to be onstage, I don't want to be hung up carrying all those things with me. When I go through, I go through clean. I'm a clean man.

Again, about Hendrix . . .
I don't know if someone sold him some bad shit or what. These days they're selling stuff, it's no longer cut with talcum powder and sugar, its cut with caustic soda, or with Ajax. England is a very healthy place in a way, or was, because they fucked it and they're gonna let the big boys in now for sure. They're blowing it by the way they're handling the drug situation. People will go somewhere else to look for junk and buy bad shit.

Once things get into powders . . . Arthur Machen wrote a story about white powder back in 1909 . . . a guy takes more and more white powder until one night he turns into a blob and drips through the ceiling. Since then I haven't touched a white powder if I don't know what they are. Even if it's for the runs.

You, though, are in a unique position. People listen when you sing, and "Sticky Fingers" is a heavy drug album, one way or another.
I don't think *Sticky Fingers* is a heavy drug album any more than the world is a heavy world. In 1964, I didn't used to run into cats in America who'd come up to me and say, "Do you want some skag? Do you want some coke? Do you want some acid? Do you want some peyote?" And then go through all those initials and names. Now you have trouble avoiding them.

People who think you're ready to finance every drug smuggling expedition in the world. "Hey listen, I'm not interested. You got the wrong idea." The cats that are into it are into it because they're good at . . . they've taken their chances at it. They're not doing it for nothing, it's either they're getting their rocks off or they're into it for bread. A lot of cats get their kicks going through customs. So what, man?

How about a 12 or 13-year-old kid who buys "Sticky Fingers" and that's the first time he hears about cocaine, or he finds out that "Brown Sugar" has another meaning?
Well, I didn't find out that "Brown Sugar" had another meaning . . . we wrote it in '69. And as far as I can tell they weren't calling it brown sugar then.

Cocaine?
Horse, in some places. Apparently what they get in L.A., it's light brown with brown lumps in it. I don't know where that stuff comes from or what it is. These people don't know what they're getting. If you don't know what you're getting, you don't know what you're putting into yourself. And if you don't know that, you're a dummy. Nobody would eat meat with maggots crawling out of it but people will shoot up some shit they don't know about.

Don't take my example. Take Jimi Hendrix. Or not. Depending on where you are and how you feel. Who says you've got to live threescore and ten years? There's only one source of information I know that says that, and even that doesn't say everybody's got to make it. Everybody can't make 70.

Do you want to make 70?
I can't even imagine what it's like, to be 70. When I was 20 I couldn't imagine what it would be like to be 28.

Can you imagine 30?
It's only two years away. I don't know, not really. Thirty still seems like a real trip to me. And I know 33 is a real trip: 33 is a year.

When Christ was crucified . . .
Everybody who reaches 33, goes through some weird things.

About "Sticky Fingers" . . .
I mean, though there are songs with heavy drug references, as people have pointed out to me. Me being completely unaware of the situation. They're all actually quite old, which maybe indicates that we were into those things a couple of years ago, three years ago. Maybe we recorded it 20 years ago, man, you know.

I mean, people, you can't take a fucking record like other people take a bible. It's only a fucking record, man. Goddamn it, you know, you might love it one day, you might hate it the next. Or you might love it forever, but it doesn't mean to say that whatever it says in there you've got to go out and do, you've got to go out and say.

There's no rules, you know. When it was teenybopper time one just despaired anyway. I mean, what was the relevance of it.

What did it all mean?
Yeah. Suddenly you're a pop star. Well, you do that because you know pop stars only last two years anyway. So you go through it: "Oh, you know, I'll be that for a bit." The thing is that things change along with it.

You understand that hardly anybody especially in America—
I thought that also along with it had changed that sort of bullshit, that authority. The establishment has its fingers on show business in this way that in fact it comes out through the mouth of justice itself. "Since you are an idol of millions you therefore hold special responsibilities."

In actual fact, you don't. There's only him that says you do. You don't shoulder any responsibilities when you pick up a guitar or sing a song, because it's not a position of responsibility.

Some people try and reflect it, don't they? Crosby, Stills, Nash and Young? The song, "Chicago"—like that.
Good topical stuff.

Which sells records?
Certainly. Mayor Daley's a good target. And there's a million Mayor Daleys in America. Why have a go at one? Sure he's cunt, you know, everyone knows he's a cunt. But there's a million hiding behind. Last time I was in L.A. I met the old lady that owns most of those head shops in the Strip, man. She's got a little home in Beverly Hills, she's rolling, you know. She's made a packet, man, and she gets those little hippies to work in there. And it's a front, man. It's all a fucking front. There's another Mayor Daley.

I mean, who knows where they are? How many times can you use those words—justice, freedom. It's like margarine, man. You can package it and you can sell that too. In America they have a great talent for doing that.

And so, as I was saying, just because it's on a record doesn't mean that you have to take it for what it is. The cat could be lying, you know, at the end of the record, you know, maybe they cut the tape off and he said, "Oh, I'm sorry, I'm lying. You know, I'm just fooling you." But they just happened to edit the tape there, you know. "I'm putting you on."

Maybe Dylan said at the end of "Visions of Johanna"—oh, I don't know, which is a very personal thing—but maybe he said it at the end of some of his earlier stuff: "But I don't give a fuck," at the end of "Blowin' in the Wind" or "That's up to you," maybe said that.

But they just, by the time somebody gets to a record anyway, they've got to realize that even our records have gone through the hands of some of the straightest people you could ever meet. Nearly all the Rolling Stones records—you know this is the first album that hasn't—have gone through this very straight English private fucking company, man. They're the people that are really giving it to you. It's not us that are giving it, we're giving it to them.

Because that's the only way you can get records out, and they're giving it to the people. So really it's coming from them anyway. I mean, we went through a lot of hassles with them, but it's not like straight from us to you. It's always going through the hands of somebody, and the thing is to try and get those hands into the same sort of sympathy. The music says something very basic and simple, man. Which, I don't know, exasperates. I mean, look at Richard Nixon and then look at your average young cat in the street, or some Indian cat. It's all there, you've only got to look at what's in front of you. And that's all we've ever been trying to do. Not trying to tell people where to go or which way to go because I don't know. We're all following. I mean, it's all going to happen. It's all coming down.

And to us it might seem, oh, world population. Before there were newspapers and radios and TV you wouldn't hear about that . . . You would never hear about that plague in India or Bengal that they're having and the cholera thing. If you was living in Wales at the time of the great plague in London you probably wouldn't get to hear about that until five years after it happened. And so, something like world population, you wouldn't even know about it.

Depends how worried you want to get about everything. I mean, how can you worry about world population, whose problem is that? You tell me.

Everybody feels they ought to do something about it. If you know the facts. On the face of it it sounds scary. But after a while it always splits into two things, one side is "Oh, in ten years there's going to be so many people on the earth and you not going to be able to do this, that and the other" and the other says, "Oh yes; it's going to be terrible for them, but it's going to be all right for us."

And then there's "Oh, the world's growing too much food and they're just throwing it all away, enough to feed the world five times over is being thrown into the Atlantic Ocean": and the only reason it's not getting to the people that need it to stay alive is either because they don't want to afford the cost of transporting it to those people or they want those people to die anyway. I mean, what about that tidal wave in Pakistan, man? Quarter of a million in one night.

No way to understand it. On the face of that, what kind of music are you writing?
I'll just keep on rocking and hope for the best. I mean that's really what in all honesty it comes down to. I mean why do people want to be entertainers or do they want to listen to music or come and watch people make music? Is it just a distraction or is it a vision or God knows what? It's everything to all kinds of people. You know, it's all different things.

OK, but the music's changing. "Can't You Hear Me Knockin'" changed because of Bobby Keyes and Jim Price. "Moonlight Mile" is a change.
Yeah, it's a gas to play. It's a gas not to be so insulated and play with some more people, especially people like Bobby, man, who sort of on top of being born at the same time of day and the same everything as me has been playing on the road, man, since '56–'57.

He was on Buddy Holly's first record. I mean he's a fantastic cat to know, for somebody who's into playing rock and roll, because it's been an unending chain for him. The first few years that he was playing around man, I was just the same as anyone, I was just listening to it and digging it and wondering where it came from. And he was there, man. Bobby's like one of those things that goes all the way through that whole thing, sails right through it.

I didn't know it man, but we played on the same show as Bobby Keys in '64, first time we went to San Antone. San Antone State Fair, no, Teen Fair, San Antone Teen Fair, 1964. George Jones, Bobby Vee, that's who Bobby Keys was playing with, playing with Bobby Vee's backup band. I remember that gig, but I don't remember Bobby.

But the reason I remember San Antone so much is waking up and this is, I mean, a young English cat never been face to face with the realities of American life. San Antone was like one of the first places we hit after Omaha and L.A. L.A., Omaha, San Antone, you know, really right in there.

I put on the TV the first morning: "15 killed last night in a brawl down on the river Brazos" or whatever it is. I thought, "God, they're riotin' down here, what's going on?' "Is it a race riot, old chap?" "Did you hear that? All these weird people with this English accent."

Turn on the TV next morning, 18 people killed last night and it slowly began to sink in, right, every night around 15 or 20 people get it done to them in San Antone, either Mexicans or spades or kids that go out. I mean in '65, I don't know if the locals are still up to it but in '64 they were very into spick hunting. You know, just go across the river on a Friday night and have a night, have a little chiv up.

I mean that's amazing. Why doesn't someone do something about that? That's what I used to think then. You know, that doesn't happen in my home town. It happens, one could find it, you could find it in any town, you could find it in my town, sure. But it wasn't *18 people* were dead the next morning, you know, and one could certainly get one's self chipped about quite easily.

You don't have to go very far to provoke, even in an English town, to get yourself done over, but 15 people dead, you know, 12 people, you know. If I'm exaggerating over the years, 12 people dead or whatever. But regularly every morning! I was there for about four or five days and every morning it was within two or three of 15. They're probably still going on now, man. I bet that morgue makes a fortune.

You going to start working on a new album here?
Yeah, right in me own basement, as it turns out. After months of searching I end up sitting on it.

How long has it been since "Sticky Fingers" was finished? How long since the band recorded?
We finished—when were the last sessions, man? Was I even there for the last sessions of *Sticky Fingers*? When did they finish it? February, January, March? Most of it was finished before the tour. And it was all finished, complete by the time we came here.

And it took over a year, did it?

Well, I mean, stretched out, the songs, one could say it stretched over two years, you know, because "Sister Morphine" comes from '68, although we cut it in early '69. Some songs were written awhile ago.

But Stones albums usually take a long time, don't they?
They've usually taken longer and longer.

Why is that?
Which really pisses me off. Because everybody's laid back a little more and everybody has other things, they do other things now, whereas when it was just a matter of being on the road and recording, that's all you did, you know, and that was it. And obviously you could do things much quicker that way.

But I mean, if we carried on doing it like that, we'd probably be doing it from wheelchairs already. Because you can't carry on at that pace forever. You know, you can do it in spurts, but I mean, even if you're young and a teenager, you get awfully drawn looking.

Do you reckon you could be doing more work than you are? More recording, laying down more tracks? You, personally?
Yeah, but you know, but you can't have weddings of the year and solo albums and you know, I mean, it's great fun.

You going to do a solo album?
No, I'm not going to do one. All I'm going to do is see if I've got enough things left over from Stones things that they don't like that I do, that I might want to put out at some time, but I'm not going to go and make an album.

Too much trouble or what?
I can't imagine doing it, you know? I can't imagine making an album just like that. I've never had an urge to be a solo. Maybe I can get together one song, two songs a year, that I really feel that I want to sing. And so I do it and I put it on the Stones album. Because it's cool. If I feel, if I become more productive, I'll just collect things. I'll just wait until I've got enough things.

Shit, man, I was just a hired guitar player when I started. Things grew out of that and I learned how to write songs just by sitting down and doing it. For me it seems inconceivable that any guitar player can't sit down and write songs. I don't see how a cat can play a guitar, really, and not be able to lay something down of his own in some way.

But that's the way I feel because I happen to be able to do it. For some guitar players it's inconceivable that nobody can play the guitar, you know, that anybody can't just pick it up just like that.

Because to them it's a second . . . you know. If it's sort of in you, and it's something that you've got together, it's simple, you can't explain it, it's easy. How do you write a song? It's fucking easy, man. I'll come back in a few minutes and lay one on you. But if you're one of these cats that sat down for fucking weeks and months and tried desperately to produce something and nothing ever comes out, it must seem like the greatest task in the world.

I mean, I've desperately tried to remain anonymous. The state the world is in today it's much more of an advantage to remain anonymous than it is to be identifiable or recognized.

As a musician?
Fucking Chuck Berry wrote "Let It Rock" under E. Anderson man, and it's one of the best things he ever did. And yet he put it out, you know he's got some tax publishing hassle, he puts it out under some middle name: Charles A. Berry, Edward Anderson, or whatever. He should have got recognition for it, and as far as I'm concerned he should definitely be recognized as the writer for "Let It Rock." Would the U.S. Internal Revenue kindly bear it in mind.

How do you feel about the music business?
How can you check up on the fucking record company when to get it together in the first place you have to be out on that stage every fucking night, you have to get out there every night in front of the people, saying here I am and this is what I do. You can't keep a check on it. Someone else is handling all that bread.

We found out, and it wasn't years till we did, that all the bread we made for Decca was going into making little black boxes that go into

America Air Force bombers to bomb fucking North Vietnam. They took the bread we made for them and put it into the radar section of their business. When we found that out, it blew our minds. That was it. Goddamn, you find out you've helped to kill God knows how many thousands of people without even knowing it.

I'd rather the Mafia than Decca.

Anita: I mean, Mafia than the CIA, man. But if you've got to be on that stage every night, there's no possible way of checking up on all those people.

Gram Parsons told me a great story about the Mafia. What they're really into now is growing tomatoes. Tomatoes is the only business in America that you can still get cash on the nail so that if you drive up with a truck load of tomatoes, you get money right off. So they have the whole tomato business sewn up.

Gram had an uncle who was growing a thousand acres of tomatoes and one day some guys came down in a limousine and got very heavy with him and said, "Why don't you switch to citrus fruits and leave the tomatoes to us."

Anita: Leave the tomatoes to us.

Keith: It gets so weird, one has to think about everything. I mean, they're running it. They're running America.

Anita: That's why in an interview with the *Daily Mirror* Keith said he was ready to grow tomatoes.

Keith: A subliminal message to the Mafia. "Come see me, I'm ready to grow tomatoes."

What is the conjunction of show business and crime?
A lot of money in entertainment. The criminal element is there for the bread. And where there's crime, there's cops. They're both in the same business, right? Who else deals with crime but criminals and cops? They're the only two that are hung up on it.

Anita: And Italians.

Anita's seen it all, from another viewpoint. I mean, I'm always in the middle. I've heard incredible Rolling Stones stories I know nothing about. I don't know if I was asleep in my room or . . . why did I miss out on that one?

5 |

AND SITTETH AT THE RIGHT HAND . . .

JONH INGHAM | 1976

In 1976, Jonh Ingham was sent to interview Richards by British music weekly *Sounds*. By this point in history, there was a general feeling that there was something profoundly wrong with rock music and that one of the reasons for that malaise was the drug-drenched hauteur and complacency of musicians of the Stones's generation. Ingham was more conscious of this than most, having recently become one of the first journalists to interview the Sex Pistols, an edgy, streetwise new ensemble who—unthinkably—dismissed the Stones as Establishment. What Ingham found when admitted to Keith Richards's lair only seemed to confirm this idea of artists too drugged up to relate or care. Although he tried to convey this in his copy, he found all drug references were sub-edited out. In February 2007, he took the opportunity on his website to revisit his experience and tell the unexpurgated truth.

April 29, 1976. Frankfurt, Germany: when I meet Dwayne he is busy crumbling golden-coloured hash from a thumb-sized block into a small, functional pipe. Like almost everyone in the first 30 feet of audience Dwayne is American and like them he wears an embroidered denim shirt covered with badges of his favourite groups, as though this hip uniform will offset his very short hair. Dwayne and his buddies are stationed at a local US Air Force base. Which one Dwayne won't say, because what he is doing is not only illegal but can get him court martialled. But hey!—we're about to see The Rolling Stones!

Dwayne is from a no-nothing town where he'd be today if he hadn't been drafted. Fortunately, the Viet Nam War is over—his older brother went and a shadow came back, eyes permanently full of tracers and incomings. Not that Dwayne has avoided carnage—he worked at the local munitions factory and one day a building blew sky high and to get out he had to scramble over some people who weren't so lucky. But in 1976 military service means a career opportunity instead of a place where every step really is a dance with Mr. D and not an inane lyric.

Of course Dwayne's favourite Stone is Keith. He is: The Riff, The Rhythm, The Rebel without Rules. Dwayne looks at me with eyes that have seen death and as the sweet Moroccan smoke pours from his lungs he says, "Hell I'm here for the same reason you are, right? Because they're the greatest rock and roll band in the world."

When we enter journalist Charles Shaar Murray's hotel room he is gluing together a generous joint. The contents of the mini-bar crowd a small round table and he gestures to the bottles in invitation. "We're on the road with The Rolling Stones!" Charles is doing the natural thing; the Stones' reputation is an undertow pulling us from the shores of sobriety, but he is willing to help us past the shallows and reefs to the outer depths because he is also playing that rockcrit game: I can get drugged up, hang with the stars, be a Rebel without Rules, and still write a better story than you.

We drain the bottles and smoke the joints. Our Stones-view is clear: Keith is the world's most elegantly wasted human being—some of us even dress like we raided his laundry basket. Mick is a social-climbing hypocrite. The new album Black and Blue is the work of an oldies band—Charles has just mauled it in print. But that's OK, because they're The Rolling Stones. "We" are the UK's rock critics, the elite with Born To Analyse Rock & Roll tattooed on our arms. We sneer at hacks like those from the two London papers the Evening Standard and Evening News, who have been promised yet-to-happen interviews with Jagger and relentlessly shadow each other, neither wanting the other to get the scoop. We will get the story just by swimming in the depths.

Shortly after a purple scarf is placed on the drum podium the lights go down and the band walks out. A spot picks out Keith as he cranks up the intro to "Honky Tonk Women" and then BLAM! It's loud, it's awesome, it's the Greatest Rock and Roll Band In The World!

The band stands still, working the music, leaving Jagger out front to pout and swagger, shimmy and blow kisses and do all those Jagger things. The stage is a masterpiece in white, which the band slowly starts to use in their various stage roles of running, jumping, standing still. The sound is dreadful, at first all rhythm, then painful slabs of trebly guitar. Jagger works really hard at being Jagger, interspersed with showbiz *shtick* that we've never before seen in rock and roll: manhandling a dragon, fighting a huge blow-up penis that half-heartedly erupts from the stage floor, swinging on a rope. It's ok, but it doesn't look cool until you see it frozen in photos. Do the Stones think that playing the world's most dangerous music is no longer enough?

The old hits remind us why we're alive; the new, ordinary songs from *Black and Blue* pull us back from Olympus. Jagger talks to us, prods us— "C'mon Frankfurt!"—trying to find the magic thread in an off night, but he does it using a preposterous Negro accent and the unwanted thought creeps into view that, really, the singer is a bit of a tosser.

They end with the crowd pleasers of "Jumping Jack Flash" and "Street Fighting Man," played fast and messy. Then, in the midst of the noise is a huge out of tune twang and Keith is . . . let Charlie Murray describe it: "You know the riffs: that when Keith Richard comes into the room rock and roll walks in the door. Yeah, well rock and roll just fell on its arse." Mick looks back and with an *"oh dear"* expression minces over, swooping on the move to pick up the dropped plectrum and hand it to Keith, who is sitting with splayed legs, hammering away with his fingers.

We are ushered into Keith and Ron's suite—large, high-ceilinged, matching bodyguards at the door. In the centre an open flight case holds two Fender amplifiers. A cassette deck on top of one playing Furry Lewis, Robert Johnson, Burning Spear. In a corner Ron lounges on an ornate couch. Against the wall on the other side Keith holds court with a group of journalists and I kneel on the floor directly to his right. The chair looks like a throne and he's draped over it like discarded clothes, holding in his right hand a foot long slab of turquoise, flat on the upper surface and jagged on the underside. If he puts it down it will tip over and spill the contents of the flat side, which he's not going to because it holds what looks like a Himalayan range of cocaine. It's a dull, flat white powder—pharmaceutical cocaine, almost impossible to get, manufactured just down the autobahn in the Swiss laboratories of Merck AG.

While he talks he twirls a small square of neatly cut cardboard, using it to cut fastidious lines out from the mountain range and then, using a silver tube on a silver chain around his neck, casually snort them up between sentences. We're there for 30?, 45?, 90? minutes. In this room someone has pushed Time's pause button. So ask a question; Keith will answer.

"Too much technology makes it more and more difficult to record rock and roll properly <*snff!*> In Russia they spend so many rubles on black market records and there's a very big scene in South America but when you try to do a tour there's so many problems <*snff!*> I miss singles but there's not a singles market anymore <*snff!*> We never sat down to write singles, we sat down to write songs <*slice, chop, shape*> I never listen to white bands because white drummers don't swing, except for Charlie Watts."

While Keith talks the mountain range in his hand becomes a mountain, a hill, a bump, a dusty memory. Nothing seems to change: his speech remains slow and relaxed, his body flops like tomorrow's washing and he sounds coherent. Only the half-baked thinking betrays him. And just when you think, God he's boring, he'll say:

"I was reading a history of Bill Broonzy nicked from Hendon Library the other day and there was a little bit there where he said that if he were to put a band together again he'd have pot smokers instead of drinkers. They don't forget their notes and they're on time."

Suddenly there's a frisson of excitement. Another pile of cocaine is on the slab, Swiss Alps–sized this time (an appropriate metaphor given the persistent rumour that every six months he gets his blood changed there), and he's neatly parcelling out eight even lines. And there are eight people around him . . . Keith is going to get us high! Now if there's one immutable truth in this palace of self-centredness it's that Keith Richards is not going to share his drugs with a bunch of journalists and sure enough, as he <snff!> continues to talk he <snff!> casually snorts <snff!> all eight lines.

Charles ambles over, kneels on the floor and licks Rizzlas. Naturally, Keith chats to his new friend until Ron walks over to hold a card in front of Keith, on which is scrawled: "You're talking to Charles Shaar Murray."

With a show of boneyard teeth Keith challenges, "Your review was rubbish."

Charles calmly rubs thick crumbs of black hashish into the waiting Silk Cut. "I stand by what I wrote."

"You need to hear it again."

"That's ok, most of my friends think it's awful as well."

"You need to widen your circle of friends."

It's bizarre to watch this schoolboy bickering—a rock god trading insults with a critic. As if our opinions *mattered*.

Charles has a smoke and passes it to Keith. When he hands it to me it's a roach. Keith is defending *Black and Blue*, but no explanation can redeem it. Indeed, the story that it was assembled during 1974 and 1975 as an audition for guitarists to replace Mick Taylor damns it further. It's just released and it's already over a year old—rock and roll is about next week. Tellingly, the cover photo is by a celebrity snapper-du-jour, the first time the Stones have followed fashion instead of leading it.

For some months I have been following four urchins busy working out what rock and roll in the Seventies should sound like and this seems the right time to speak up. "Keith, there's a band in London called the Sex Pistols." He looks bored. "They think you're old and should stop playing and get out of the way." He jerks forward, ultrasheen eyes glaring and just below the surface a volcano is erupting.

"Just let them try," he snarls, jabbing the joint at me. "We're the Rolling Stones. No-one tells us what to do. We'll stop when we feel like it." Emotion spent, he sinks back into his throne, realises he's holding a roach and passes it to me.

Indefinably, a wave of charisma washes through the room. In the doorway stands Mick Jagger. He is stationary, hands on narrow hips, head

slightly tilted and looking up, the King ready to acknowledge our wor-
ship. Only everyone looks up, thinks, "Oh right, Mick," and goes back to
what they're doing. His shoulders slump and he stalks over to the couch.
No one goes over to him. In our journalistic japery we've assigned them
roles like some cliché vaudeville gang; one critic had said earlier, "Who
gives a shit what Mick Jagger thinks about these days?", and it seems to
be true.

But we do care what Keith thinks and as he tells us he wipes his nose
with a finger and scrapes it off on his trouser leg. A foot from my eyes,
stuck to the corduroy, is a thick line of cocaine mixed with a little snot
and for a mad punk minute I think of leaning forward and with a quick
"Excuse me Keith," snorting it. But manners prevail and I wonder how
much more pharmaceutical-grade powder is lodged undissolved in his
nose.

Charles is now on the couch sharing a joint with Ron while Mick
broods next to them. Cutting through their talk come the distinct Jagger
tones, now clothed in Cockney, "I fort your review was blaahdy stoopid."
Charles ignores him and Mick repeats himself. Same result. Mick sulks,
then gets up and talks to a mountainesque heavy, who in turn talks to a
record company man and then it is announced: we must leave. Charles
is now building joint number four and continues work while we're shep-
herded out. Keith follows.

"Jagger," he sneers with contempt, "wants to go over a few songs and
change things around. But later on we'll go up to Billy's room. There's
going to be a party."

He waits and chats while the joint is finished and the touch paper lit.
Charles savours his work with a connoisseur's appreciation, watching the
smoke exhalations, small-talking to Keith, having another draw, finally
handing it to Keith, who opens the door, backs through it and with a
cheery "See you later," waves the incriminating hand and shuts the door.

Three weeks later, the Stones start their first English tour since 1973.
Driving to London after a show in Stafford, Keith drives his Bentley off
the road. As the press jubilantly report, the police search his car, find "a

substance," arrest and then release him on bail while forensics determine what it, "obviously a drug" according to the police, might be.

Their canter into London for six nights at Earls Court triggers press adulation. Hold the front page—MICK IS A GODFATHER! MICK MEETS PRINCESS MARGARET! Every night sees a private party, from pubs to Sothebys. And Ron Wood has his salary held while Deltapad, a management company, sues Promotone Productions over causing Ron to breach contract by playing with friends. A few miles away in a crummy club, fifty people watch a scrappy group called the Sex Pistols work on a sound to change the world.

6 |

NO ONE SHOT KR: KEITH RICHARDS 1980

KRIS NEEDS | 1980

This interview with Richards was conducted at a point between the negligible but high-charting *Emotional Rescue* and *Tattoo You*, which though mostly composed of dolled-up discards would transpire to be the final landmark Rolling Stones album. Already perceived by many as over-the-hill or even betrayers of a generation's ideals, the Stones were assuming a curious simultaneous position of irrelevant and commercially colossal.

As such, this would be just about the final time Richards could command a cover of an alternative publication like *Zigzag*. Yet, even at this point, *Zigzag* would probably not have put Mick Jagger on its cover. The street cred Richards still retained derived partly from his outlaw image, which had been underlined by a 1977 Toronto drug bust that saw him theoretically face a life sentence for heroin trafficking. With his eventual suspended sentence partly dependent on cleaning up, a smack-free Richards was now at liberty to talk completely candidly about the drug for the first time.

When this piece first appeared, some columns were pasted in the incorrect order. The author has now corrected the resultant sequential mistakes so that more than three decades down the line the feature is appearing for the first time the way it was originally intended to be published.

Note: for "MacLagen" read "McLagan."

for "Pallenburg" read "Pallenberg."

One Saturday evening in 1963 an eight-year-old perched on a chair, peepers glued to a small wooden telly. Wheezing out of the tube was "Thank

Your Lucky Stars," the now-extinct weekly showcase for Pop Stars of the day. The wide-eyed Beatles rubbed Rickenbackers with heart-throbs like Cliff, Dusty and Pat Boone. Safe for kiddies.

This particular Saturday a new sensation came bursting through the cleancut cuties. Five shaggy unknowns called the Rolling Stones, ill-fitting suits a reluctant compromise, bowled on and savaged the nation's blood pressure with raw, wailing blues.

That was it. I was grabbed. Watched every TV appearance, devoured the records and sowed all the seeds of what I still believe as the Stones carved a chaotic swathe through convention and petty values. I didn't wear me cap to school cos I knew Brian Jones wouldn't and revelled in the effect liking the Stones had on Beatles-fan friends. Cheered 'em through the court cases and finally saw me first gig at the 1968 NME Poll-winners concert.

Gradually sheer fan-fixation grew into total addiction to the monumental music they steered us into the 70s with.

The pre-and-early-teen me thought Jagger was The Man. But by "Beggars Banquet" and "Let It Bleed" it'd dawned that the entire Stones thing now laid square on the spikey head of Keith Richards. If Charlie Watts was the engine room, Keith was the machine and its inventor, whipping up the body-riffs with that churning guitar.

Amidst all the gloss and pompous irrelevance of the early 70s, here was this geezer who didn't care so long as he could play and live the way he wanted.

I saw him persecuted and prosecuted as they tried to do a Brian Jones and batter him into the ground with litigation. Doing a Houdini out of all that by cleaning up the bad eggs, Richards then found himself taking the Stones through a flakbarrage of punk (Ironic seeing's a lot of 'em merely took old Stones blueprints and speeded 'em up!).

The Stones were charged with everything—irrelevance, old age, being jet-setting tax exiles, dinosaurs . . . dirt. But the records still sold, even though some of the recent stuff ain't matched up to Stones-scratch— blame that on pressures and growing apart as Keith Richards fights to get it down fast and out, the feeling intact (with ballsups), while Mick Jagger polishes away. Compromise can stifle and it riddled "Emotional Rescue," but they can still shine (and I know who's on *that* particular case).

This interview took years to come and was in reach for months before Keith was in the right place and right mind. He's really gone off interviews, you see.

We met at his hotel but had to go to the Stones office in Chelsea—a ten-minute drive . . .

"Oops, I'm going the wrong way," remarks Mr Richards. "I'll have to do a U-turn!" The big blue Rent-A-Merc curves across three lanes and he blows kisses at the surprised motorists going home from work.

We end up talking for nearly three hours. Keith would spout about anything in his slow, deliberate, laugh-peppered croak. He talked a bit like his driving, going where the bourbon-fuelled thought patterns took him.

The 1980 model Keith Richards is devoid of Rock Star flash, maturing like a caring, kindly old blues musician. But he still possesses an indefinable swagger that makes any of the preening idiots that still profess to be R 'n' R stars look the pathetic buffoons they really are. In a grey RAF sweater too!

Talk kicks off: Jack Daniels in hands and my fags going fast. The ailing Music Biz and its Major companies provides a jumping off point.

KR: . . . I think they're squealing like fat pigs—there weren't as much in the trough this year as they expected. No way is the record business declining, it just ain't growing as fast as they'd all got used to expecting. You know—30 per cent more in America almost every year for the last few years. Suddenly they only get 20 per cent more so they start squealing and start axing everybody and giving the artists a hard time. "Aw, I was going to buy a new Rolls Royce this year and now I can't afford it because we're only 20 per cent up and not 30 per cent up on business," and they start screaming "Recession!" use that as an excuse, come down heavy on the musicians.

ZZ: It hasn't really hit you lot though, has it?
KR: No, since we have our own label they turn round and think "oh you've got a label, you're one of us." Bullshit, man! We're not. We're just gonna do what we do anyway. It don't affect us that much, at least not noticeably. We're still gonna try and get this label off the ground slowly. Apart from just ourselves, Peter Tosh has done real well, much better than anyone expected . . . he's just broken in South America real big. He did these

big festivals down there and suddenly we're getting this demand for Peter Tosh records and we ain't got 'em! Factory didn't press enough.

ZZ: Anyone else coming out?
KR: Yeah . . . Earl McGrath, who's been running the label for us found this good white kid from New York called Jim Carroll. I did a couple of numbers with him in New York but I was drunk so "yeah alright!" Actually Mick was supposed to join me but he chickened out at the last minute. Cunt. That album should be out soon. We haven't got enough staff to work on more than one album at a time, so they're waiting until they don't have to do as much work on "Emotional Rescue" or whatever, and when that's over they'll put out Jim Carroll's album. I heard it a couple of times—he's good, and he gets better cos he cut the album once a couple of years ago, and I said you should do some gigs for a year and think about it again. So they recut it after a year of working, and it's a good record. It's a fairly basic sound, he uses his voice kinda like Lou Reed, almost half-talking. He'd written a couple of books before he started writing songs so there's some good lyrics.

ZZ: And you've got another Stones album coming from the "Emotional Rescue" sessions, you said earlier.
KR: Yeah, they sent me six C90 cassettes full of stuff, not all finished, but ideas for songs, a few demos, here and there and a surprising amount of finished stuff, a lot of instrumentals. Some of the stuff went back into the Mid-70s, stuff with Billy Preston just jamming, riffs . . . but there's an album there, although we'll probably put a basic album together and see what we need to finish it off. Then we might go in and record for a couple of weeks to cut a couple of new ones, to add.

ZZ. When "Emotional Rescue" came out there were a lot of disgruntled "oh it's taken them two years to do this"—type criticisms.
KR: They're quite right in a way. Having so much stuff, we've just had songs coming out of our ears lately. Also you do write quite a lot of songs in two years—try 'em out. Some songs actually take a couple of years to get out of the mind and onto tape. You try it three or four different ways

over a few months and it doesn't quite work, and then one day later some-one says, "remember that one?" and you remember it slightly differently and you get it in one, things like that.

ZZ: So were you happy with what eventually came out?
KR: Yeah, I mean it's almost as bad as not having enough—not quite, that's the worst feeling (laughs)—but having a lot it takes so long cos you've gotta listen to everything you've got and that takes up a load of time because you've got so much stuff. Then you cut that down to a short list, eventually get it down to album length as far as songs go, and then start editing them down, cos some are too long. That album's not by any means the best of the stuff that we did, not like, "that was the best and this album's the second best of what we've got." It's just, up to a point, what was ready and what we could finish in time, because it had to be ready by March or April or whatever it was.

Keith's track, "All about You" was unanimously lambasted when "Emotional Rescue" came out, but it stands out as one of the moments of real emotion on the record. Unfortunately it seems that Mick Jagger has slipped to trotting out mainly superficial parodies of himself or other artists (the Bee Gees on the title track, boozy punk on "Where the Boys Go", etc.). Meanwhile Keith's contributions can be traced through the years as sources of genuine raw feeling: "You Got the Silver" ("Let It Bleed"), his strained attack on "Happy" ("Exile"), the pained "Comin' Down Again" ("Goats Head Soup"), the stumbling "Harder They Come," "Run Rudolph Run," most recently "All About You." Though the guitar never falters, the voice cracks, but it's from the heart not the wallet or the ego. "All about You" is an aching but bitter love song, Keith slurring and whining a put-down. But any stereotyped sexist jibes are dispelled by the last line's, "how come I'm still in love with you." A million miles more real than "she might be the alien."

ZZ: "All about You" is my personal favourite.
KR: (Seeming a mite taken aback) Ah good . . . hur! (short laugh). I enjoyed doing it. That was another of them songs which must've been around for

three years, maybe even a bit more. I wrote it in some soundcheck, Charlie was keeping time. I was convinced myself because it came so easy, the actual basic song—"this is someone else's song and I can't remember what it is." For ages I was hawking this tape and saying "who's is this" and they go, "uh hold on . . . um . . ." Nobody could put their fingers on it so after three years I thought, "well . . . I must have written it!" So I went ahead and finished the lyrics and that.

ZZ: It sounds like you sat there at the piano when everybody had gone home and plonked it out then added the horns and stuff later. . .
KR: When we eventually cut the track and put the horns on it last year I still wasn't entirely convinced exactly how it should go, so I had the track and everybody was saying, "you've got a song to put on it then we should put it on the album." But I still hadn't written it. Then, as you said, everybody went home and I sat down by the microphone and started it on the spot. [I] hadn't written anything for it, I just started doing it and after two or three hours started to take shape. I put harmonies on it . . . although when I was doing it I still wasn't thinking necessarily of me singing it, I was just sort of writing it and doing it to keep it for myself to remember how it went, and to play it to Mick if he wanted to do it. But when it was finished everyone said it should stay like that so I said fine, okay.

ZZ: You sound pissed!
KR: . . . (chuckles) yeah. I didn't try to clean it up, if I'd tried to change it I'd have probably screwed it up. I like it as it is.

ZZ:. I read about some conflict between you wanting a raw sound on the album and Mick wanting to clean it all up . . .
KR: Well . . . I always get a bit obstinate, "specially towards him when I think "'Christ, we've been working on this thing nearly two years and if I don't watch it it's not gonna come out unless I start kicking the fuckin' walls down and stuff.'" But that happens. with every album . . . (laughs). You ain't gonna get through two years in the studio without somebody getting shirty.

ZZ: What tracks did you have most to do with on that album then?
KR: Er . . . Eventually all of 'em, but I had more to do with . . . obviously "All about You," "She's So Cold," "Let Me Go" . . . Fffff . . . gimme some tracks, what else is on there?

ZZ: "Where the Boys Go"?
KR: "Where the Boys Go," yeah. That was a real band effort, it was Mick's song, and "Summer Romance," but we'd played 'em a lot. Pretty much everybody was into those. "Indian Girl" was Mick cos I just played piano on that. I enjoyed doing something different. "Send It to Me" and "Emotional Rescue" are both Mick's songs but we all worked on the tracks.

ZZ: I thought "Send It to Me" was pretty lightweight when you consider the Stones' deep immersion in reggae (and Keith playing so well on corkers like "Shine Eye").
KR: There you get on another of my beefs on the making of this album: alright you got ten tracks, but it's the first one in two years and I thought "Emotional Rescue" and "Send It to Me" were just a little too similar—not necessarily musically, just in the sound—that mid-tempo sort of . . . I just thought we were giving a lot of plastic vinyl over to a very similar sound and I was saying, "You should have one or the other of those two—then you could put a couple of other tracks on, couple of other rockers that we had almost ready. But I gave that one up: 'Cos originally "Dance" had a whole vocal thing, it was swamped with vocals. Mick had decided he'd got to write this song to this track. He did a lot of work on it and he did a good job, but it *totally* nullified the track. I said "let's make it an instru[mental', to which he replied,] 'I can't waste time on an album with only ten tracks and instrumentals' . . . instrumentals have got a dirty name. Everyone thinks it's just a filler, but some of the best rock 'n' roll records I can remember are instrumentals—Johnny and the Hurricanes, the Ventures, Bill Black's Combo . . . instrumentals used to be a regular part of your diet. *We* used to put out instrumentals from the very first album —"'Now I've Got a Witness'"—just let a band have a blow once in a while. Sometimes you can screw a track up by putting a vocal on it, you lose some of its impact cos it's neither a song and it's no longer an instrumental.

ZZ: Also I heard Bill left for a couple of months while it was being done.
KR: I dunno. He said something about retiring to somebody and then he got a new manager, but Bill, as far back as I can remember, is never there when we finish an album. For a start there's too many people in the control room . . . we play for months and do it, and then he leaves it to us.

ZZ: Do you wanna talk about any of the new songs?
KR: There's so many. I'm still trying to sort 'em out into tracks that are finished—there's a few that are mixed and done—then there's some which are good songs where the ideas are pretty much there but we need to recut 'em. Some have no lyrics yet, people humming away over the top of the track or the drums come in halfway through cos we started it when Charlie was in the bog, all those sort of things. There's some stuff I've totally forgotten about.

ZZ: You played on Ian MacLagen's album recently, didn't you?
KR: Yeah . . . I was on "Truly" and a recut of a song on Ronnie's first album ("Mystifies Me"). We did it at the end of the Barbarians tour.

ZZ: Another one—that Black Uhuru single.
KR: Yeah. "Shine Eye." That was those sessions I did with Sly and Robbie. It was just a backing track when I did it, then somebody said it'd come out with Black Uhuru singing on it.

That was one of the best things I did, to hang about in Jamaica after we'd done "Goat's Head Soup." I stayed there for nearly a year. I don't get down to Jamaica as much as I'd like to—every time I go down there I have a great time with this little band of Rastas I've played with for years. Just drums and chanting. They really kept me at it.

ZZ: Are you itching to get back on the road again?
KR: Yeah, I am a bit. I thought when we finished this last album that we'd get on the road now, but now I've sort of gotten over that and got used to the idea . . . I'm into finishing this other one, making it as good as we can, at the same time trying to set up some gigs, not waiting till we finish the album again before we think of what we're gonna do, but try and

work it so we've got something to do when we finish the album. I wanna get them on the road because, Mick and me have been playing one way or another—working on this album—but you forget we haven't played together with the other guys since we stopped cutting this time last year. It's a year since we even played together! So, get this one done as efficiently and quickly as possible (laughs) . . .

I know I wanna tour Europe. I can't see that until about March or April cos the weather screws up tours. In the winter you can't ever be sure of making a gig, not every one. There's a lot of places we ain't played for a long time. We want to play here but they just make it very difficult for us, y'know—taxes, there's a lot of red tape for us to play here. On top of that you don't get promoters and tour managers saying you gotta play England' cos you don't make any bread out of it. We don't expect to make any, but if they're not gonna make any bread they're not gonna push us to play England. We have to say, "look, we wanna play England, set it up." Otherwise it just doesn't appear on the list of things to do, which is dumb because there's no reason why we shouldn't play here more often.

ZZ: Yeah, cos I wondered how you still related to the kids here, the people who buy the records and all that.
KR: Well that's why I try and come back here as much as I can, just to see what's going on. Just soak it up and hand around, go and see bands . . .

ZZ: Do you talk much to the fans, geezers who come up to you? (IE: Is he really an untouchable 'cept for the jet set a la Rod Stewart, or—as I suspected anyway—did he still care what the kids thought, if they existed)
KR: Yeah. All different kinds, that's the whole thing innit? Half the time you find you're surrounded by middle-aged guys—"I saw you in the California Ballroom, Dunstable." You get surprising people coming up. Kids too. If I had longer time to spend I'd get into it a lot more.

ZZ: The Stones are often presented as a bit cut off.
KR: Remember who cut us off. It weren't us. We were kicked out. It was that or . . . they tried to put us in the can. They couldn't do that so they

decided to force us out economically, which they did. They just taxed the arse off us so we couldn't afford to keep the operation going unless we got out. Nobody's out through their own choice. I mean, we can live with it. By now, after travelling all these years, it doesn't really bother me where I am as long as I know I can come back occasionally. If we hadn't been kicked out I've no doubt we'd all still be here. It wasn't a matter of choice it was a matter of no choice. Get out. That was it. I mean, it's understandable—yeah the Stones are rich, tax exiles, blah, blah, blah, but it's only alright if you can live like that. Charlie came to live back in England, has for a year or two. If we hadn't been used to being on the road all the time I don't s'pose any of us would've wanted to go, wouldn't have gone. But we wouldn't have been able to keep the Stones together and stay in England, so it was a matter of having to get out. Now I've got used to it. No point in moaning, the only thing I wouldn't do is what they've tended to do over the last few years, bugger off to Los Angeles and live in that weird cut off climate out there. That Rod Stewart syndrome. I probably could've have got like that if they hadn't rubbed my nose in the shit so many times so that I never forgot the smell of it (laughs). In a way I don't really mind all the shit I've had to go through. At least it kept me in touch with reality when I could well have gone off the realms of . . . anywhere for a while! Eventually it got to a point where . . . if I was Joe Blow I probably could've stayed on dope forever as long as I could just sit in me little corner and have nothing to do but it had to reach that point in Canada where I thought, "I don't wanna be busted anymore, I don't wanna go through this shit anymore, knock it on the head," y' know.

(I'll just butt in 'ere. Before the interview, I made a mental note not to dive into the murky realms of Sunday paper "shocking Truth about Drug Fiend Keith" obsessions unless he brought this well-dredged skeleton up himself. So much has been written and speculated on the man's private life hobbies it would just seem predictable and brainless to try and prise more juice out of his weary and battered reputation. On the other hand, dope has been close to his heart for years. Now he's brought the subject up as the conversation gains momentum, so that's alright).

ZZ: You'll always be lumbered with the rock 'n' roll junkie chic number, won'tcha Keith?

(The man passes a hand over the thatch, which remains standing up in that position, lights another of my fags and the bourbon drawl creaks on.) KR: Yeah . . . I ain't gonna get rid of that one easy am I? (laughs) Maybe if I keep my nose clean as long as I kept it dirty they'll forget about it.

ZZ: Do you still get hassles about it?
KR: No . . . no. S'funny. (leans forward and whacks table) Touch wood! It's like they've said, "oh we've had a go at him he's done his bit, we'll leave him alone, he's kept his end up" . . . which I certainly didn't do for them. I did it for the Stones and for myself, the kids, whatever . . .

ZZ: They pry into your private life, put all the dirt in lights . . . then say you're a bad influence on the kids.
KR: Right. Not only would you get done for what you got done for, you get done for setting a bad example. If they hadn't have come smashing through my front door no-one would've known what example I was set-ting! They made it public, not me. I could understand it if I'd gone round saying, "oh yeah have a needle and a spoon, go off and have a good time, that's what it's all about." But I wasn't about to go round advertising it, they advertised it, then I had to pay for it. But fuck it, it happens to lots of people.

I don't know how much the powers that be all work together or com-municate with each other but it was like, how many more times would they have done me without it looking really like a bit of, "let's pick on him," y'know? I was an easy target. They knew I was on the stuff. They could've come round every day! That's why I eventually had to say "no more." I don't wanna see 'em anymore. I was seeing more of cops and lawyers than I was of anybody else. To my mind in the business of crime there's two people involved and that's the criminal and the cops. It's in both their interests to keep crime a business, otherwise they're both out of a job. So they're gonna look for it, they ain't gonna wait for it to 'appen.

ZZ: I just read Tony Sanchez' book . . .
KR: Ohh . . . Grimm's fairy stories, yeah! Unbelievable, that. When it got to the blood change bit I thought, "oh, here we go!" Marvellous. "Then he sprouted wings."

(The book, "Up And Down with the Rolling Stones"—so far published just in the States—consists of the "memoirs" of Keith's old bodyguard—right-handman Spanish Tony, who really lays on the heavy Dope exploits. Keith emerges as a hard, selfish doper who changes his blood more often than his socks. The gutter press has already serialised bits, Tone makes a packet. Keith dismisses it with a grin and a shrug. What's the point getting steamed up, launching injunctions and losing sleep. More "past acquaintances" have made more money out of the Stones than anyone else.)

KR: It wasn't him who wrote it, just some hack from Fleet Street. I'm the nasty, dirty, yellow schnide—oh nice, Tony, thanks, you're my friend! Actually it's quite clever. The actual incidents all happened, but then halfway through each chapter the description takes off into fantasy. This guy says Mick and I buried Brian, we made sure that nobody would ever see him again . . . the guy's gotta make an angle or how ye gonna sell the book? The Fleet Street hack thinks in terms of headlines. Spanish Tony had been with us for a long time, and a lot of the incidents in broad outline happened, but some of the details . . . I just gave up on the blood change! It's surprising the number of people believe all that. No doubt some people do it.

That one came about like this: I'd been in a clinic in Switzerland. Spanish Tony came to help us move into a house—I was still in the clinic. Tony: "What did they do to you up there?" Since I could hardly remember anyway and I'd only been in there about a week—I'd just crashed out virtually, went around puking in the ashtrays, ripping down the furniture and fittings for a couple of days and then I'd sort of got better, as usual. So I couldn't explain all this to Tony so I said, "ohh, they took all my blood out and gave me some fresh blood, all cleaned up." And slowly over the years that one sentence has become one huge . . . "oh the blood-change man," y'know? It's funny, one remark because you can't be bothered to explain and before you know it that's what you are. They probably wouldn't have sold any books without that.

ZZ: *What about Brian though? (In the book the hapless original Stones guitarist who died mysteriously in a swimming pool in 1969 is depicted as a drugged shell beaten into the ground by police oppression and paranoia fostered by heartless colleagues stealing his thunder. No-one will ever know the true circumstances of his death but it remains one of rock's biggest tragedies—and most ironic, seeing as he was on the way back up with a new band and healthier outlook.)*

KR: He was getting in a real state towards the end. That was the main reason he eventually left the band. He was just no longer in touch with anything. Although he was real strong in lots of ways, he just found his weakness that night, whatever happened. I still take all the stories from that night with a pinch of salt. I've no doubt it's the same with anybody when those things happen. There's a crowd of people, then suddenly there's nobody there. Instead of trying to help the guy, they think of their own skins and run. It's the same as what happened to Gram Parsons—someone gave him a turn-on, he passed out and they all got chicken and ran without even calling the ambulance or anything.

ZZ: Anyway from the morbid subjects . . .
KR: Industrial accidents . . . I dunno, either. In my own head I think about it and reach the same conclusion as last time, or I start to think about it again and get another idea on it. If you're not actually there when those things go down you can never say . . . I don't know what really went on that night at Brian's place. I know there was a lot of people there and suddenly there wasn't and that's about it. Yeah off that subject, right?

ZZ: Okay. Back to the album. Do you think people didn't bother to listen to "Emotional Rescue" properly before slagging it away?
KR: I dunno. I remember "Exile on Main Street" being slagged all over the place when it came out and then the SAME guys six years later holding it up and saying, "oh this new album's not as good as 'EXILE ON MAIN STREET,'" I read about two or three reviews when they come out and that's it.

It's a number one record, and it sold well. We've done what we intended to do—put out a record; after all, it's popular music. Unpopular music is about the worst thing you can make. I'd rather it be popular. So I'd rather use that criteria than two or three writers slagging it off.

ZZ: . . . They say the Stones don't stand up to the groups around today (you know who).

KR: (With a tinge of cold irritation) Well that's the bands they like. A lot of the bands they like don't mean fuckall anywhere to anybody. Whether they might in the future, I ain't slagging the bands. It all depends where you live. No doubt if we'd all stayed in England we'd be playing and doing things differently than the fact that we had to move out . . . you start picking up music from wherever you start to live or where you start to move around, y'know. A lot of it didn't turn out to be that different, whether I was in England or not. We've been playing reggae between ourselves and into reggae for over ten years, just about since it really started to emerge as its own form, So that kept us in touch with a lot of what's happening in England just by coincidence in a way. We just happened to be in Jamaica. And at that time soul music had taken a dive cos Disco had taken over. That was about the only black music we could find that was still fresh. They gave us something we used to get out of American black music. So it was just a natural substitute, in a way. At the same time a progression. But when we started listening to reggae *nobody* wanted to know, 'specially rock 'n' roll musicians—they couldn't understand it cos the beat's turned round. Now a lot of kids have grown up with it, on the street, there's a lot of Jamaicans here and they've brought their music with 'em. Now it's mixing up and you've got black guys coming out and playing supercharged rock. That's what's interesting, that's what keeps music going. If it just stayed the same as the three or four reviewers people read wanted it to stay, or just because it isn't like their pet favourite of the moment . . . people say the public's fickle but critics are ten times more fickle than the public!

ZZ: "Some Girls" got a favourable reception compared to "Emotional Rescue."

KR: Yeah, "Some Girls" . . . just because of the time it came out, etc etc, and the circumstances—very favourable reaction there, but you know that the next one's gonna get slagged, "oh they're just marking time again." But we've just done what we've always done, we'll go in and make a record. We'll go in and make it as good as we can in the period of time that we've got to make it in—which is a long time sometimes, but the bigger a band gets and the bigger its organisation gets, the longer everything takes. This is one thing I'm always fighting against, saying "it shouldn't be like that," but it's just a fact of life. The more people involved, the bigger the size of the record company, the bigger the importance . . . it just takes longer. I mean we made the first one in ten days, and several of the others too. But now it's A Rolling Stones Album and you feel you've gotta work and work on it, polish it up . . . and eventually you give in to that pressure a lot of the time, then afterwards you wish you'd just slammed it out like this rough mix on a cassette. I always try and push it. F'rinstance "Dance" on "Emotional Rescue," I wanted to keep instrumental. The track's dynamite by itself. Putting the vocal on it I felt—and I still feel in a way cos I've got the instrumental track at home—just detracted enough from the track for nobody to really listen to the vocals either. To me it was a kind of compromise. I'd have much rather kept the track as it was.

It became a compromise - do the vocals again but rewrite it. You win some, you give a little, you take a little, and I wanted "All about You" on there. But if I wanna listen to "Dance" I play the cassette of the track!

(I'm steadily building up this picture of the Stones at Work. Keith with his bits bartering with Jagger over what goes on "well if I can 'ave "All about You" and you take those ridiculous vocals off "Dance" you can keep "Emotional Rescue" AND "Send It to Me" on the album, 'ow's about that, Mick?" There's the nagging irritation that "Emotional Rescue" would've been a KILLER if Keith'd had his way more.)

KR: But it's always a compromise, because it's for a specific reason. You're saying this is it, but we all know there's lot of stuff left on the floor which a lot of people like as well. The trouble is you just can't please everybody with one album, it's not possible. Everybody wants to hear their idea of what the Stones is. There's the old-timers who remember from the year dot, then you've got the ones who believe we popped out of the ground with "Satisfaction," then there's the lot who joined us with "Beggars Banquet," the "Brown Sugar" lot. There's people who didn't get into us till the 70s. Everybody's got their own idea of what the Stones are about, which I suppose gets more and more confusing the longer you exist.

ZZ: It gets impossible to live up to all that.

KR: Well it gets impossible if you *try* and live up to it. We just do what we do and hope they like it. I mean usually you find more and more that people come up with interesting ideas on an album a year later. Me too. It'll take that long to get a little perspective on the last album. I'm too close to it right now. I've only just healed up from the last sessions! (laughs). Beat me own record—nine days on a stretch! Once you get in the Studio it doesn't really matter. It's timeless, like hibernation (giggle)! One tape op drops, you wake another one up!

ZZ: How dya keep awake then?
KR: I dunno, I can only do it when I'm working really. I've got a cycle of it by now, I get up and I'll be up for two or three days, but when you're working—I mean, Ronnie and I, when we were doing the '75 tour in the States at Madison Square Gardens—six nights in a row—we didn't sleep from the first gig till the end of the sixth one. I guess it was because we were stuck in the same place suddenly—same hotel, same theatre—and you feel like you're a record that's just got stuck! You don't think of sleeping. I don't remember the last three gigs. We'd just go off somewhere and turn up at the Garden for the next gig. God knows what we did, we just wandered about! We were well out of it I know that! It gets down to the point where you go round and bug people—you don't just go and visit someone, it's "let's find someone we really don't like and go round and bug 'em!" It's just so rare we find ourselves at the same place for a week in a tour. It's like a summer season at Great Yarmouth pier. (Keith goes on to bemoan the lack of decent venues in Britain, 'specially London. Obviously Hammersmith's a bit small and he don't wanna do the monstrous make-shift Earls Court. "London's eleven million people, you'd think they could rake up enough for a decent stadium, five thousand seater or something." He mentions the buzz he got when the Stones did some three thousand seaters in the States. "Kept us on our toes. It's a totally different way of playing."

"Put an ad in—anybody wanna bug a lotus-shaped stage. That's as far as I want to take *that* one!"

He's still with Anita Pallenburg "she's in good spirits nowadays, she's been through a lot of shit too." Son Marlon's at school—"he's too fuckin' bright, I'm trying to retard him"—and the Richards are on the move again cos their lease has run out.

ZZ: Thought any more about doing a solo album? What's happened to all these tracks you laid down in Canada?

KR: People always ask me cos they know I did those tracks. I mean I do 'em because the opportunities there in the studio. For some reason nobody else has turned up . . . at the time I do them I just do 'em. I'm still in the same state of mind as always, like Mick. I'm not interested in split-ting meself up to the point where I'm going "I'm going to keep this for me, that's a nice song I won't give it to the Stones": put yourself in that position it's stupid. One thing at a time—if I'm in the Stones I'm in the Stones and I make Stones records. If I'm not in the Stones, I'll think about doing my own record. I don't wanna split my loyalties.

ZZ; What about your solo single, "Run—Rudolph Run"?

KR: Oh yeah. I put that out, I just wanted to put out a Christmas record, why not? I had it around for a while—stick it out. And the other side "Harder They Come" is an even bigger jumble. It was like a quick snatch of tape we'd done between two other songs—did it during a break. But there's nothing on the actual record that was on the tape. Eventually we overdubbed it and wiped everything that was on there off. There's noth-ing left of the original tape. Ronnie ended up doing most of the drums on it. There's a couple of mistakes in it, I don't care. Some of the records I like best have got mistakes all over 'em. So we put it on the "B" side of "Rudolph."

ZZ: You've been involved with Ron Wood's solo projects.

KR: Yeah, he doesn't have the pressure like me 'n' Mick of having to write for the Stones. I mean, if he's got a good song we do it, some of his ideas and riffs and stuff we have used, that's fine, the pressure isn't on him to come up with stuff for the Stones and at the same time I know he enjoyed doing the first one and I enjoyed doing it with him ("I've Got My Own Album to Do"), but after that it's really been, "you owe the record com-pany an album." And that's what he's still doing. He's doing it cos he's got to now, not cos he wants to. It's ultimately his own fault in a way, he let himself get in that position, but Ronnie's not the sort of bloke to understand what they're all doing behind the scenes until they've got him tied up in a nice neat parcel and he's got to cough up with the songs and an album, which he'll enjoy doing while he's doing it but it's not something he would've done unless he'd had to do it. There's nothing worse than making an album just to fulfill a contract. That's like work! You stop playing and start working. I mean, we call it work but to meself, working . . . that's something I've tried to avoid all my life! (laughs) I've always tried to avoid feeling like I'm working anyway.

ZZ: You must be quite pleased how it turned out. There's lot of kids start playing the guitar for fun.
KR: Yeah right, that's what I thought when we had two gigs a week—oh great! No more schlepping around this artwork trying to get a job in an advertising agency and I chucked it. "I'm making a tenner a week, en 'I ? I'm alright! As long as I don't break strings or a valve goes in the amplifier I'll come out with a fiver at the end of the week. Be alright!" So it was always like that, they just added more zeroes on the end as it went on, but as far as I'm concerned it's the same attitude since we got our first gig— "fine, great, wow, I'm doing what I really wanna do, and they're paying me to do it!"

ZZ: What's your favourite thing that you've done? Is there any one thing you can pick out?
KR: Ohh wow . . . umm . . . that was easy to answer years ago when there wasn't so much to choose from or remember! Fairly broadly speaking, without picking out particular songs or anything, going backwards as albums go. I was very happy with the last one. I like it, and "Some Girls." More and more now I've been listening to "Black and Blue." Quite like some of that, considering especially that I know the ins 'n' outs of how it was made—that album was put together while auditioning guitar players, trying to find a new guy (to replace Mick Taylor), It's interesting for me to listen to "Black and Blue" because there's a different guitar player on virtually every track, Wayne Perkins, Harvey Mandel, other people came

round and played with us—even Jeff Beck, who I get on with now but at that time we were sort of glowering over the guitars.

ZZ: Another classic from 'round then was "Time Waits for No One" (more under-rated Stones emotion—this time on the passing of time—they ain't just a rock 'n' roll boogie squad, y'know. Mick Taylor's solo is a classic.)
KR: That was the last thing Mick Taylor did with us. Why don't Mick Taylor kick himself in the arse and realise what he is? He's a fuckin' great guitar player. If he'd stop pissing about trying to be a songwriter, a producer, a bandleader. At the time it was probably the right thing for him to do (leave the group), for him and us. But he hasn't done a thing since he left which he couldn't have done with us. It was his decision to leave. If he'd decided to stay he could still be with us now probably. What's he come up with? One album and a couple of gigs with Jack Bruce.

ZZ: His album was pure crap.
KR: That's what I mean. If only he'd realise what he is, a damn good guitar player. He should find somebody to play with. He's a bit lazy and while he's still got our royalties coming in he'll just indulge himself—produce, write, be the drummer . . . he's not a guy to make quick decisions and if you produce a record you've gotta be able to say even if you're wrong, "rub that out." That's why albums take so long these days. That's the other side of recording—the technology. Every time you do four more tracks you put another two months on the album. When we started if the record didn't sound right at the playback, tough shit because that was it! There was nothing else you could do!

ZZ: When you play live that's it too.
KR: Yeah, you've still gotta be able to do it, but it's the other way round. You write the song and record it then work out a way of doing it live. That's not the natural way to do it is play it live until you've got it honed down real good and THEN record it. But then nobody wants to hear you play material they don't know. That's the other thing with being in a band like the Stones—you've always got 'em down the front going "Satisfaction!," "Play with Fire"! Everybody's got their old favourites, they don't

wanna hear the new stuff—until it's out on the record and they've bought it and got it at home, then they wanna hear it. Wanna shot of this?

Keith offers his bottle, realises what he just said and adds into my recorder, "when I say shot of this, it's a drink!" We take a break to find a light switch.

ZZ: How's your guitar style going—still pretty much sticking to rhythm?
KR: Me 'n' Ronnie should play more together, but finishing the record has put the mockers on it recently. I enjoy playing with Ronnie a lot because . . . I think the main thing about making records is to produce a sound. I've never been that interested in being a guitar-player as such on my own, by myself. Sometimes I surprise meself, sometimes I disappoint myself. I'm more interested in what sound you can produce. This is why I've never really been interested in bands with only one guitar player, unless they've got something else going. Bass, drums 'n' guitar just ain't enough for me, there ain't enough to make a sound. Ronnie knows that and we can get into that a lot, especially if we play a lot together. But we're gonna have to do a bit of swotting up cos we ain't played lately!

ZZ: He mainly takes the lead lines, doesn't he?
KR: A lot of the time. Mainly, I guess, cos if I'd written the song then I'll get into knocking out the chords with Charlie so everyone can learn it, so by the time we've got it together the roles are pretty much fixed cos of that. Usually there's a lot more than two guitars on any of our records. I overdub, and usually you can't distinguish the overdub, you might only hear it as distinctive sound once or twice in the record—I'll just mesh it in with the other guitars and pull it out here and there. We're more interested in the sound—that's being made rather than who's playing what.

ZZ: Still got that guitar with the daggers and devils on it?
KR: That went up in flames. We had a fire in my house. Ronnie had that made for me, I used to use it a lot. It was a custom job, Zematis. There was a fire—didn't even get me trousers on, just jumped out the window! There were all these neighbours worried about the flames catching their houses. I was standing there—"wadya want me to do, pee on it? Forget it!"

Keith leafs through a recent *Zigzag* and notices the embarrassing American Heroin Scene overview, which I'd tried to keep out cos I thought it cheap, superficial and irresponsible (I was over-ruled). The first line went, "Heroin is not chic" and a quote about Stones drug references in songs is blown up as a headline. As Keith scans this gutter-scraping I cringe and foresee an abrupt termination of our conversation. He reads, grim and tight-lipped. Looks up . . .

KR: There's no way of writing about anything like that. It doesn't matter which way you angle it or state your case. Somebody's going to get turned on by it. Saying it's "not chic," that means it's chic. If you said it was chic . . . there's no way of writing about it because it's such an emotional and sensitive subject. The main thing is, why, especially in this business, do people go on to it in the first place? What are the pressures? Is it the one guy above you that you dig the way he plays. Charlie Parker has done more to turn lots of horn-players into junkies just because it happened to be known. If people had left him alone and nobody had known he was a junkie, maybe it would've been better. Why go searching out making sensational stories when you know that, just because the cops bust somebody if they're popular musicians or a superstar, there's gonna be somebody, no matter what that guy's going through himself, who's going to try and emulate it in some way? There's no right way of writing about heroin. There's plenty of wrong ways and it's difficult to know. Ever since I kicked it and cleaned up I've been bombarded with requests and offers to make a statement about this, or address judges—I've been asked to do lectures for judges! What would I say in front of 800 judges? The chance I've been waiting for—FUCK YOU! What else am I gonna say to them about dope? I'd just be embroiling myself and keeping myself in the same bag and attaching myself to the same thing that I'm trying to get rid of. Probably the only thing that might have any effect is, once everybody knows you're a junky then yeah, you are an example. They've made you one, whether you wanna be or not. So the only example I can be now is to say, yeah, I've done it for longer than most people and luckily came out the other end and I'm still here and I'm alright. Even if you're into it already and you need to kick it, at least you know, because I'm still 'ere. If you want to you can kick it and the sooner the better, darlin'. If there's one thing I can talk about more than Music and guitars, I can talk about dope (laughs). It's like guns. There's nothing wrong with the gun, it's the people who're on the trigger. Guns are an inanimate object, a Heroin needle's an inanimate object. It's what's done with it that's important. I think of all these people doing it and not even knowing what they're doing. That to me is the dumbest thing. At least by the time I got on it I knew as much as you can know. The one thing I've realised more than anything since I kicked it is that the criteria you use when you're on it is so distorted from what you'd use normally. I know the angle—waiting for the man, sitting in some goddam basement waiting for some creep to come, with four other guys snivelling, puking and retching around, and you're waiting for something to happen, and it's already been 24 hours and you're going into the worst. How does it feel, baby? You don't feel great. If I was Joe Blow maybe I'd still be on it, I dunno. I wouldn't take any notice of what I was saying if I was listening to it or anybody else, cos when you're on it you don't. The only thing I can say is, if you want to, it's no big deal to kick it. Everybody wants to make like, "oh, I've been to Hell and back." You've only been half-way, baby. Nobody's been there and back. Anyway, here I am. Ten years I did it and then I stopped and I'm still 'ere. I've still got two legs, two arms luckily and a bit of a head left, and that's about it. If examples count at all that's the only statement I can make: I'm still here.

In America it's even worse cos you have doctors coming on TV, discussions about the drug problem. These doctors—the more patients they get on methadone (heroin substitute), the bigger federal grant they get, so it's in their interest. They tell people who've been on it a few months, a year, "your body can never do without heroin, you'll need methadone forever." Bullshit. You can kick it in three fucking days. That's as long as it stays in ya. After that it's up to you. I might oversimplify it in saying that, but that's the way it's always hit me. It's a physical thing for me in almost every way. If I can kick those three days . . .

The other big problem is not cleaning them up, just sending 'em back. The same with me. The times I cleaned up and went back to exactly the same scene I was in before. What else you gonna do? You've been doing it for years. Everybody you know's doing it, you're kind of locked in. Unless you can break out of that circle afterwards—that's the next step.

You're back in that same room as five years before when you were on it and they're still calling you up, some people are coming around. It's a total drug, like total war. It takes over your whole life, every aspect of it eventually.

I used to clean up to do a tour, cos I just didn't want to be on the road and have to be hassled. But physically having to readjust when a tour just stops. (snaps fingers.) "*Now* what do I do?" I'm physically readjusting to then going home and living a quiet family life for two months. That'd do me in. Boredom, I'd go back on it. But if I had to work I'd clean up. But what a hassle! But when you're on it you'll go through any hassle to get it. "First get me the dope then I'll do what I have to do."

ZZ: I bet you had a never-ending stream of fawners who gave you stuff so they could boast they supplied Keith Richard.

KR: Oh sure. It was "great to see you man, I need it and you got it." You've got that to deal with as well, people stuffing it at ya. There's no way I could explain that in Aylesbury court. The things that are given to us. But I knew there was no point in trying to explain it to straight jury and a judge, even to my own lawyer. All the time, they think they're doing you a favour and probably at the time I thought so too. Some kid sends me an envelope with a quarter of an ounce of smack in it, y'know, "have a good time, Keith, thumbs up, yeah right, whaay." If you're on it you'll go "yeah right, whaay" back, cos you need it and you're not gonna say no.

But really nobody's doing anybody a favour.

Once I cleaned up and viewed it all from a bit of perspective . . . dealers would still be coming up to me. I'd dig just watching their faces. One thing that got me over that second period of cleaning up the environment was seeing these dealers' faces when they realised there was no sale! (laughs) It was a perverse way of going about it but it got me through the period.

The morbid mood lifts again as the talk drifts back, this time to the earliest days of the Stones. Keith's highly amused when I tell him that the Bricklayers' Arms, the pub off Wardour Street where the Stones rehearsed for their earliest gigs, is now a violin shop, and ("must've had some influence somewhere") retaliates with a tale about original pianist Ian Stewart forgetting the breaks cos he was eying the Soho strippers out the window. The laminated elbow-grasping Mike Yarwood doing his "Cor I could shaft that!" impersonation of Stewart is a far cry from the Devil's right-hand man of popular repute.

Keith described how he and Jagger initially developed their prolific songwriting partnership. I'd never heard this one before . . .

"I can thank Andrew Oldham (their first manager) for many things, but more than anything thank him for forcing me to sit down and write these horrendous songs, cos when you start it's always the worst. We'd farm them off to somebody else cos we didn't wanna know. Gene Pitney, Marianne Faithfull? Sure, have this one. You've gotta get all that shit outta your system before you can really start writing. At the time you write 'em you're even amazed you can write that. 'I'm just the guitar-player.' Hats off to Andrew for that one just for making me find out I could do it."

ZZ: Your first composition on record was "Tell Me," right?
KR: Yeah, and that was a demo. Andrew stuck it on the album because we needed another track. It was cut as a demo and Andrew was gonna try and flog it off to somebody. But we bunged it on. In America it was the first thing we did that got pulled out. Then we realised about songwriting. Apart from playing, that's the other thing I enjoy doing more than anything, trying to hammer out a new song.

Keith had to go so I trotted off, well pleased. He's a good geezer and he still cares. Who'll shoot KR? Not me.

7 |

TATTOO ME

GIL MARKLE | 1981

In July 1981, Keith Richards made a quick decision to locate the Rolling Stones' rehearsals for their *Tattoo You* tour at a sprawling, picturesque complex of recording studios located deep in the countryside of Massachusetts called Long View Farm. Studio owner Gil Markle made copious notes about Richards's inspection visit and the subsequent six-week stay of the Stones at the facility, eventually collating these into the book-length Internet monograph *Tattoo Me*. This entertaining cyber-volume has remained unpublished, save for the excerpts that follow here. Also unissued, incidentally, is the lengthy compilation of classic songs, some dating from the 1930s, that Markle found himself engineering for Richards who accompanied himself on piano. This widely bootlegged collection has come to be regarded as the definitive statement of the "solo" Richards.

"This is Cessna 75 X, intercom to base. 75 X, to base.

Tell Gil we have Keith plus four. Alan Dunn and wife, Jane Rose, and some knockout named Patti.

We're twenty miles out. Will call back over the Outer Marker.

Tell Gil to get the Cadillac cooling. We've got his man."

That was pilot Bob Adams. I switched off the scanner, grabbed my leather briefcase, and began the procedures for turning off the lights at our company headquarters at the Worcester Airport. Convenient, having your offices at the Airport, particularly if you have a twin-engine airplane. Long View shares its office space with the large student travel company

123

I started as a graduate student at Yale, and to which I have continued to devote myself over the years.

One bank of lights went out after another. Mailroom, sales cubicles, computer room, overseas offices, travel agency, financial offices, acceptance division, finally Gil's office. I scooped up my gin & tonic, locked the stainless steel double doors, and lurched out into the warm summer night, toward the car, the arrival gate, and my night's work.

It had been a long day—the day of the Keith Richards creeping delay.

No, Keith could not possibly make it at two. He had a dentist's appointment at two. Keith was late for his dentist's appointment. No, Keith did not leave for the airport directly from the dentist's; he had to visit a friend first, on the way out of the city. What friend, or for what purpose, unknown. It was now suppertime. Keith was still at the friend's house, expecting to leave soon for Teterboro, but hadn't left yet. Keith finally leaves for Teterboro, it's thought. No one knows for sure. Gil calls Teterboro; no Keith, although the plane's there and waiting. Gil calls Teterboro a half-hour later; still no Keith. Gil calls Teterboro a half-hour later still; now 8:30 PM, or thereabouts.

"Charlotte. I'm glad it's you this time. It's Gil Markle. Listen, I've got some high-level clients meeting 75 X-Ray, any minute now. I'm calling to see if anybody's showed up yet."

"Who this time, Gil?"

"Never mind, Charlotte, it doesn't matter. Should be a group of four or five, some English. Seen anybody like that, Charlotte? Charlotte? You there, Charlotte?"

I heard a loud noise, as though Charlotte had dropped the receiver onto the floor. Commotion. Charlotte's voice, high pitched and squeaking.

"Gil," she gasped into the phone. "You'll never guess who just walked in the door. Je-sus . . ."

"It's not Keith Richards by any chance, is it Charlotte?"

"Gil," she said with determination, "I hate you."

That's when I first knew we had our man. Also, that's when I first knew, or felt, that my meditation was projecting itself out into the world in conformity with the manifest wishes of others, and hence the Grand Design; I mean, that the Rolling Stones were coming to Long View Farm.

I looked at the clock, switched on the aircraft scanner, and went down to the bar for a gin & tonic.

I had now only another hour or so to wait.

Keith ambled out of the airplane, legs stiff from the 45 minute trip from Teterboro. He smiled. Keith looked like warm, friendly leather. Soft eyes.

"I'm Gil Markle, Keith. Welcome here."

"Hey, yeah. Nice, man. Nice trip."

"And I'm Alan Dunn, Gil. Sorry for the delay, but here we are."

I was then introduced to Jane Rose, who was talking to Keith and looking at him while shaking my hand, to Alan's comely wife Maureen, and to a smiling Patti Hansen, who looked me right in the eyes.

"Let's go," I said. "Black car, over there."

"We all going in one car?" Keith asked.

"Yes," I said. "We'll all fit." I made a mental note to investigate the purchase of a second black Cadillac. (Except they didn't build big ones anymore.) We squeezed into the car. Keith, Patti, and Jane Rose in the back seat; Alan Dunn and his wife up front; me driving.

"Car got a radio?" Keith shouted up.

I flipped to WAAF, The Police; then to WBCN, an old J. Geils cut; then to some Hartford station, Jerry Lee Lewis.

"Yeah," Keith erupted. "Yeah."

I turned up the volume, and by the end of the tune, which was "Personality," we were gliding up Stoddard Road, past the Long View pond and rowboat, and up the long gravel drive. The Farmhouse glistened white, and the enormous barn glowed cherry red under a dark but very starry summer's night sky. There was a new moon. It was silent, except for the crickets.

"Welcome to Long View, Keith," I said.

"Yeah," Keith replied. "Nice place."

We were scarcely inside the house, drinks ordered up but not yet in hand, when Alan Dunn motioned to me and took me aside, behind the fireplace. "Look," he said, "this has got to be quick tonight. I've got to be back in the city for a day's work tomorrow. So does Jane Rose. Keith's got to be in Rome before the weekend, and he's nowhere near ready to go. Just got evicted from his apartment, and there're a lot of loose ends to tie up. So give him a quick tour, and let's take a look at your plans for the loft. Don't get your hopes up. There's just not time for us to do much tonight."

"Here's your wine, Alan," I said. "And here's a screwdriver for Keith. Where'd he go?"

"Into the control room, I think. With Patti. Let's meet up in the loft in ten minutes, and you better call your pilots and tell them to be ready to depart Worcester for Teterboro at eleven, at the latest. Sorry it's got to be so rushed, but this was your idea, not mine."

"Ten minutes, Alan, in the loft."

It took us twenty minutes to get up there, not ten. Keith was in no hurry, and neither was I, if you want to know the truth. We hung out in the control room for a while, and I explained to him how we have tie lines between the two studios, and how we sometimes record over across the way, in the barn, but mix here in Control Room A. We then took a look at the bedrooms upstairs, the balcony overlooking our antique Steinway, and our collection of records.

"You keep all your fifties in one place, too," he remarked with apparent relief. "Easier that way, isn't it? That cassette deck work?"

"Sure does, Keith. What you got there?"

"Bunch of stuff all mixed up. Starts with some Buddy Holly, I think."

Keith slammed the cassette into the cassette deck, which hangs at eye level just as you enter the kitchen, and hit the "go" button.

"Select tape two on the pre-amp," I shouted over to him, which he did.

On came Buddy Holly, as expected. Keith turned it up, loud, very loud, until it began to distort the JBLs hanging overhead, then down just a notch. Maximum undistorted volume, that's called. He extended his glass to me, which now had only a bit of yellow left in it, way down at the bottom of the glass. He needed a refill.

"Good idea," I said. "Then let's go across the way and I'll show you what we have in mind for the stage."

"Yeah," Keith said. "Let's go over to the barn. Got to find Patti, though. Hold on a minute."

Patti materialized, and we headed out, through the library, under the moosehead, past the fish tank, and out onto the driveway.

"Look down there, Keith," I said. "Those lights down there are Stanley's, and he's our nearest neighbor. Farmer."

"Hope he likes rock 'n' roll," Keith laughed.

"He better by now," I said. "He's been hearing it from us for almost eight years now. Up these stairs here, and straight ahead."

Alan Dunn and Jane Rose were waiting for us in the loft, and had already been briefed by Geoff Myers, who was talking in an animated fashion, and moving his arms in wide arcs. He was explaining how deep the stage was going to be, and how strong. Keith listened for a moment, then walked over to one of the massive support beams, and kicked it. He looked up, whistled softly through his teeth, and spun around slowly, on his heel.

"Yeah," he said. "What's down there?"

"Come on, I'll show you," and I scrambled down the rickety ladder into what we now call the Keith Richards bedroom suite. Keith followed, with Jane Rose telling him to be careful.

"We don't really know how strong that thing is, now, do we? Gil, are you sure you need Keith down there? Why don't you just leave Keith up here and you can talk to us from down there. Keith, are you all right? Keith!"

"Figured we'd do a bedroom and living area down here," I said. "Right beside the chimney here. A place for people to hang out during the rehearsals, but still be out of the way. Look up there. The stage will be on the level of those transverse beams. You'll be able to see the whole thing from down here. We'll build staircases, fix it up nice. Cassette deck will be over there; speakers hanging so, on either side of the chimney. Should sound good down here."

Keith looked up at the chimney, then back at me. I saw a gleam in his eye. We had this one.

Keith and I made our way back up the ladder, Keith first, much to Jane Rose's pleasure and relief. Geoff Myers was jumping up and down on the plank floor, trying to make it move.

"See? And this is just one layer of two-inch pine on top of two-by-eights. Nothing compared to the strength of the stage, which will have three layers: beams of hemlock, pine sub-flooring, and oak finish. You could drive a truck up there and the floor wouldn't give a bit."

And that's all Keith needed to hear. He walked up to Geoff, and gave him a friendly slap on the lapel with the back of his hand.

"It won't bounce, right?"

"No bounce, Keith."

"We're coming, then. What a place I found!"

"We're what?" Alan interrupted.

"We're coming to this man's barn. Where's Mick now?"

"India, Keith."

"Let's go ring him. What a place I found!"

"How's your screwdriver, Keith?" I asked. It was plainly down to its ice cubes, and needed refreshing.

He looked at me, and at my screwdriver, which was still quite yellow, and full of Stoli.

I poured my glass into his; he laughed, and we walked back across the driveway to the Farmhouse. Keith and I were getting on just fine.

"Oh, Keith! Keith!" Jane Rose tends to shriek a bit when she talks. Her job is to take care of Mick Jagger and Keith Richards, and she's very protective of them.

"Oh, I knew I'd find you in here, in this ice-cold control room, talking to Greg and listening to records."

Keith hit the "mute" button on the console, lowering the volume level in the room.

"Gil's his name," he said.

"Gil, then. Listen, Keith-eee, we simply must begin to think about getting on our way. Greg, here—Gil, I mean—has those two pilots waiting inside that gorgeous airplane, and we simply can't keep them waiting, can we? You know what you have to do for tomorrow. There's the dentist again, and there's the Consulate, and there's Renaldo, in Rome, and we're way up here in goodness-knows-where. And I know Patti must get back to the city, too, mustn't you, dear, and I know . . ."

"We're not going anywhere," Keith said, returning the level of the studio monitors to full, undistorted blast.

"We're not going anywhere," he said again, I think, judging from the way his lips moved.

I smiled, having only moments ago taken Keith behind the moose head in the library with our two full glasses of Stoli and orange juice. "You don't have to go anywhere tonight, Keith," I had said. "It just starts to get fun here after supper. You can hang out, listen to some records, fool around, anything you want. The place is yours."

"Yeah," he muttered through a smile. "I don't have to go anywhere, do I?"

"No, Keith," I said, "you don't."

And he didn't go anywhere. Jane brought the word back outside to Alan, who was tired and just as happy to stay, and the pilots were released from any duty within Gil's gorgeous airplane. Keith stayed, and stayed largely inside the control room, playing and listening to music, for the better part of three days.

"Get Jane up," he said at one point. It's always dark in the control room, particularly when the black velvet curtains are pulled, and so it's difficult to tell what time it is, or whether it's night or day. I think it was about 5 AM. We had just gone through a half a dozen versions of Merle Haggard's "Sing Me Back Home," Keith singing and accompanying himself on the piano.

"Tell her to get Woody on the phone, and Bobby Keys, too."

"Keith," I asked, "do you know what time it is? I don't."

"Doesn't matter. I never get a chance to do this. You don't understand. I suppose you think it's all fun being me. Listen, I never get a chance to sing by myself like this—play the piano—without some bastard weirding out and asking me why I wasn't playing the guitar, and looking mean. People have their ideas about me. I bet you didn't think I could play the piano, did you? Or sing classics from the thirties. Well, I can, and I want to talk to Woody. He'll love it here. Where's Jane?"

"Upstairs, Keith, in the Crow."

"I'll go, Keith," volunteered Patti Hansen, and she slithered out the door and up the staircase to the bedroom we call the Crow. Muffled female voices indicated that Jane had not been sleeping all that soundly, if at all, and that she had some reservations about calling Woody and Bobby Keys.

"I know what you mean, Keith," I continued down below. "It's not all that great when you get what you want. Me, I've got a lot of things happening, but also a lot of screwed up relationships, like with my girlfriend, who's the mother of my kids."

"Me, too," Keith said, slapping his vest pocket and looking about for something he had obviously misplaced. "I did the same thing. Her name's Anita. Kid's Marlon."

"Here's what you're looking for," I said. "Use the razor in the editing block."

"People think I get my way a lot more than I do," Keith continued. "You don't know what it's like dealing with the people I have to deal with. If it wasn't for the music, I wouldn't be doing it."

Sniff!

"Let's do 'Dream' next, what d'ya think?"

"Let's do it, Keith. Gimme a minute, though. I want to put some two-inch tape on the big machine for this one. Something I want to check on the machine first, too."

"No hurry, man. No . . . hurry." Keith stretched out the "no's" until they wouldn't stretch any more, and addressed the mirror once again.

Sniff!

Patti Hansen leaned her full weight on the heavy studio door, opening it a crack and looking in on Keith and me.

"Look at the two of you. I mean, I can't leave the room for a minute. I need to talk to you, Gil. Come here, will you?"

"What's up, Patti?" I asked, a bit blinded once outside the door by the early morning light. "What's up?"

"You've got to invent some excuse, Jane says. He may never leave here if you don't. You don't know Keith. He likes it here, too much maybe. But he's got to be in Rome before next Monday to get his visa fixed. Jane's worried. Can't you say something about the plane, or something? Really, Gil, he may not ever leave here, at all."

Patti Hansen is a very beautiful woman, and it was clear that she was asking me to take action, too. Not just Jane.

"Something about the plane?" I asked. "Like there's bad weather coming in, and we'd better make a move soon."

"That would be great," Patti said, eyes flashing.

"Not before the Everly Brothers' tune," I said, somewhat automatically. "He wants to do the Everly Brothers' tune, and he really should. That's next. Don't worry, Patti," I said. "He's really doing fine in there."

"O.K., Gil, that's all great. But what do you think, I mean, what should I tell Jane?"

"Tell her after the Everly Brothers' tune," I laughed.

"O.K., Gil," Patti said, smiling. "You know, you're not bad for forty-one. That's how old you are, right?"

"You read the article in the magazine in the plane?"

"You put it there for us to read."

"Yeah, I guess I did. Listen, don't worry about Keith. I'll get him out of here somehow. Just so long as it's not before we do the Everly Brothers' tune, O.K.?"

"O.K.," Patti said.

I was true to the promise I made to Patti Hansen, although it took me a day or two longer than expected to deliver.

"What d'ya think, Keith," I began. "We've been in here for days, it seems. I've got to do some things in Worcester. You've got to go to Rome. Why don't I call Bill Mahoney, the pilot, and get you and Patti out of here before the front comes through?"

There really was a lot of bad weather on the way, and it's best not to fool around with that unless you really have to.

"Sounds O.K. to me," Keith said. "Sounds O.K. to me. Either that or you've got to give me a job banging nails with those lads out in the barn."

Wouldn't that be something, I mused. Last remaining superstar guitarist knuckles down with North Brookfield country strong hands—building a Sound Stage for the use of his band, the Rolling Stones.

That didn't happen, of course. Instead, we called Mahoney and set up a departure out of Worcester for Teterboro at 11 AM the next morning. And I set about doing some rough mixes of the two-inch recording tape I'd made the night before. The piano demos I'd done with Keith. As luck would have it, our Chief Engineer, Jesse Henderson, had taken a week to do some engineering chores for Sha Na Na, in California. And so I had to engineer myself, leaving Reed Desplaines, Night Manager, to play assistant engineer—running back and forth to the tape library for more reels of virgin tape. This for studio buffs: we used three Neumann '87 microphones on the Steinway, which Pat Metheny left with us two years ago. The piano, I mean. Mikes in our top-secret positions. Another Neumann '87 on him, close up, with a pop filter; voice highly compressed using an Eleven-seventy-six limiter set at twelve-to-one. Finally, a good measure of live acoustic reverb on either side of his voice, in stereo. Lots of E.Q., on everything. I had only one shot at this, and I wanted it to be right the first time.

The live mix was great all by itself, and the best results of that extraordinary session were in fact recorded directly onto our Studer mastering deck, and not the 24-track. 30 ips; no noise reduction, very hot on AMPEX 456 tape.

"Listen to this one, Keith," I said, just before driving him to the airport.

I selected the live stereo tape of "The Nearness of You," a classic Hoagy Carmichael ballad dating from the late '30's. Keith Richards playing the Steinway, and singing, too.

"Far out, Gil. Voice sounds great. Sounds great."

"ZIP—BUZZ . . ." There was a loud, familiar noise on the tape.

"What the hell was that?" Keith asked, with a look of anguish on his face.

"Jane Rose taking a picture of you with her Polaroid camera," I replied.

"Bloody well ruins that take, didn't it?"

"No, Keith," I said. "I think I can razor it out later. We've got this tune about six times, anyway. So don't worry."

Recording enthusiasts will be interested to know that the eventual edits on these ten or so tunes—classic Keith Richards piano demos—took nearly two weeks' work. I found the time to do it only a month after the Stones had finally gone, and performed the edits on a 7½ ips dub inadvertently left behind at my house on Cape Cod. Editing at 7½ ips is no fun, as you may know. Several hundred cuts were required, since Keith never really bothered to begin or end any of the tunes. He'd just keep on playing, and singing, with me scrambling to keep tape on the tape machines, late at night in the A-Control Room at Long View Farm.

Studio A at Long View is the one people travel considerable distances to use, and I think you'd hear it said at the Farm that I can make it work pretty much as well as anybody can. Mixing tape is what I like to do. I can make really good, live, super-present mixes. That's what got me into all this, back in '72, when I was still teaching Philosophy at Clark. I figured I needed some time off to build a studio to make some mixes in. And that's how Long View came about.

So when I tell you that the live stereo tape of Keith Richards sounded good, you better believe me that it did.

We drove Keith Richards and Patti Hansen to the airport the next day. 300-foot overcast; visibility a quarter of a mile in rain and fog. Mahoney couldn't make it in, missing two instrument approaches in an attempt to land 75 X-Ray. So Randall Barbera, who works for me, as you may remember, offered to drive Keith and Patti over to Westfield in the Cadillac. Westfield was still operating, and only about 45 minutes away. They had a wonderful trip, I learned later. Cruising along on a light powdering, Stoli's and orange juice, and a fantastic compilation of fifties rock 'n' roll classics played at high volume on those wonderful-sounding Auratones mounted on the rear deck of the car. Pete Wolf of the J. Geils Band had left this particular cassette behind. By mistake, I'm sure, because it was a real beauty. "Earth Angel," "Good Golly, Miss Molly," "Tears on my Pillow," and songs like that.

"Take this and listen to it on the way to Westfield, Keith. Only remember it's not mine but Pete Wolf's, and he's certain to want it back."

"O.K." Keith said laughing. "I'll bring it back with me. See you."

"See you, Keith," I said.

"Bye, Gil," Patti said, and then they roared off.

And you take it from here, Pete, if you want that cassette back. He won't give it to me.

Let's all pause for a second and note that Keith Richards said "O.K. I'll bring it back with me." Meaning the cassette of course. Meaning also that he intended on coming back to Long View. That this gig was going to happen, after all. It was during Randall's trip to Westfield with Keith Richards that I figured it out all over again—that the Rolling Stones were coming to Long View Farm.

Maybe I'm just a bit slow, sometimes.

It must have been a new moon, or close to it, because the tide was way out, exposing an extra quarter mile of beach, just outside my old Coast Guard boathouse in Truro, on Cape Cod. It was a weekend, a Saturday, and the sun was directly overhead. I had just come down in the Twin, from Worcester.

"Gil, you look terrible."

"Thanks, Bill," I said. Bill's my brother, and had just rented the house up on the bluff for two weeks for himself, his wife, Viki, and his two kids. We were standing on the sandbar—halfway out in the ocean, it felt. Great for kids, let me tell you. Good for big people, too. Particularly somewhat burnt big people.

"I don't feel so good either, if you want to know the truth, Bill. I've been in the control room for three days with Keith Richards. That's what it does to you. Look. Notice the grey pallor to the skin, the bags under the eyes, and the ringing in the ears. That you can't hear—the ringing in the ears—but my ears are ringing, too."

"High volume levels?" my brother asked.

"Yup. Also lots of talk about rock 'n' roll. About other people—half of them dead now, or dying. Lives lost to rock 'n' roll. Decadent, tired stuff. Stayed awake all the time. It was sad in a way. Thrilling in a way. Just happened, you know. Haven't yet figured it out—what exactly happened, I mean. Looks like the Stones are coming to Long View, though. That much looks clear now."

"You just get here?" Bill asked.

"Just now. Haven't seen Nancy or the kids. They been here?"

"About an hour ago," Bill said. "Then she took off down that way with Abby and David. Some other guy with her, too. Don't know who. They all went down that way, towards Brush Hollow."

"Thanks, Bill," I said. I needed some exercise, to get the poisons out of my system. Better than jogging on the road anyhow, low tide was. And so I set off, running along easily on the salt flats, down past the lifeguards and the tourists, south along the beach to the place we call Brush Hollow, and which most new people or visitors call "the nude beach" at Truro.

It wasn't long before I could see them in the distance. That was Nancy, all right. Couldn't tell who it was with her, though. Except for the two little forms, which were almost certainly my kids.

I broke from a jog into a run. Nobody seemed to have any clothes on down there.

About a quarter of a mile away from Nancy—I could tell it was Nancy now, for sure—I see her walk up to where the blanket is, pin her little bathing suit on, and stalk off toward the right, up and over the dune, toward the path that leads through the Hollow and back to the road.

I'm really running now, pounding along at the water's edge, thinking I might still get down there before she disappears over the dune. No way, though. She disappears. Couldn't tell it was me, I figured. So I let off a bit of the steam, dropped back into an easy jog, and thought some thoughts about the Rolling Stones. Much of this book was conceptualized that way. Whenever I relaxed enough to let my mind roam a bit. Whenever I fantasized.

That, of course, is meditation. It's meditation in action; meditation in situation. The repetitiveness of your feet, slamming one after the other into the hard surface of sand, each making a sound like the sound before—like the sound after. It hypnotizes you, and for a second you forget yourself. That's the "window." The window on the future. The person you re-remember is a person with a game plan for tomorrow. A solution to the current dilemma. It's the window that makes the difference. "Zen and rock 'n' roll," if anyone asks you.

Today, running easily along the water's edge, feeling loose, and stronger with each step, it's Keith Richards I'm hearing in my head. It was the song we recorded the night before, or was it two nights before? I don't know. A country tune. Keith Richards singing a country tune with great pain in his voice—great expression. I made the tape play back in my head—something I wasn't able to do at all before turning thirty—and adjusted the speed so it would play along with the sound of my feet on the sand. Keith Richards, loud and live on the studio monitors at Long View Farm; me jogging along a Cape Cod beach under an August sun.

Another great meditation; take it from me. A meditation in situ, which is the best kind; ask any guru.

8 |

THE ROCK SURVIVOR

ROBIN EGGAR | 1983

Robin Eggar's 1983 chat with Richards was for the *Daily Mirror*. That this is a UK tabloid newspaper perhaps explains why the interview is so revealing about things that often get short shrift in the copy of music press journalists eager to assert Richards's edgy credentials, namely love and family.

He has old, old eyes. They have enjoyed great triumphs and indulged in worse squalor. They have seen everything, done everything, travelled to hell and back . . . and survived.

Keith Richards is just a few weeks short of his fortieth birthday. The haggard face is being held back from collapse by force of will.

He could be just another pathetic has-been old pop star junkie.

He chain smokes and tipples Jack Daniels as if it were tea. His voice is slurred, his thought processes appear to ramble.

He shows all the signs of the ex-drug addict searching fruitlessly to replace the one great love of his life—heroin.

But Keith Richards does have replacement loves. He has his band, the Rolling Stones; his fiancee, American model Patti Hansen, his parents and his children.

He also has a throaty, infectious laugh and a caustic wit which quickly slices through his apparent mumblings.

Keith Richards is very much more alive than he has been for the last 15 years.

He has survived everything twenty years at the top of the rock 'n' roll tree can throw at him. And he's proud of it.

Keith says: "I've never regretted going through heroin—especially coming out of it. It made me what I am today.

"I've been through the furnace and out the other side.

"Whether you've got millions or whether you've got nothing heroin is the great equaliser.

"I used to have to go down to Manhattan's lower East Side to score. It's as bad as it can be down there. I'd be carrying a shooter in my pocket.

"Nothing mattered, except getting the dope.

"You only get high the first few times, after that you just maintain the habit.

"The money, the whole way of life you go through to feed it, is so time-consuming and boring.

"But the money wasn't a waste. It was a necessity.

"I'm glad I got out of it," says Richards, draining his whisky glass. "Some of my best friends didn't. Some never will."

The six years since the Mounties entered his Toronto hotel room and arrested him on drugs charges have seen other crucial changes in Keith's lifestyle.

He split with his long-time girlfriend—and the mother of his two children—Anita Pallenberg.

The Rolling Stone who has always refused to gather any marital moss is finally getting married.

"I am going to marry Patti Hansen," he smiles mischievously, "But we've had Mick and Jerry up to here, so I want to let them get it over with first.

"I've only just had the engagement ring made. I'm doing this properly. I'm only doing it once. I'm really old-fashioned that way.

"I presented the ring on bended knee a month ago, in Paris at the Ritz hotel. It was fairly romantic, I can make anywhere romantic.

"Patti and I will have kids eventually. But we've got to find a suitable venue to get married first."

Richards' daughter Angela, 11, lives with her grandmother in England. Marlon, 14, lives in New York with Keith's father.

"The pair of them are terrible together. They go round the local Hell's Angels bars. My dad's got this protector, The Weasel. He's seven foot tall and makes sure they get home safely.

"Dad's 68 and he'd never been on a plane before last year. We only got together then. I hadn't seen him for twenty years.

"I left home 'cos we couldn't live together. After that he separated from my mum and, like a good boy, I took care of her.

"I'm real glad we're friends again. People need their families."

For two decades Richards' only real family has been the Rolling Stones. Like a repentant schoolboy he regrets the heroin days because he let down the band.

If they had ceased to exist back then, he probably would have, too.

"There was never a time when I wanted the Stones to end," he says. "There was for Charlie when his father died just before the 1981 American tour. He was griefed up. We made him keep going to help.

"He hasn't stopped drumming since. He gets better and better—it makes me sick. And Charlie just thinks he's a mediocre jazz drummer.

"We couldn't give Charlie 15 million dollars to continue if he didn't want to. If he stopped I'd stop too.

"But we continue because the Stones aren't as good as they could get. Maybe they never will be."

Richards is adamant that the Stones are still relevant and not just a bunch of ageing, rich rock stars.

"We have always been a mirror of society at the time. Mick is brilliant at articulating the disquiet people are thinking or feeling.

"The new *Under Cover* album has a political feel that dates back to the *Beggars Banquet* era.

"I'm not the person I was in the past. But people won't let me forget. 'He was the junkie. He's still the junkie, the pirate, the rebel, the meanie.'

"In my middle twenties I was confused by my image. I used to wake up in the morning and ask 'Who am I today?' 'Am I the dark side of the Stones mirror?'"

The whisky bottle is empty, the ashtrays full. Keith is still in control. And happy, too. The Stones are still rolling. While he is alive they always will.

"Please spell my name right. With an S," he asks, ancient eyes smiling. "Our manager took it off in the early days to sort of link me with Cliff and the Shads.

"When you're a nobody, that's not a bad deal. And we both survived.

"I know who Keith Richards is now."

9 |

GLIMMERINGS OF IMMORTALITY

BRUCE POLLOCK | 1986

That Keith Richards is a guitar icon and a rock god are givens. Less noted are his contributions to the repository of classic songs. While it is of course understood that he composes, less reflected upon is the fact that he and his collaborator Jagger were, along with John Lennon, Paul McCartney, and Bob Dylan, among the most important songwriters of the 1960s and hence among the most important songwriters of all time. This 1986 interview shines a spotlight on that important quadrant of Richards's talents.

Like a politician on the podium, whistlestopping across the boondocks on a flatbed, Keith Richards has his share of timeless bromides, comfortable answers his tongue slips into after years in the public eye. In the midst of a searing query, or a deft, seven-tiered multiple choice essay question, you can pick them off like sand fleas.

"My first job is to turn the band on."

"When we go into the studio we spend the first few hours just playing the Buddy Holly songbook."

"I have a good feeling about this new album . . ."

"People haven't covered our songs too much, but I take that as a compliment. You don't really hear versions of *Heartbreak Hotel* either. What it means is that your version is pretty much seen as the ultimate."

"More than half the people running record companies are just executives, guys who can sell a whole lot of baked beans. To them a record is just another unit. They couldn't care less about music."

The story about waking up in the middle of the night with the riff for *Satisfaction* is a chestnut, as is his well-documented affinity for the acoustic guitar. "I firmly believe that there ain't a good guitarist around who just plays electric guitar. You can do a lot of tricks on the electric, but as much as I love to play it, a guitarist can keep his chops together on an acoustic, where there's no tricks like sustain. It keeps your wrists and fingers strong. You can't fake it with feedback. You just have to play the thing."

Perhaps his opinion of heavy metal has also made the rounds. "I hate heavy metal," he said. "It just bores me to tears. It sounds like this plane we have in England, with fifteen engines on each wing. It was designed for fantasy. When they built it, it did a great job of charging down the runway, but it never took off."

Certainly you don't think his attitude about the new album, **Dirty Work**, is a freshly-minted burst of enthusiasm, prodded out of him by the reporter's perspicacity or intuition. "Instead of working old formulas here," I noted about the title cut, "it looks like you're adding a few new ones. It could be the sound for the Stones in the 90s." I was falling right into his trap, I sensed, buttering him up with an easy one, but how could I resist? He was such a friendly, elfin sort of guy, smiling at me like a rock 'n' roll Dudley Moore.

"My favorite theme at the moment is that after all these years, rather than marking time, the Rolling Stones are in the unique position of seeing if we can get this thing to grow with us. Rock 'n' roll is just about the same age we are, so nobody's really had the chance to take it this far, not as a band anyway. All of the kings are dead—Elvis, Buddy, Otis Redding. Maybe the most obvious example of how a guy can play a guitar in pretty much the same form as what rock 'n' roll is based on and make it grow up and mature in an interesting way, is Muddy Waters. So for the Stones one of the most interesting things is to see how rock 'n' roll grows up, and see if we can grow it up with us."

So how do you pierce this polished exterior? How do you mine new territory on the much-plowed fields of Rolling Stone history, myth and nuance? The answer proved simple, as obvious as the glimmer in Keith's eyes. So, fans of their rabble-rousing exploits, look elsewhere. Strings and picks fanatics, turn the page. For herein rhythm-cruncher supreme turns orator, nasty scourge of the earth becomes sage, as Keith agrees to expound at length on one of his most overlooked yet favorite subjects: songwriting. With a catalogue of million sellers as vast as it is unrelenting, surely the Stones' output ranks up there with the best that solid rock has produced. No need to give these monsters names, because for twenty years we've welcomed them into our kitchens and bedrooms and hot rods, one after another, chiseled gems of the form, consistently on the mark, lyrically compelling, absolutely rock 'n' roll.

"The hardest thing to write is a really good original rock 'n roll song," Keith said, "because the form is musically very limited. So much depends on the feel and the enthusiasm of the playing. The song is virtually almost an equal partner to the performance. Then there's that indefinable thing that makes rock 'n' roll what it is: that thing that somehow gets in there and nobody knows how."

As a songwriter, Keith Richards is first and foremost a guitarist. "To me songs come out of being a musician, playing. Personally, I cannot write to poetry, rhymed couplets and things like that. I can write a song out of a chord sequence, a riff, and eventually come up with lyrics to fit onto it, but the other way around, no way. The important thing to me is to sit down with an instrument. You might spend three, four hours going through the Buddy Holly songbook, and then out of nowhere there'll be a little crash, and there it goes. All it takes is a split second. It might be an accident, a mistake that sets you off. It's a matter of sitting down and playing, more than with any definite intention to write. All you've got to do is be receptive and recognize when it happens, because it can come from the weirdest angles. Rarely do I write a song totally by myself. Even if I actually do write it by myself, I always like to have someone around just playing along with me, saying, yeah, yeah. I'm a band man, a group man. I can't sit there alone in a room and say, it's songwriting time—ding, ding, ding."

In a very real sense, Keith views the songwriting experience as somewhat metaphysical, although he'd be the last to put such a label on it. "I never think I have to put anything down," he said. "I never care if I have it on tape, or if the tape runs out and the song disappears, because they all come back eventually. I've written songs and lost them and found them ten years later. Once it's there, it's there; it's just a matter of how long it takes before it comes back out again. I find the more I play, the more I'm into it, the more the songs pour out. I don't have a problem with being non-prolific. That's all psychosomatic. Music isn't something to think about, at least initially. Eventually it's got to cover the spectrum, but especially with rock 'n' roll, first it has to touch you somewhere else. It could be the groin; it could be the heart; it could the guts; it could be the toes. It'll get to the brain eventually. The last thing I'm worried about is the brain. You do enough thinking about everything else."

In the studio, Keith relies on the rest of the Stones for valued collaboration. "When we're doing an album, I come in with a handful of riffs and some songs. One or two will be fairly well-defined. Others it would be, this could be dynamite for the Stones, but I have to wait until I get them in the studio and all together in order to really find out. I can't take it any further by myself as a song or a structure or an idea until I've got their input on it. On *Dirty Work*, for instance, we had the hook. The bridge didn't come until we were in the studio trying out various ways of breaking it in the middle, trying to find something that wouldn't be too obvious. I decided, let's just go Jamaican and turn the beat, and suddenly everybody looks around and says, yeah. And that's the way a song is made. It's in the studio that you get those final things that give it something extra."

Songs can also die a death under the caustic glances of his bandmates. "If there's no kiss of life, there's nothing you can do," Keith said. "If everybody walks off to the toilet, then you know you've got to drop that one and go on to something else. But when you just sort of pick up your guitar when the studio is virtually empty, people are telling jokes in the back room or playing dominoes, and then within two or three minutes they drift back, they pick up their instruments and begin whacking away, you know they're into it.

"What a songwriter loves more than anything is a sequence that comes with a hook. Once you get that, you try to expand it. You've got a hook and the first verse, you start to think of the second verse, how to expand the idea. Or do you want to turn it around? Do you want to leave it ambiguous, or do you really want to make a certain kind of point? Bobby Womack and Don Covay have been writing songs even longer than I have. Ronnie has a great tape of them writing songs together one night, and it's ten minutes of chords and a first verse, and then this incredible conversation of: 'Yeah, but she's gonna. . . or, is she gonna be the one with him or is he gonna. . .' And there's a whole soap opera going on. It's like writing a movie script. 'Well, he wouldn't do that because he's got to come back, and that's why you're saying . . .' One of the great things about writing songs is to leave a certain area vague. Even if you're being as specific as you possibly can, somebody else is going to take it totally the other way anyway. It all depends on what they were doing when they heard it."

Keith works differently with Mick than he does with Ron Wood. "When Ron and I sit down together to play, we're two guitarists, whereas with Mick and I there's maybe more of an idea in our heads that what we're after is a song at the end of what we're doing. When Mick comes in with a song, usually he's got it worked out pretty much. He may need a bridge to be written, or a different beat, or turn it around a little bit. Over our whole period, maybe 50% of the time he writes the lyrics and I write the melody. But that's a far, far too simplistic explanation. We write in every conceivable combination of ways. It's really an incredibly elastic arrangement, especially when you're writing with a partner for a band, a specific unit, rather than just writing a song to see who you could sell it to. Some songs hang out for years before we feel happy with them and resurrect them and finish them off. Others, in two takes they've come and gone and you've got to relearn it off your own record to play it later. It happened so quickly you've forgotten how it went. In a way I'm like a guitar maker. Some songs are almost at the end, others are hanging there waiting for that special coat of paint—you can't find the right color for them right now. Lots of times you think you've written four different songs, and you take them to the studio and you realize they're just variations on one song."

These days the Stones have a lot of luxury in the recording studio, the ultimate luxury of using it as a rehearsal hall and sounding board. "When we go into the studio we have to knock the rust off," Keith explained, "because you're either working at top speed or you're training or on the road or in the studio or it's nothing. Nobody ever stops making music, but when you go back in to make an album, the first two months are spent just getting chops and sound together."

In the early days there were different forces moving the industry; in order to even qualify for an album deal, a band had to make its mark in the singles world. Like the Beatles, the Animals, the Who, the Kinks and the Dave Clark Five, the Rolling Stones were first and foremost past masters of the art of the 45: every three months they were required to produce another superior example of the three minute genre made heavenly with the perfect combination of hook and crook.

"I remember after *Satisfaction* got to number one—bang bang at the door. Where's the followup? I mean, every 12 weeks you had to have another one ready. The minute you put out a single you had to start working your butt off on the next one, and the bigger the hit, the more pressure there was on the followup.

"But it was an incredibly good school for songwriting, in that you couldn't piss around for months and months agonizing about the deeper meaning of this or that. It kept you writing all the time. No matter what else you were doing—like touring and recording—you had to make damn sure you didn't let up on the writing. It made you search around and listen for ideas; it made you very aware of what was going on around you— because you were looking for that song. It might come in a coffee shop, or it might come on the street, or in a cab. You get a heightened awareness. You listen to what people say. You might hear a phrase at a bus stop. Instead of accepting life, you start to observe it. You become an outsider rather than a participant. You're listening for it every moment, and anything could be a song, and if you don't have one you're up the creek without a paddle."

For instance, *Ruby Tuesday*. "I saw this picture in some fashion magazine that a chick had lying around her apartment. It was this great photograph of a great chick—she's probably a housewife now, with 15 kids. It was an ad for jewelry—rubies. Also, it happened to be Tuesday. So she became *Ruby Tuesday*. I was just lucky it was Tuesday I guess."

In the sixties the Beatles played Pat Boone to the Stones' Elvis, the essential and elemental rock 'n' roll struggle for good and evil in the minds and hearts of men. The Beatles came to be known as the World's Greatest Songwriters, the Stones as the World's Greatest Band. Off to the side of the fray, the World's Greatest Lyricist, Bob Dylan, lifted the stakes higher.

"I'd say that Lennon definitely felt a strong urge, not so much to compete with Dylan," Keith surmised, "but Bob did spur him to realize he could dig deeper. Mick and I felt that, too, although maybe we didn't feel it as strongly as John. The differences between John and Paul were always greater than between Mick and myself." Keith cited *Sympathy for the Devil* as the Stones' most Dylanesque song. "Mick wrote it almost as a Dylan song, but it ended up a rock 'n roll samba."

But with songs like *Sympathy for the Devil, Street Fighting Man, Gimme Shelter* and *Stray Cat Blues,* the Stones broadened their bad-boy reputation into a decidedly warped young manhood. To some they were the Devil incarnate. None of this was lost on the Glimmer Twins, as they concocted the image for its greatest benefit. "You use every available tool in the kit," Keith said. "To a certain extent you play on your image. Oh, that's the general perception? And I'd just come up with a line or a song and lean on it, push it, go for it. You get a general feel for what people want to hear from you and when you're good at providing it and they like it— oh, you want more? Here's more. When you first strap on your guitar you just want to play it like so-and-so. Then suddenly you're up there with the spotlight on you and you become aware of the pressures. You have to try and gauge your perception of what you're doing. Nobody writes a song or makes a record to put it in a back drawer."

So although the Beatles and Dylan have catalogues ensconced in the bosom of pop literature, here's a vote for the collected works of the Stones as meriting inclusion on that sacred mount.

"I don't write songs as a diary," Keith said. "None of them are auto-biographical, but in some sense they're a reaction to certain emotions. Some of the best songs, some of the happiest ditties in the world come out because you're feeling exactly the opposite. Sometimes you write to counteract that feeling. I was feeling anything but happy when I wrote *Happy*. I wrote *Happy* to make sure there was a word like that and a feeling like that.

"I work best when the sun goes down, I've eaten, had a few drinks, and I've got some good buddies around. I love sitting around with an acoustic guitar and whacking out songs with friends and family. Somehow they never sound as good as they do that first night on the living room couch."

10 |

KEITH ON KEEPING ON

CHRIS SPEDDING | 1986

This 1986 interview with Keith Richards upon the release of the Stones' *Dirty Work* album is surprisingly lacking in references to what Richards termed "World War III": the furious disputes between Richards and Jagger about the latter's solo career that were known to have marked *Dirty Work*'s gestation and would come close to splitting the band permanently. This turns out not to be a demerit as interviewer Chris Spedding finds another entertaining level of communication, speaking English-guitarist-to-English-guitarist with the man radiating the sort of rock iconography that infused Spedding's 1975 UK hit single "Motor Bikin'."

It has to be said that Richards's new mantra—present for neither the first nor last time in this anthology—about using the Stones' unique longevity for the benefit of rock music (". . . see if we can make it grow up with us . . .") has contrasted painfully with the reality of the progressive deterioration of the band's art.

There was a time when the Rolling Stones gleefully played up to a shameless need among certain of their disciples for some kind of hedonistic role model. All very fab 'n' groovy at first, I suppose. Except I have this feeling that the Stones themselves, after a time, must have got heartily sick of it! Just think for a minute . . . These guys have been consistently delivering the right stuff, both on vinyl and in person, for twenty-five years. "The Greatest Rock 'n' Roll Band in the World" is at once both your mandatory show-biz hokum and a prosaic statement of fact.

So I guess it is some kind of tribute to the enduring seductiveness and potency of whatever bizarre tableau they evoke that no one ever stops to ponder how they can possibly still be out there—as prolific, creative and compelling as ever—if they're all supposed to be your lovable ol' burn-outs! Well, that's show business, folks! And I'm sure they must still get a kick out of it.

Now, at this point I'm hoping some of the more perceptive among you will have divined what all this is about. It can mean only one thing. Yes, you got it . . . there's a new Stones album out. Called *Dirty Work* (the first single off it being "Harlem Shuffle"). And since the first hint of a new Stones product usually generates an unseemly stampede throughout all they survey, I must say I find it greatly reassuring that the guys still *care* enough to come out and do the rounds of interviews. They're checking in with us, making contact. Hey, these guys like us!

So on the appointed day, at the highly civilized hour of three-thirty in the afternoon, I presented myself at the Stones' New York office, just a Stones' throw from Columbus Circle. While most of Manhattan was ago-nizing over whether (a) to observe Lincoln's Birthday (b) Valentine's Day counted as a public holiday and (c) we could take the whole damn week off because of the snow, there was none of *that* kind of nonsense at the Stones' office. Very much business as usual.

Keith had phoned ahead with apologies: He'd been delayed leaving the house and would be a few minutes late. A small courtesy, but kind of pleasing in a way. And since the "delay" turned out to be only two or three minutes, it might even score more points than arriving on the dot!

I was shown into a room dominated by a large conference table, the usual vulgar display of framed "platinum" discs refreshingly absent. No need for such ostentation *here*. Wonder where they keep 'em all? Prob-ably in storage until the recording industry designs awards eye-pleasing enough to be worth wall space.

Off in another room a redundant telephone warbled soothingly. One left secure in the knowledge that someone, somewhere, would attend to it.

The door opens. Enter, Keith.

Nattily turned out in a dark blue pinstripe suit, the effect artfully soft-ened by a loosely fitting creamy silk blouse.

Coffee is brought in, and an ashtray for Keith. The scene is set.

So here it is, then. My tête-a-tête with Keith Richards. And a pleasur-able experience it was, too. For me, anyway. Ask the guy a straight question and you get a straight answer. But then, you'd expect that, wouldn't you? I mean, you can't get much more direct, incisive and unpretentious than a Keith Richards riff. It's almost as if the guitar had evolved to the stage where it needed a Keith Richards to come along and reach in and give us a glimpse of part of its true essence, its proto-soul. Keith's unique view of his relationship to his instrument is revealed when he talks (below) of how he first came to ". . . *touch* the guitar." Oh, sure, we've had more flamboyant players who, in varying degrees, have worked the same magic—Jimi Hendrix and Jeff Beck come immediately to mind. But with Keith it's not just a guy playing the guitar; the guitar sometimes appears to be playing *him*—drawing, as he does, on a solid and still-vital blues tradition, sifting and nurturing that rich harvest with just the right sensibilities, thereby becoming the medium—our medium—for its expression, and contributing in the process to some of the more significant songs in our rock repertoire!

The Rolling Stones have carved themselves a sizable niche as the spearhead of a movement that awakened the American consciousness to that neglected part of its own musical heritage—the blues. In this respect their influence has probably been more far-reaching than that of that other flank of the British "invasion," the Beatles. Plus, the Stones are still very much with us!

When Keith spoke of Muddy Waters at the close of our interview, I like to think he was unconsciously expressing hopes for his and the Stones' future.

Chris: So you've just finished a new Stones album, right?

Keith: Yeah. *Dirty Work.*

Chris: Gonna tour?

Keith: Good question. Can't really give you a definite on that. I think so, though.

Chris: Why haven't you done a solo album like other members of the group?

Keith: I've never had a clear enough idea of what I'd want to do. Something's been forming up in my mind over the last three months. Stuff I've been thinking of doing for years. It's sort of coming together. But I'm waiting for the little internal clock in me that says, "Now!", you know. I may well do something when this Stones thing is on its way—after the record and the tour—I may do something later this year. Make a start of it anyway.

Chris: What about producing?

Keith: Yeah, it was interesting doing Peter Tosh and Max Romeo, but the thing that stopped me doing more of that has always been the time thing, you know, sort of being able to say to somebody definitely that I can spend . . . give all my time for as long as it takes, you know. I don't think I'd like to take something on a schedule like, "We've only got four weeks in the studio here." I wanna be able to promise, to say I've definitely got the time, let's take as long as it takes and get it right. There's quite a few people fishing around, a mention here and there if we can put it together. I enjoy working with other people very much and, given the time, I'd work with just about anybody, really. As long as I can get along with them and they've got some good stuff to do.

Chris: Did you enjoy working on the Tom Waits album?

Keith: Yeah. Very much. I'd never met him before. He asked me to do one track and we were having such fun we tried a bit on this one and a bit on that one. A good lad! I didn't realize how complex his stuff was till I started getting into it. 'Cause on the surface it sounds very casually thrown-together blues, but some of the times are very sort of jazz.

Chris: Since the first Stones album was cut on a two-track recorder, what is your reaction to the ongoing rampant technological explosion in the recording studio?

Keith: A lot of young bands that come and see us in the studio can't believe there's an actual band in there playing all at once. They think it's some new technique for recording, 'cause with those guys it's the drummer Mondays and Tuesdays and the bass player goes in on Fridays or something—they never see each other!

Chris: And drum machines that are judged by how like real drums they sound, and drummers who are judged by how like drum machines they sound!

Keith: That's true. So much technology has flooded in in the last seven or eight years—not that it ever stopped, but it's speeding up a bit now with all the possibilities—and everybody's going a bit berserk. What you eventually end up with, right, is that you've got five million more possibilities of what you can do with all these different pieces of equipment with the result that all records start to sound more and more alike—and most records are made on the same three or four pieces of equipment. A studio will buy a new piece of equipment even if it costs a billion dollars, because it keeps you in the studio. They know that every time they give you another possibility or a choice to make, you have to be making these decisions in the studio and the clock's ticking and money's going around. I mean, you can make a movie with the budget of a record for a big group.

Chris: But you made records on two-track when you didn't know half what you know now. You have the knowledge and technique to make records without all this stuff. Don't you think that might put something into the music, might be an actual *advantage*? With the *Let It Be* album years ago the Beatles made a conscious attempt to get back to basic recording techniques.

Keith: Well, "Street Fighting Man" was cut on a cassette player and you know what they were like in those days! The first little Phillips ones, you know. There's a million possibilities—like overloading an acoustic guitar instead of using an electric guitar. You can get that lovely acoustic dryness and feel but with an electric sound. To make a rock 'n' roll record, technology is the least important thing. As far as technology is concerned we keep it to a minimum. We're the kind of band that you don't . . . . We sound terrible if you try and make it techno-pop with us!

Chris: I did notice on the last couple of albums you've been using a kind of rockabilly slap-back echo on the lead guitar, which I quite like myself.

Keith: Yeah, right, that analog-delay thing, yeah. The only new technology that interests me is when it sort of throws me back soundwise. And I can think, "Wow, that means I can go onstage and sound like Scotty Moore now and again!"

Chris: Looking back, what first got you interested in music?

Keith: I was twelve or thirteen in 1957 when rock and roll first really hit in and as you know, up to that time living in England it was "How Much Is That Doggie in the Window?" But my mother always had good taste in music. At home I can remember listening to Billy Eckstine, Sarah Vaughan, Ella Fitzgerald and stuff every day, 'cause that's what my ma would play around the house, singing away doing the dishes. And then her father, my grandfather, Gus Dupree, had a dance band in the Thirties, and whenever we'd go visit granddad there'd be a piano, fiddle, guitar, you know. He was probably the one who got me on guitar. I wouldn't be surprised if he had a long-term plan for it, 'cause I always used to think this guitar was always sitting in the corner of his room, and then I found out only a few years ago that he only used to bring it out when he knew I was coming. So I sense a conspiracy there.

But I didn't really start playing an instrument until, really we're talking about '57–'58, when I started to actually sort of touch the guitar. Although, as I said, I was brought up not unused to having musical instruments around and just going sort of plink-plonk-plonk and, you know, bang-bang wallop.

Chris: But when you first heard rock music, didn't something inside of you *click*? I know it did for me.

Keith: Exactly.

Chris: . . . and everything prior to that seemed to be a time of total innocence and then suddenly there was a whole new thing going on.

Keith: And you wanted to know where the fuck it came from. And because there wasn't so much of it, you weren't swamped with it and you would say, hey, I really like that "Sweet Little Sixteen" and trace it back and you find out that this guy Chuck Berry comes from a record label that also has these guys like Muddy Waters, and it made us English guys a little more conscious of the history of the music just because it was such a bombshell when it first hit.

Chris: And in the Fifties in England, we used to be embarrassed about not being able to come out with a good rock record.

Keith: There were only a few guys that could sound convincing.

Chris: And then all of a sudden with the Stones and the Beatles . . .

Keith: Yeah, 'cause we were the ones who were twelve or thirteen when rock first hit, so it took those six or seven years for it to seep through and get the chops right.

Chris: Did it surprise you when you realized that America was picking up on this stuff that you'd . . .

Keith: Oh yeah, we couldn't believe it that we were actually going to come to America and work. To most English guys at that time, America was this half-fabled land. And then later to actually work and record at Chess in Chicago, the same studio that Chuck Berry recorded in—amazing.

Chris: What was the attitude of those guys at Chess to you guys?

Keith: Pretty much disbelief on both sides. They were just knocked out that some white kids from England knew more about their music than American kids, they just couldn't believe it. So it was a little bit of a shock all around. We didn't know how long this thing would go on so we went for it gung ho! Charlie came to New York and hung around at the Metropole and Birdland fulfilling all of the old dreams.

Chris: I saw an old clip of one of your live *Ed Sullivan Show* appearances recently on MTV and it made me wonder just exactly what Brian Jones' role was in the early group. 'Cause when we started getting original songs it was always Jagger/Richards, never a Brian Jones song, and although he was obviously a charismatic performer and had this great image thing, when it came down to writing and performing it was always you up front with Mick and you were usually playing all the leads. Was this a gradual change that came about when you and Mick started writing? It was surprising to see him in such an obviously subordinate role.

Keith: Yeah. He never got 'round to writing. I sat down with him a couple of times and tried to write with him, but . . . . You see, I personally believe that most people that play an instrument would be able to write a few songs here and there. But they say, "I tried, I can't do it" and give up and don't try it again; they get too discouraged. But for myself and Mick it became a matter of, almost, necessity. It was Andrew Oldham who made it very apparent very quickly. He said you really got to buckle down and try and start writing songs because another album or two and you're going to be forever at the mercy of other songwriters. You're always gonna be hunting around for material. So the first song, "As Tears Go By," was a great encouragement because, moldy old ballad as it was in its way, it did come out as a record and did all right. And that's all you need to be able to say "Okay, I'm a songwriter as well." But Brian was the one who was most affected by becoming a pop star. One minute he was a real back room jazz boy and then within a very short time it seemed to me he felt his main job was to be a pop star. He got less into playing and more into flitting around. He became very adept at leaping onto a vibraphone or xylophone in the studio and being able to knock it out. And in that way added a lot of interesting texture to some of the earlier records. It seemed he thought, "I've made it, I'm a pop star, that's really what I do." I suppose a bit of him inside, well, maybe there was a little bit of self-contempt: "I've sold out, therefore I'm not gonna concentrate on playing anymore."

Chris: Well, he was always the blues purist, wasn't he?

Keith: Very much so, yes. He would never even listen to Jimmy Reed, and hardly any of Muddy Waters' electric stuff. We turned him on to Jimmy Reed and Bo Diddley. He was into guys like Sunnyland Slim and Tampa Red. Elmore James was about as far down the road as he'd gone with electric blues. Even people like Buddy Guy—I think he thought they were too showman-y. Chuck Berry, too. But he did get into it. I had a lot of trouble in those days, and I nearly didn't even get in the Stones because I insisted on banging out Chuck Berry songs. "We don't want no rock 'n' roll 'round here," he'd say. But I got through that one pretty quick. For a while he was ostracized from the blues purist societies of London for that. Mind you, so was Muddy Waters for a while.

Chris: So how did the group come about?

Keith: Well, there wasn't really a group first. We all sort of met at Alexis Korner's club, you know. Brian knew Alexis and he'd played in a couple of bands in Cheltenham, whereas I'd only done the odd dances and a country band at art school and a couple of rock 'n' roll gigs for fun. Brian was more into "A gig—we can get fifty bob for this." Get a guest slot down the Red Lion or something like that. He knew a little bit more about the musician scene in London. Stu was the first guy I saw when I went to the first rehearsal of what turned out to be the Stones. He was just sitting there at the piano. Mick and I had done a couple of numbers with Alexis. It was good experience and we got off on it. And then Alexis had offered Mick a couple of gigs to come and sing at some of these deb jobs he was doing.

Chris: Yeah?

Keith: Yeah, 'cause he saw a certain amount of commercial appeal to use Mick for four or five numbers to give it a bit more variety, I guess.

Chris: Another thing I noticed on that old Ed Sullivan clip was that Mick was just *standing there singing*—nothing like what you see these days!

Keith: To me, as long as we've known each other, I've always thought Mick's most brilliant thing was that he could work in an area two foot square and give a very exciting performance. I keep saying to him, "Don't worry about it, save your breath, you don't have to look upon it as an athletic stunt anymore. Just stand there and sing."

Chris: Do you still enjoy playing live?

Keith: Yeah. There's no substitute for live work to keep a band together.

Chris: Yes, almost every other band from that era has faded away. It's almost as if you'd all consciously made a kind of pact with each other to keep it together. You're getting to be like an institution.

Keith: Yes, I find it very interesting to still be together after all this time, and in a way it's put us in this unique position. Since nobody else has got this far with it as a band, let's see if we can take this English rock 'n' roll fab group/mania sort of thing it started as and see if we can make it grow up with us. Without having to get hung up on the Peter Pan aspect of it.

Chris: Well, rock came about as a sort of musical expression of the post-war baby-boom generation and it was originally an adolescent thing you were expected to grow out of. There *were* no rock musicians over twenty-five and the idea of still doing it when you're forty . . . and yet look at guys like Muddy Waters.

Keith: Muddy is the example I always use when talking about this. He commanded all the respect in the world and did it in a mature and graceful way. So it's really up to you. None of the great ones ever sort of . . . stop.

THE GREAT LOST KEITH RICHARDS INTERVIEW

IRA ROBBINS | 1988

After opening with the issue of what new questions one could possibly ask an interview veteran like Keith Richards, Ira Robbins unpromisingly poses the most clichéd Stones question of all (the one about group shelf-life that plays on the title of their hit "The Last Time"). However, the ex–*Trouser Press* publisher comes up with a fine interview, containing little-known facts (Richards's almost-involvement in *Midnight Run*), candor (Richards's almost suicidal honesty about the quality of CD versions of Stones product), and reflectiveness (how the music business has changed beyond recognition from the small entertainment sector it had been at the outset of the guitarist's career). Amazingly, this is the interview's first print appearance. It was intended for *Creem* in 1988, but said American monthly ceased publication before it could run.

19 SEPTEMBER 1988
JANE ROSE'S OFFICE, NYC

You've done a lot of interviews lately. It's hard to pick questions you haven't been asked . . .
It's hard for me to find other answers. How could I now possibly remember the lie I told somebody a month ago?

If the Stones get together next year and make a record and a tour, does everyone agree that it will be the last time?
No, not at all. In fact, that would mean it wouldn't happen. This is no last

killing. For the last ten years, to my recollection at least, it's always been "the last tour" but that's just promo hype bullshit. I find the Stones now in the most interesting period since either they first got to make a record, or since "Satisfaction." Here's this band that people really love to see and are a part of a lot of people's lives. For millions of people, there's the sun and the moon and the air to breathe and the food we eat and there's the Rolling Stones. A part of the world as far as they're concerned. You can even be 25 years old and not know a world without the Rolling Stones.

The interesting thing is to get this thing to grow up. This music is still going through its own growing pains. I think the Rolling Stones are on the cutting edge of pushing this music and making it grow up, making it mature. The same as the audiences that have grown up with it. If you can get it this far, let's see how far else you can go. That's a very exciting idea, an essential thing to do. This is uncharted area. All we've got to do is grow up with it. There's no reason we don't know if you can get mature rock'n'roll. Since you're growing up there's no way you can pretend you're a teenager anymore so you might as well go ahead rather than back.

I always figured the Stones would be the first rock band to retire as champs . . . This isn't a marathon race. You obviously have to have a certain stamina or sturdiness about you in order to do this gig, even for two or three years, but if you can do it for 25 years, then you're pretty well conditioned to do it. It just depends how you do it. If you can make it grow up believably then I don't see why you can't get mature. Rock'n'roll is a hybrid of gospel and blues and country music and all of the best exponents of those kinds of music manage . . . My man Muddy Waters, right, they had to refund tickets for the show that he didn't make the next day and he was still powerful, he wasn't just pretending to be Muddy Waters, he was Muddy Waters and he was playing some great shit and also encouraging new guys. There's no rules in this game, no certain age when you've got to stop—only when you die.

There's a high rate of industrial accidents in this game. The guys you don't need to disappear disappear real quick. Buddy Holly had 18 months, maybe two years of recording; Ritchie Valens had only three records out of any consequence; Eddie Cochran was only just getting started and Otis

Redding—Jesus!—the guy was just starting to feel his way. Most of the big cats have gone down by accident rather than self-induced stupidity. Jimi just overdid it. I won't include Janis and Jim Morrison cause I don't consider them driving forces in this game. They're very good periphery, but to me they're not the meat of the matter and the guys I'm talking about are.

James Jamerson and Benny [Benjamin]—the Motown rhythm section—worked to death. When you wonder why Motown suddenly didn't happen anymore—it's usually a matter of two or three guys. Same with Hi Records—Al Green—Al Jackson died and the whole thing fell apart. I was there, I worked with Willie Mitchell and the Memphis Horns and he's still got Al Jackson's drum kit in a closet, covered in cobwebs. It's like a shrine.

Most of these things happen by accident and if you're fortunate enough to be around—the core of the Rolling Stones is still around—it's a fascinating prospect.

I thought perhaps you might view the end of the Stones as a chance to do other musical projects.
I don't see why you can't do both. They let me out of the cage and I've done this one and I kind of enjoyed it and I love this band I'm working with. These guys are too much—they don't take any bullshit from me at all and they kick me up the ass and make me work. They're that good.

Hiring and firing top hands doesn't matter. The guys might be the best players in the world, but that doesn't mean they're gonna click together. It's finding the right people.

With the Stones' legendary insanity and excess seemingly behind you, do you see yourself being past some point, at a new level of maturity about your life?
I've a fairly good idea what image most people that were around then had, and it was nowhere near that level of debauchery. I wish it was, in a way. It was really more desperation. One minute you're a blues band looking for regular gigs in London and the next minute it's Stonesmania. Suddenly it's happening in America and the next thing you're picked out by the authorities—as long as they can put you away they've solved all their problems.

Suddenly you're thrown into so many different areas. You write a couple of songs and suddenly you're a threat to society. Then you realize in a way how fragile even some of the oldest and strongest societies are set up, i.e. the British government, to name just one. How actually fragile they are, how uncertain about what the hell they're doing. They made us a threat to their society just by their perception of us. It gives you a lot of insight into the way things are actually run. Suddenly, license is given to lean on somebody. It's no fair. No matter what it was anybody was doing, the way. . . . it was set up and framed. Yeah, I was doing the shit, but half the time I was busted the stuff I was busted for wasn't my stuff, it was the stuff they brought with 'em. They couldn't even find my stuff—it was hidden too well.

What are they so desperate about? A guitar player is this big a threat to a thousand-year-old democracy, so called? By doing that, because they're not successful at it, they don't really know what they're doing, they hand you this weapon to wield which is far bigger. . . You're looking for a weapon to wield and they give you one on a plate. Suddenly they make you a cause, they make you a focal point of all this stuff, which is the dumbest thing to do. You realize how stupid and how fragile our society is. We live on the thinnest thread of civilization. It's so fine. By doing that kind of stuff to you, you wise up a little quicker than you would normally, if you were doing another job, 'cause they wouldn't need to lean on you. You find out a lot of things behind the scenes because you've got to deal with important lawyers and barristers who tell you a lot of things. All this information is coming—they're writing your songs for you. All you've got to do is find a riff and pick out a phrase here and there.

They tried to put us in jail and they couldn't do it—it wouldn't stick. Somebody screwed up. Then you've got cops looking for promotions. If you're perceived as a threat, you are a threat. It doesn't matter if you want to be one. You can't go off and become a gardener. They've increased your importance in society just by leaning on you. It's juvenile, dumb. The way to deal with something like that is to defuse it, and absorb it or lay off of it and just let it run its course.

Between the fans and the media, your image was amazing.
We sort of set ourselves up for it without realizing it. It took a few years to

percolate down to the point where the authorities would take any notice, if they could find a focus. And of course the focus, the easy one, is drugs, which is always a handy one: war on drugs, very convenient. But who let all the blow in the last two years? As long as a few guns went back to Nicaragua, you can bring it in for nothing. The cost of blow went [pfft]. Guys I know go we can't get rid of the shit . . . this is primo quality and we can't get rid of it, there's so much of it. And now they want to revive their war on drugs but it's all such a big lie. The drug itself is a fairly harmless thing, it's just something to toss around in the public arena and make a deal of. You only turn people on by making a big deal out of it.

If they'd have left me alone, you wouldn't have half these freaks thinking that's the way you play guitar, by taking that crap. It's got nothing to do with it. To me it was an entirely personal thing, a problem that I had to deal with in my own way. By splashing it all over, all they did was turn it into a them-and-us situation. The distance of most governments from the people they're governing is just so enormous. That's the worrying thing to me, I don't care what country you're talking about. They get so far away they actually think anyone's going to look at this bullshit and fall for it. You've got to kiss a baby here and there and you go so-and-so and talk about crops because you're talking to a load of farmers and the next day you hope to say the right thing about fish because you're talking to fishermen. It wouldn't play in Peoria—it's like the scum end of the entertainment business to me.

Does it bother you that people have written and discussed so much about the Stones over the years?
It can't really bother you. Obviously, if you bother to check it out, the more that's written the greater the percentage of on stuff as opposed to rubbish. I think it's pretty obvious to most people as to what stuff's been written about the Stones that has just been made because some guy was given some money to spill some beans and weave a new tapestry. As opposed to somebody who's writing to try and give you an insight into the way things are done and the difficulties that are forced on you by doing it, and the brilliant moments and the terrible moments as opposed to somebody's who's just trying to make some bread.

As the person who's lived through it all, do you ever look in a book and say, so that's what happened that month? Is it nice to have people taking notes while you're living your life?

Stanley Booth's book, I think, because he took like 15 years to write it and it was still very authentic and accurate. Also, the S.T.P. one was very good, as opposed to, say, Spanish Tony Sanchez's book, which is like Grimms fairy tales, where every chapter would start off yeah that's how it started and then you turn the page two or three times and he went off into fairy land. Maybe he would incriminate himself if he would tell the real story.

Are there projects you'd like to try doing in between bouts of being a rock star?

Nothing that I can tell you definitely, but anything that came up that I thought I had the time for. For instance, they asked me to do the music to *Midnight Run*. But I was in the middle of making this record. As much as the idea of doing that intrigued me, I had to say no. They'd finished the movie already, and to me the music for movies should be planned further ahead than that. And there was no way I could devote enough time to it. I'd have to clear the decks totally to get into something like that.

The people that I've got to work with me in the last couple of years has been one of the biggest surprises. I'm going to say surprises rather than thrills, because the cats that wanted to work with me are guys that really turned me on, like Maceo, Bootsy, Buckwheat. Bootsy's another guy that doesn't like to fly—he drove from fucking Ohio for one night. It never occurred to me that a guy would do that for just one track for me, not even knowing if it would ever come out. It's heartwarming. Maceo runs James [Brown]'s band—you don't just go up to James and say I'd like to borrow Mr. Parker. You gotta go round the back door. But the fact that Maceo is ready to come up from Carolina for just an overdub is too much.

Guitar heroes don't play rhythm guitar anymore. You and Townshend stand as the two best rhythm guitarists in rock. Does it worry you that these new guys just play solos?

It's the Fastest Guitar in the West syndrome. As a musician it bothers me, because that's not really what rock'n'roll is about. Jimi Hendrix could play great rhythm guitar as well as great lead. Most people who revere Jimi forget how great a rhythm guitar player he was. They think it's all just a matter of speed up on the top end of the fretboard.

Also, video has a lot to do with this, posing—you've got to spread your legs wide, shake your hair around and wear this plank round your neck and get down on your knees . . . But then rock'n'roll has always been a bit circus-like and theatrical, so you can't really knock it that much.

It's harder to be a good rhythm guitar player than it is just to wail away and just become very fast and scream. To me, any electric guitar player that doesn't play an acoustic guitar is already blowing his whole gig. If all you do is play electric guitar and you're suddenly given an acoustic, you're lost, because there's so many tricks in the bag, so many easy ways out with an electric guitar. If you don't keep up your acoustic work, you're blowing an awful lot about guitar playing. You have to forget all the toys and just play.

A serious guitar player—someone that loves to play guitar and wants to get better—should play a bit of acoustic every day and keep your hand in. You can use that to build up on electric guitar work but you can't do it the other way 'round.

Chuck Berry is another brilliant rhythm guitarist . . .
Even his leads are rhythm. It's all two-string stuff, it's beautiful. To me, there's no such thing as rhythm guitarists and lead guitarists. The musician does that to himself by doing too much on one end and letting the rhythm section carry the rhythm. A guitar player is somebody that can play rhythm and lead. Chuck Berry's solos take off as an extension of his rhythm work without losing the drive or point of the song.

His style developed out of horn riffs from the '40s—Louis Jordan and his band. Nat King Cole is his ideal vocalist. Everybody passes it on. If Chuck passed it on to me, for instance, who turned Chuck on? Louis Jordan and Nat King Cole. Who turned Nat King Cole on? Who turned the cat who turned Nat King Cole on? It goes back and back and back, probably to Adam and Eve. That probably means there's only one song in the whole world. In the last 100 years, you've been able to record it. Imagine if Beethoven could have had playback . . .

The most amazing scene in the Chuck Berry film is where he's arguing with you how [to] play his bends in "Carol." It struck me that this was probably the first time in ages anyone had argued with you how to play guitar.
You're right. The rest of the band behind me, the guys that are with me, if you look at their faces, are going "he ain't gonna take much more of this, watch out or you're going to get stabbed or that guitar's gonna go round your chops." I was willing to take all of that. I ate the bullets and chewed lead. If I could show the rest of the guys that I'm willing to take any amount of crap to do this gig, then I've got that much of a better band. Also, it's gonna fox Chuck. He's trying to provoke me, and I ain't gonna go for it.

He's never rehearsed in his life. He thought the rehearsals were for the band. He didn't realize they were for him. He needed rehearsing. The band knew their shit.

The cameras came in real late—there were some bits a week earlier where Joey Spampinato is showing Chuck how to play, and what really happens, in "Around and Around." Chuck would go back and listen and— to give him his due—would come back and say "you're right." After playing for 20-odd years with pickup bands, he didn't know how to play live any more. It was bugging him that this band was really kicking him up the butt and suddenly he realizes he's not really cutting the mustard.

If I'd turned the gig down, somebody else would have done it and I would have been kicking myself, it would have been a sore point with me for the rest of my life.

You've been working with a lot of American musicians. Are there any British players you'd like to work with?
I'm not there enough really to know. There's a couple of great pub bands: the Dirty Strangers from Shepherds Bush, a great straightahead rock'n'roll band, one of the guys is a really good songwriter. I like U2, Bono especially. I like individual guys: Johnny Marr's playing, Glenn [Tilbrook] of Squeeze. But I don't know a lot of stuff out England right now. The business has got the clamps on in England.

There's too much charity work going on right now. I wonder how much of this is a race for knighthood. When you're talking about the

Prince of Wales Trust and the fact that the Prince of Wales is going to be the next king, are we talking about Sir Phillip Collins? There's too many doubtful areas: [at] the Wembley gig for Nelson Mandela, there's Whitney Houston—she doesn't even know who Nelson Mandela is—and they cover up his name while she's playing and put up Pepsi-Cola or something instead. I don't trust it too much—there's too much ass-licking going on around England for my liking.

The bigger a business gets, and the more money involved, the more entrenched and conservative the whole game gets. It's only the public that'll eventually let them know that they're sick to death of being pumped full of shit—like disco in the '70s—they thought that formula would last forever and suddenly in two weeks they couldn't get rid of them, the returns are coming back. And they're wondering what the hell happened. For ten years, this worked. And their immediate answer is look for a new formula.

Do people ever underestimate you?
I don't know—I can't tell. Charlie and Bill and myself and Ronnie take immense pride in the fact that we can back up a guy who doesn't have to keep looking over his shoulder and wondering if the machine is gonna stop. Even if they pull the electricity, Charlie is gonna keep going. We give the guy enough confidence that he can go half a mile down a football stadium and not worry about the machine behind him—the beat's gonna be there. Whether he takes it for granted or not, that's another story.

I don't work in a highly technical way—we just throw the band in the room. To me it has to do with ambience and everybody plays at once. It's not "drummer on Monday" and "bass player on Tuesday." The Stones have always recorded in the same room [at the same time]. It's the only way I will record. That's the only way to make a good rock'n'roll record—eyeball to eyeball and making the moves on the spot. You can't manufacture it. You can pretend to, and you can fool the public, they don't have a lot of time to check it out. They'll get sick of it eventually, and then people wonder why. Especially the guys that are trying to sell it—suddenly it doesn't sell. To them, selling it is the most important thing. The most important thing to me is making it.

What was the effect when all the Stones began living in different countries?
That was a very important point, one of the reasons why the quality of
the Stones' work went down the drain for a few years, specifically because
of that very problem. Exile on Main Street was the first record we made
out of the country but we all moved to the same joint, so there wasn't any
difference. After that, things started to disperse and it had nothing to do
with being super fat and rich jet star bullshit, it had to do with the difficulties not being able to call up your friend and say "I've got a song, an
idea, I'll be over in ten minutes." Somebody's three thousand miles away
instead of ten minutes away.

A lot of that had to do specifically with just geographical distance.
You'd have to wait and come together and then try and pull it together on
the spot all at once, instead of having this percolating thing happening,
which is the way it should happen.

*That was a turning point in rock music, when extremely successful bands
were affected by new forces that drastically affected their lives.*
The [rock] music business began to break wide open in the early '70s.
Before that, it was quite a small business—a tax writeoff for electronics
firms. It was just a way of subsidizing recording classical music. It's just
fuckin' music. Beethoven and Mozart rocked—those buggers rocked.

Even the Beatles and the Stones in the '60s weren't enough to change
the basic financial structure of the companies that own record companies.
Suddenly, in the early '70s, it became a business on its own.

*When did you realize that you as a group held the deck in the balance of
power with the record company?*
For us, luckily, straight away. We only got a record contract because
Dick Rowe who worked for Decca had turned the Beatles down, and he
couldn't afford to make the same mistake twice. We didn't ever record for
Decca, we recorded for our own company and leased the tracks to Decca.
This way, we could retain control. They just got the finished product. They
couldn't interfere in it in any way, especially if it was successful.

What the Beatles and the Stones did in the early years was to take
control of the product more and more out of the hands of the a&r men,

who—at least most of them—don't know shit. The Beatles were lucky, but George Martin is an exception.

Now it's not so cool as it was in the mid-to-late '60s and early '70s. We'd almost got it to the point where if you took a band on, you just let 'em do their stuff. In the '70s the money started to get so much bigger and, as usual, the more money, the more conservative, the tighter the controls. The record business is now firmly back [in control], especially with videos. The investment involved now of putting on a new act is a big deal. It used to take ten grand to make an album. Now you're talking movie budgets to make a record. And to go through the whole thing—the p.r., the video, to make the record—you're talking really big bucks. And of course the more money involved, same as any other game, the more wary and the less chances the people in control of the money take. Which is usually their downfall.

What about CDs?

I've been listening/checking them out and I don't like the *Emotional Rescue*—it's really crappy. Some of the others—I thought the *Sticky Fingers* was pretty good, the *Beggars Banquet* is really good and *Exile* I thought was pretty good. I haven't really checked 'em all out, but those three I thought are good. But I thought the *Emotional Rescue* one was really crappy, but then I haven't checked it against the original record. I never did like the mix on that record at all, 'cause I had nothing to do with it. Maybe that's the reason I didn't like it. It's thin and bitty. I have the original tapes at home from it and I say "where did it go?" That's the same as with *Love You Live*. Mick is a great performer but what he doesn't know about he thinks he can buy. So he buys a guy and the guy don't know shit maybe. He mixed that record [*Emotional Rescue*]. Except for "All about You," he mixed the whole goddamn record. Even if you listen to the CD there's an immediate difference when "All about You" comes on. It happens to be my track, but I got to mix that one because no one else wanted to deal with it.

Interestingly, that was recorded on fairly recent technology, as compared to some of the earlier . . . I was more worried about your *Beggars Banquets* and *Let It Bleeds* and *Exiles*. I thought that that might not trans-

fer too well to CD, rather than a record of the date of *Emotional Rescue*.
But that's the only one . . . I've got to go and check the record again and
see if they really did screw up there or not. There's that CD radio sam-
pler, *Start Me Up*, which is incredible. Maybe it's got to do in the transfer.
It's hard to say. You can make a great record and blow it all just on the
mastering. Or even in the sequencing sometimes. You take a great record
and shift two or three songs around and it's down the drain, somehow it
doesn't work.

Would you be a Stones' fan if you weren't in the band?
Yeah. I think so. That's a very hard one to answer honestly, but I think so.

Are there any Stones albums you regret making?
Not regret . . . *Satanic Majesties* was just kind of hanging in while you were
out of it. We'd been on the road for a long long time and really we were all
just looking for a break but we had to make a record. In retrospect, I find
some very interesting things on there. Soundwise, we could have done a
better job on it. Also, *Between the Buttons* we were a little tired. I like some
of the stuff and I like the way it was going, but we'd been on the road for
five years nonstop by then and there was a certain lack of concentration,
me on the mixing more than anything else. We let it slip a bit.

I've gone back and listened to the original, which was in four-track.
We could have done a better job on that. Not so much on the playing or
the songs, 'cause that's what was happening, but on the mixing and the
mastering.

I understand Jagger's touring Australia.
Yeah, he just got there—he starts tomorrow or the next day.

Who's he playing with?
I don't know the cats—some ersatz Stones version . . . What's scary about
Mick is that he's done two solo albums and he goes out there with chick
dancers doing "Tumbling Dice." Maybe in Japan you can get away with
that, because they haven't seen you before and they don't know, but he's
going to do four or five weeks in Australia. They're a little hipper there,

and all it needs is for somebody to say "ouch" [embarrassed grimace] and it's gonna be a rough time for him. But I did tell him, what did you make two solo albums for—to go out and do Stones songs? I mean, it's okay out of sheer exuberance to throw in "Jumping Jack Flash" now and again on a show, but if you're going to make a break with something . . . that murky area, that's what's always worried me about being part of something like the Stones and then doing solo stuff. To make a clean break is so important.

Put it this way: if no one in the Stones could tell you anything about what to do, would you do stuff differently?
No, I can only do it the way I do it, anyway nobody in the Stones ever told me what to do—except for Mick and I, they'd ask me what to do. The Stones are such a weirdo chemical mixture of people, such an unlikely bunch. Charlie's been totally embarrassed for 25 years—it's not his idea of himself at all, having chicks scream at him and being in a rock'n'roll band. His idea was playing the Village Gate. If you try to figure out the chemistry and the makeup of a band then you go mad. Even if you found the answer, it would probably be destroyed at the same time. It's better unknown.

Tell me about Brian Jones.
Brian and I worked very hard on two-guitar stuff for a year or so before the Stones even got to make a record and then we carried on working very hard on guitar for another couple of years. But he lost interest in the guitar very early on, once the Stones got on a real roll. Brian was the first one to really get on the star trip. I don't know if he lost interest because he got on a star trip, but it seemed to coincide anyway with his lack of interest in the guitar.

Some of the things he did with marimbas in "Under My Thumb" and sitar in "Paint It, Black" were fantastic, amazing touches [that] gave the band a whole different area of color. When he started to play around with the bells and marimbas, it was great but I couldn't get him back into the guitar. I'd end up doing all the parts, which made it a little difficult on the road because he'd have to relearn . . . there's no marimbas onstage in 1965 [laughs].

He got more and more interested in being a star and what that meant. Not so much anything to do with the job, the music or making records, but what it meant behind the scenes, like "hey you, c'mere" or "I want her—bring me her." All that to me is despicable and still is and always will be. You can't be that way. It's too easy to do and it's not going to do you any good to give into yourself that easily. I'm not saying that I ain't ever done it myself now and again, but [not] to get into it as a habit, as a way of life.

Brian became quite a problem. You were always getting kicked in the balls by Brian when you least needed it. He was quite a manipulator, angling one clique against the other. We were working so hard, that eventually no one had the time for it. That's what happened to him—mainly giving in to weakness in his character. No one in the band had the time to deal with this—what did I call him? —this fragile monster. You see this diabolical weakness in somebody but you don't have time to deal with it. Everybody has to bear their own weight. If one gives way, either you collapse inwardly or you cut the fucker out and ignore it and just carry on.

Did he understand why he had to leave the band?
I don't think by then he understood much at all. Not by the time it went down. Brian just went on a trail of debauchery. I'm not trying to paint myself as any saint—everybody knows my story, what I've done and what I ain't done. "Satisfaction" hit number one and that was enough for him. "I don't have to do any more except satisfy my desires whatever they may be and everybody had better buckle down or they get shit on."

We didn't see it as his problem, we saw it as a problem for ourselves. When you're working 340 gigs a year and you've got ten [days] to make a record and the other three or four days free, the weak go to the wall. Brian had a lot of weaknesses that nobody had time to deal with. If he'd have hung in for a bit more and people grew up a little and a bit more understanding might have been . . .

In the early days, you and Mick wrote songs like "Blue Turns to Grey" for other bands.
Mick and I were still learning how to write material for the Stones. The first song we wrote together was when Andrew Oldham locked us in the kitchen

and we were both dying for a crap and a pee and decided we'd better come out with a song or it's the sink, sweetheart. So we came up with "As Tears Go By." Meanwhile, we'd go onstage and play "Hoochie Coochie Man."

You tend [at first] to write stuff that's totally different from the stuff you're actually playing. It takes a while. I think "The Last Time" is the first song we wrote for the Stones that we could actually record ourselves. Before that we'd written "That Girl Belongs to Yesterday," which Gene Pitney had a hit with, and "As Tears Go By," which Marianne [Faithfull] had a Top 10 with. It took us a year or so to find our way through all that and find songs that we could feel comfortable about recording ourselves.

Lots of people over the years have looked up to you and not realized that they had to work things out for themselves.
And that it wasn't me that said this is how I do it. It's a totally peripheral thing to me, and my own problem. It's the same thing Charlie Parker had to deal with: these young kid horn players that come up and think they have to mainline in order to play and he'd say no, that's my thing, it's nothing to do with it—it's not gonna help. You've got it or you ain't got it. You ain't gonna inject talent into yourself. It's just something I'm into and I've got to deal with one way or another. Everyone looks for an easy way in or an easy way out.

You've certainly been emulated by musicians in numerous ways. Drinking Jack Daniels . . .
I should have made a deal with those guys.

One picture of you in a magazine, passed out backstage after a show, is the kind of thing people want to aspire to. That must be a strange feeling for you.
You suggest to me what I can do about it except say look, you've got it wrong, that's got nothing to do with it. One strength I have is a fairly sturdy constitution and a pretty good self-knowledge of who I am and what I'm capable of. I'm not always right, but to me that would be the thing to work on if you really want to do this gig.

You can die doing this shit—it's not kid stuff, this isn't some panto-mime. Once you get into this game and you're on the goddamn road and you've got to make records and write songs and deal with all of this shit, it's not nursery time anymore. It's for real. Unfortunately, a lot of cats find this out just too late. It's a battleground out there, whether you like it or not.

I never looked for my personal way of life to be exploited—it was a decision of policemen and authorities. As I've said many times before, I didn't have a problem with drugs, just cops. Most of my cases were thrown out straightaway because it was obviously a setup. But still I've got to go there and face this shit and plead guilty 25 times to something that I know I'm not really guilty of.

Is it amusing to be in your position?
Life is amusing to me, it always has been. To me, one of the most precious things in this world is sense of humor. A good laugh. To take it too seriously—and the older I get, the more I believe this—you can worry yourself into the grave by taking everything too seriously. Obviously there's some serious problems here, but without a sense of humor you aren't going to be able to deal with it. It's a sense of humor and a certain disregard for certain norms—given the fact that you're living a life which is basically outside of the norm anyway just by the very virtue of the job that you do—that if you can't laugh about it, if you can't see the funny side of it, then you're not going to be able to deal and you're not going to be able to make any impression upon what you think is serious. A sense of humor to me is one of the most serious things in the world.

How do you like living in New York?
I love New York. In actual fact, I live in Jamaica and I've just found out today that my house is one of the few that didn't get blown away [by Hurricane Gilbert]. A few trees lost and everything. I'm checking up on my people there to make sure if they need anything. The funniest line I got was from this Rasta guy that works for me there he said we don't need food, but we need ganja, though—the crop's washed away! I'm just gonna send him some bread and hope he can figure it out.

New York can be an anonymous place for musicians, can't it?
For sure. I just live like anybody else. I don't have anybody taking care of

me. I take the kids for a walk, I take the dog for a walk in the middle of the night. And it's very cool: "Hey Keith" from all over the place. I sign a couple of autographs, no big deal. Most of it's just a smile and they're glad to see you and they ask you when the record's coming out or if you're gonna get the band back together. Cops give me a ride home when it's raining and I'm out with the dog. "Don't tell me fucking captain and we'll give you a lift home." That's very heartwarming.

That would be different if the Stones were playing Madison Square Garden this week. You'd be surrounded by ten bodyguards.
If you're in town doing a gig, the whole windup becomes such a thing that it is different from just living around the neighborhood and not actually working. Now and again I do run into a gang of avid Stones fans and I'll do a runner. I'm still fairly swift on the legs.

My feeling [about bodyguards] has always been you can't trust anybody to look after you except yourself. You can't pay a guy to take the blows for you. It's bullshit to abdicate control of your own life. You're asking for trouble. Who's going to take shots for you? I don't care how much you pay! Most of this bodyguard shit is either to make these guys feel great about themselves or show off. I don't need a bodyguard. I can spend that money in other ways.

It'll be interesting to see the Stones tour next year.
It's an interesting proposition. I've been working for two years nonstop now, so for me it's no problem. What I would love them—especially Bill and Charlie—to start to play now together. It's six, seven years since we've been on the road, three years since we've even played with each other. And it's time. If they want to get it together next year, they can make it a whole lot easier by starting now. I've got some other things to do, but if they just start playing together then it would be a breeze.

How do you find England these days?
I'm a little out of touch with England, but it's still home to me. There's a lot of skyscrapers going up in places where there just used to be slums or docks. I still know just about every street [in London]. I'm there maybe

six weeks a year. I take a couple of long walks, early morning, I just walk around, smell it, check it out.

What do you think of Albert Goldman's John Lennon book?
I've only been asked this once before and I'll give you the same answer. I think it says more about Albert Goldman than it does about John Lennon.

Do you think he'll ever turn his focus on any of the Rolling Stones?
He can try and find my garbage can if he likes, but if I catch him, god help him. I find Albert Goldman a despicable character, especially when he picks on guys that can't answer back. Albert won't turn his focus on me until I'm dead and gone, but I wonder if he'll live that long. I'd much rather what happened to John happen to Albert.

What did you think of the Who in the old days?
They were fascinating. I never liked Daltrey much, but I thought Pete and Moonie were fascinating together. I thought that the reason Pete went into book publishing was because no matter what drummer you got you were never gonna find . . . Moonie to other drummers was all over the place—you'd say off-beat to him and he wouldn't know what you'd mean. But he could play with Pete a treat. I think Pete's always just missed him and never got over that incredible energy that Moonie had. He would only play good behind Pete. But I loved "Can't Explain" and "Substitute" and "My Generation" and that shit I thought was some of the most original and right-on stuff that came out of England in that period.

What about the single they did of "Last Time"/"Under My Thumb"?
Thanks for doing it, boys. I needed the help. Thanks a lot. To me, the magical thing about that was just Moonie and Townshend together; the rest of it was peripheral. The Ox and Daltrey were just window-dressing, compared to those two, for me.

They're talking about getting back together . . .
I wonder who they're using for drums? To me that's the important thing. The only other important thing is, of course, I heard Pete's got itchy again.

He's started working instead of publishing books he wants to play. Good on you, Trousers, we need you.

I think that they lost half of their force with one guy, whereas the Stones have had three different guitar players. The Stones are a bit more adaptable, I think, and a little bit more of collective combination. I've heard tapes of whole Who albums Townshend's done by himself and then cut with the Who and the original one was better. The power in that band was weighted to Moonie and Townshend and the other two, as much as I like John—I don't know Roger Daltrey real well, I've never liked his attitude towards certain things, I've never liked his come-on. As a lead singer, it's never impressed me—that style of singing or anything. I don't want to knock the cat, but I think he's just another LV (Lead Vocalist) that wants to be a star, basically. The LV syndrome.

How did the "s" in Richards get detached in the first place?
Andrew Oldham knocked the "s" off at the beginning of the Rolling Stones' recording career because I think he thought there was some press to be grabbed out of the English press because Cliff Richard was still a really big act at the time. Since my first name had the same consonant sound as his, he thought that the confusion might help. He was a devious motherfucker, anything to intrigue people. After about nine or ten years [I said] "Bollocks! I'm Keith Richards and I put the "s" back on, but there was a long period when people couldn't decide which one was for real and which one wasn't. I think that mainly came about from that.

Have you ever worried about dying?
I'm no fonder of the idea than anybody else—I'd like to stave it off for as long as possible. I'm intrigued by it, actually.

12 |

KEITH LOOKS BACK

MARTIN ASTON | 1989

This 1989 Richards interview marks the period in which the Rolling Stones reassembled after a three-year hiatus. Said hiatus was one that many genuinely thought heralded the end of the band in the wake of Mick Jagger pursuing his solo career and refusing to tour *Dirty Work*. Richards's joy at working with the Stones again is evident in his answers. The discussion of the three-year break, though, is striking in light of the fact that over the past couple of decades that would represent quite a short gap between Stones activity.

Despite Richards's intelligence, a certain self-deception is also on display in him allowing the suggestion that current negligible album *Steel Wheels* compares favorably to Stones classics. However, it's also interesting that he concedes the Stones' hiatus had provided him a new maturity and self-discipline.

Originally published in Dutch, this interview here appears in English for the first time.

It's not unusual, but The Rolling Stones' publicist is getting worried because Keith Richards is over two-and-a-half hours late—"they were recording until six o'clock this morning," he excuses on Richard's behalf, but that only makes the two journalists even more worried that they'll only get a fraction of the interview they wanted. "Don't let him see any of the tennis at Wimbledon on television," the publicist pleads. "That will just divert his attention." Keith Richard, a tennis fan? Isn't he meant to be the world's most decadent man? The rock'n'roll star that you would have bet your life savings on dying before his time. The man who rumour says has had more blood transfusions than hot dinners. The man who one British magazine called The Man Who Just Said Yes. Finally, Richard arrives, wearing tennis shoes, and apologises for the terrible traffic that delayed him. The hotel suite television is turned off but another of his vices is immediately announced. "Hello, how are you . . . hold on a second while I raid the mini-bar," is his second sentence. He pours himself a large Jack Daniels and the publicist smiles.

Richard is already drunk and his voice slurs over some words, but he is remarkably lucid and sensible. He even has a tan, and looks very relaxed. The BBC Television crew who have followed Richard and fellow *Glimmer Twin* Mick Jagger around for a documentary about the preparation for the first Rolling Stones album *Steel Wheels* in three years, and the first tour since 1982 don't bother him at all. It's business as usual, and drunk or not, Richards happily accepts the camera and microphones set up to record our first five minutes of conversation. He's obviously not bothered about reputations and setting a good example at this stage. It's 26 years since The Rolling Stones' debut single "Come On"/ "I Wanna Be Loved" was released. The longest-serving rock'n'roll band in the world . . .

Do the Rolling Stones have an insatiable desire to be in the Guinness Book of Records *as the world's longest serving group?*
"I thought we probably already were! I'd like to keep them going for as long as possible because I think there's loads still left in them. Playing with them and making this record so far this year has been very impressive—everybody has a second wind. A little ventilation helped, I think. The fact that I'd been working consistently during The Stones' three-year break, and Mick's been working a lot, we came in well-oiled. When you're with The Stones all the time, it's very difficult to get a consistent playing continuum. You don't—you work frantically or you do nothing, and as much as you promise you'll keep your hand in there, you don't keep it in enough. It takes a long time to knock the rust off and to get back to the point you reached two months ago. This time, it's very interesting because since we're all very well-oiled, it's been very fast and easy. Charlie's playing fantastically and there's been some good songs, it's been fun to do. That's the answer to that!"

If you don't see Mick that often and haven't been best friends for a while, how easy is it to get back and write songs together?

"It's strange because even though you haven't seen each other for ages, sometimes months at a time, once you get in a room and start working again as the two of us, you just slip into that groove. I mean, we have been doing it for a while! You just click into gear. It's been a lot of fun writing with Mick this time. We've just sat in this little room in Barbados with these 50-50 arrangements and then recorded in Monserrat."

Would you find it hard to record in an urban environment like London?

"That depends on financial considerations. I'd love to record in London and we are mixing the album down the road. I can't remember when we last recorded in London but it's financially they made it so difficult for us, tax wise. Also, working in a city isn't necessarily the best thing for a band because always somebody's going to dinner or somebody's in town who someone's got to see, so you have to round everybody up, whereas if you have a little island and you're living in the studio, then you get a lot more done, quicker, and focused in without too many other distractions."

The three tracks I've heard sounded alive and kicking, and other opinions vouch that the songs have a renewed vigour, recalling the group's classic early seventies period. Pete Townshend recently said the album was the best he'd heard for ages.

"Well, that's encouraging. Thank you, Trousers! I think there is a feeling in the band although nobody is saying anything, that this is one of the special ones, when everything falls into place. It's probably the best since 'Some Girls' because 'Tattoo You' was pretty good but wasn't recorded as an album but just as a collection of tracks."

The television crew give us the sign they've recorded enough and start to pack up the microphones. Richards lights another cigarette.

Are you still smoking 100 cigarettes a day?

"No, I never have smoked that much. I tend to smoke a lot more when I'm working. It's about a pack a day. It depends. Sometimes I go off them. But you know, Aretha Franklin and Dionne Warwick both smoke loads more and have wonderful voices, so maybe I should."

Where does the new album fit into the Rolling Stones track record? "Hold on to Your Hat' is reminiscent of "Exile on Main Street," while the second "Terrifying" is more Stax-influenced, but with the Nassau feel of the "Some Girls" album.

"I don't know. There are a few echoes and a couple of previous Stones eras in there that maybe I recognise. The way this album was cut was very much the way 'Exile on Main Street' was, although that was a double album, which was fairly fast and very simple. Everybody plays in the same room at the same time, which is unheard of apparently in some circles. To me, it's the only way—if you want a group to sound like a group, then you have to be able to look at the guy in the eyes. You can't just overdub and have the drums done one day and go for some imaginary perfection of sound. There isn't such a thing. It's a matter of everyone playing together. I think that's the reason that people ever liked The Stones because the guys can play well together. God knows why, but it's evident to us all when we're in there and it's working, for some weird reason, this bunch of guys get together and something really basic and true happens."

Why have you called it "Steel Wheels"?
"Since we're touring this year, we wanted to give a feeling of motion. Of *rolling*. That's one reason. There's also this kind of idea of cog wheels as a symbol of 'everything's in gear,' although it's a very ambiguous idea. We also just like the words. I can't remember who came up with the title but it was a working title for a song that's now called 'Between a Rock and a Hard Place.' And people started calling us up from the record company, needing an album title, so we thought of going on the road, sprawling, blah blah blah . . . it's all packaging (laughs)."

How do you feel about being packaged and sold?
"We've always been packaged one way or another. You just try and keep as much control as possible and stop people screwing around with you. It's like being a frozen pea though."

Was there competition between you and Mick on the album in writing and singing?

"There always has been to a certain extent. That's how we work together. To see who can work together. But it's a pretty healthy one. Having worked apart for a couple of years, we've both learnt and developed slightly different styles, so we say, 'OK, you do that one.' It's the same way we worked on stuff like 'Happy' or 'Before They Make Me Run.' We recognise what each does better. Mick's playing quite a lot of guitar on this album. He's a good rhythm player. I'm singing two or three songs. He sings more rhythmically when he's playing, kind of like Aretha Franklin. If you can get her to play piano and sing at the same time, you get this extra kick. When I worked with her on the 'Jumpin' Jack Flash' video, I told her I'd appear but only if she played piano and sang. She said, "Nobody's asked me to do that for ages' and then she said she couldn't fly anywhere because her fear is too great, and I said, 'that's OK, you play piano and I'll bring the band to Detroit and I'll do it there' so this was a 50-50 deal."

Did Mick really call you up just as you were about to start your solo venture and agree to getting the Stones back together?

"For a moment, I thought he was deliberately trying to screw me up, (laughs) but in order to be working now, the subject would have had to be broached then, but there's always that part of you that thinks, 'you bastard, I know why you did that.' I never queried him. I just had a laugh about it. All I said was 'sure, after I've done what I want to do,' and that worked out to be the beginning of this year. But I initially told him to fuck off."

What were Mick's reasons for starting up again?

"You'd have to ask him that really. I would imagine that first off, he realised something I always knew, that this thing, The Stones, is bigger than both of us, and what else was he going to do was probably the biggest question in his mind after his own tour."

Doesn't that infer that the Rolling Stones becomes an institution and a place to hide rather than a purely creative grouping?

"There's certainly a danger of that, and I was worried about that going into it early this year. When I planned to go to Barbados to work with Mick for two weeks, I said to my old lady, 'I'll see you in two weeks or two days.' After the third day, she phoned up and said, 'OK, it'll be two weeks.'"

When a group first starts, you tend to think of them as three, four, five people who spend a lot of time with each other and share one goal. Does the Stones still feel like a group?
"There's a very common strong bond between all of us, which sometimes implies that you don't see a guy a lot of the time. I don't see Bill (Wyman) very much but when I do, we're friends. We like different things but we're still friends. When we're working together, you can feel it very strongly, especially as we are for the rest of the year. Also, in that respect, I think Mick feels the same as I do, that there is a lot to The Stones and it's not something you toss off lightly. OK, we took a three year break, but maybe the ventilation up to now has been very healthy. Maybe people just need a break after 20 odd years of working together. It doesn't mean you can't get back together. At the moment, it feels very positive. I'd be the first one to say it wasn't."

What made the difference?
"A little realism on everybody's part, maybe. It was also very important in those three years that we didn't just lie around. We all worked more consistently and continually than we have done since the late sixties. I've had to be up there, being responsible, for three years, whereas with The Stones, there's a five way split and you can fob it off and divide it between you. For the last three years, everything I've done, like working with Chuck Berry, the buck stops here with me. I've probably got a little more self-discipline than I had up until 'Dirty Work' just from having to sit on top of things and making sure they came off and worked. You have to deal with all of the problems, and Mick has had to do that as well."

How did Mick react to some of the criticisms you directed at him in a recent British interview? That he, "wanted to compete with Michael Jackson and Prince—why do that when you have years of integrity and respect behind you?"?

"He didn't like them and he said, 'Why do you keep having a go at me?' and I said, 'Because you deserve it' (laughs). I think The Stones can grow old gracefully—to be more mature and make it stronger doing it that way, instead of him trying to be all young at heart."

Does he feel there is a semblance of truth to your comments?
"I don't know but I don't think he would admit it to anyone else. Maybe on the odd night when he has insomnia and he's lying back and wondering whether it might be a little valid, but he'd never let me know."

Your disagreements came to a head over the "Dirty Work" album when Mick wouldn't tour after it was released. What was the general feeling about the album?
"It was a hard album to make, and usually Stones albums are fun. Everybody was having a bad year. The album was built to go on the road by being deliberately structured to play the songs live, simply and easily. I think there were good songs on there and that when we go on tour and eventually play the songs live then it might become more interesting. I think it's a consistent album—it doesn't do much but it hovers around the charts somewhere down in the hundreds all the time. It's a sleeper. I have a kind of soft spot for it but it was a real struggle to make, with people not being there, and Charlie was having a very bad year because he felt the untogetherness of Mick and myself very strongly, and Charlie responds very dramatically to that—he can't play with people who are antagonistic and it was disturbing him a lot. All of us actually. And then Stu died just after (December 12, 1985) and that really did it. The glue fell out of The Stones, which was the final nail in the coffin. Stu was the one who held us together. It devastated everybody."

But you played a concert of blues covers as a tribute to Ian Stewart in February 1986 which was the first time the Stones played in almost five years so he also unified the group.
"In a way, although the idea of actually going out and doing a big tour without Stu was totally out of the question. In a way you felt like it was Stu's band—one of the first rehearsals I ever went to, I walked up the stairs

at The Bricklayers Arms, just off Wardour Street in Soho and the only guy there was Ian Stewart. In a way, we felt like we were working for Stu. We can get sentimental about it, but we all miss the old sod."

Why was Ian never an official Rolling Stone?
"He actually was, until we started going into the packaging business, that is, making records. When you look at a six piece band, it can look unwieldy to a public relations officer, and also Stu didn't exactly look like a teenage idol, with his baggy grey suit and his civil service tie! Brian took on the task of saying so, which to me, says a lot about Stu. Unlike anyone's normal reaction, like 'sod you, I'm off, you ungrateful bastards,' he understood, saying he would take care of things, that he'd still play on the records, which was all he was interested in. He didn't want to be a pop star anyway."

Did Brian make sure Ian left the group because it would bring him even closer to being the centre of attention?
"Brian wanted to be a pop star. He didn't start off with that idea but nor did Mick, because you don't think it's possible, and we weren't playing music that you could ever imagine at the time would get us there, because it was just Chicago blues. We weren't writing our own songs then. But when it suddenly became feasible that you might be able to turn yourself into a pop star (laughs) . . . because if you get a chance to make a record, there's always a chance. The Beatles had opened that door, which put the gleam in Brian's eye."

Did Brian want to be a Beatle?
"He had to be as much of one as he could. But he couldn't control that desire. One little taste of fame and Brian was up there. But you can understand it. I didn't mind it either at the time but I don't think I had the same insatiable desire as Brian did. Maybe he never imagined that it could happen. You don't think when you're growing up that you'll have thousands of chicks wetting their knickers and screaming at you every night. It's a heady notion!"

You went back to Morocco to play with the Pan Pipers of Joujouka who Brian Jones recorded.

"Yes, for a track called 'Continental Drift' that we overdubbed using the Joujouka tribesmen who Brian recorded with in 1967 when we were virtually living in Morocco off and on for months. I was in Marrakesh for about seven months and Tangiers for two or three."

Didn't the Joujouka Pipers send a letter inviting you back?
"Yes, they suddenly got back in contact because they got organised a little now. They're like a national folk troupe with a government grant. The song we used them on is 'Continental Drift' which is really is an attempt in its own way, to cover the fact that everybody's music is connected. One minute, these guys are sounding like Irish pipes and the next, Indian . . . we wanted to get all of these different kinds of music in one track—African, American, English, and so on."

Is the song a recognition of the growth of world music?
"'Continental Drift' started off when Mick had this synthesiser organ sound that had a very North African riff but the beat behind it was very Western. I thought that tribal drums or pipes would be good with it, which he thought was funny because he'd just had a letter from the Joujouka people. Sometimes you wonder, you're just there and when a song decides to come together, it provides all the ingredients for you. I never think that I've written a song or created it—I was just around to pluck it out of the air. But we've used percussion many times from a very early stage. We love it—maraccas, tambourine. We'd fix them onto the hi-hat or bass drum, like for 'Sympathy for The Devil.' We just felt this song needed it. 'Continental Drift' was actually Mick's song and we just let him roll with it. I was just the guitar player who suggested the riff and the changes in the middle. In a way, it's dance music and has nice echoes of 'Miss You' in there. I don't mind tying things up. I like continuity, at least if it's done properly without trying to parody yourself. There's always a fine line there."

The freedom of drugs in Moroccan culture must have been inviting after Britain and America's hypocrisy.
"They had to carry me out! I went to Paris and a doctor had to give me vitamin injections for about a month (laughs). I was paralytic. It was the custom of the land—you go to visit a carpet dealer to buy a rug and he'll

get you stoned and get you to look at it, and the colours start to vibrate and he's giving the spiel that you'll never get anything like it. It starts from going shopping!"

Did you ever write what you think are your best songs when your were totally under the influence of drugs?
"A lot of them! There are so many! You fall asleep, and suddenly wake up after dreaming something. 'Satisfaction' I dreamt and just woke up, and it was all there in my head, you know, (sings guitar riff) 'I can't get no. . . .' usually, I'm together enough to have a tape recorder and a guitar next to the bed and get 30 seconds down, and I must have fallen back asleep without turning the tape recorder off, because the rest of the tape is me snoring for about an hour! In the morning, I didn't remember recording it but I looked at the tape and I saw it had run through, and then I suddenly remembered the dream had actually come awake. I think this was in the Kensington Hilton, before Morocco, so obviously you see I could already do that. You didn't have to go to Morocco! The latest one I wrote was for my own album, 'Talk Is Cheap' called 'Make No Mistake.' I woke up and put it down on tape one night, trying not to wake the old lady up!"

Have you ever released anything that you later regretted?
"No, they never came out. Maybe there are some but I can't think of any that did get released, although there were plenty that we just threw away when we realised that all we were trying to do was make a Rolling Stones track instead of playing it. Sometimes you don't realise it until the track's finished. It's not apparent to you until the end."

In the last few years, bands and artists of your generation have been producing some of their best work. I'm thinking of old masters like Lou Reed or Roy Orbison. Rock'n'roll and its audience are obviously getting older together . . .
"Demographics, you mean." (laughs)

Maybe Mick was spurred back into action because he saw everyone getting back in on the act . . .
"You've got a point there. I hadn't thought of that but, yes, Mick does keep

a very keen eye on what's happening and maybe he's catching a drift there as well. I shouldn't imagine that at the outset of getting the idea of getting The Stones back together that Mick felt it particularly attractive to himself. There must have been other reasons apart from love of The Stones and me (laughs), so that's probably another factor. I think it's a mixture of all those factors, and to be honest, I probably still am his friend. OK, I've beaten some of my best friends up. Sometimes you've got to. That's what a friend's for . . . , like, '*you stupid idiot*' and then, *bang*! Who else is going to do it? Everybody else will be saying 'yes' to you instead of 'wake up!'"

Do you think that either yourself or for Mick, that you needed to attract attention and win recognition? That you weren't able to let your egos rest for good?
"I don't think so. I think we feel recognised enough. I don't think it's any attempt to be recognised even more. You don't know what it's like being recognised! Sometimes it's bloody awful. Sometimes you just want to go out and the luxury of being anonymous is something else."

I meant more as a group and for your achievements.
"I understand that but for us, the idea of recognition starts on a very basic, personal level! The idea of The Stones being recognised for their achievements? I think they've had enough for what's they've done and that it stands us in very good stead. While I can't speak for everyone else, to me it's more the feeling that there is more in this band and it would be really dumb not to find out what it is, not to try and dig for it, because it's a pleasure to do and when it comes out right, there's no feeling like it in the world. And then there is that other feeling of what the hell else are you going to do?"

Decca are rereleasing all your singles as a CD collection called "The London Years." Were you or the group personally involved in the compilation?
"Quality control. Listening to them and saying, 'yeah, re-cut it.' I was incredibly surprised because I thought the older tracks would suffer with the pristine quality of CD but actually it reproduced them dirt-faithfully. It was actually more 'Emotional Rescue' or 'Undercover of the Night' that I thought was really weak on CD. But 'Come On' sounded like 'Come On,'

still with all the grunge on it and stuck together. 'Aftermath' and those albums sound really good."

What do you think of when you hear that grunge and your first tour in 1964 with the Everly Brothers and Bo Diddley?
"When I think of that tour, I just think I had a very, very compressed education! Having at first starved all day and listened to the blues and trying to get gigs, we had played the club circuit, and then when we were just out of the clubs, I was working with these guys that I'd listened to when I was growing up. I'd get the best seat in the house. I'd watch from the wings or climb the rafters, even stand out right front, and watch and see how they worked. In those six weeks, we learnt what might have taken us a couple of years to figure out if you hadn't worked with people like that. It was on that tour that we knew we were going to be successful. We saw how the audience reacted and how the girls on the street were in their best clothes. It all started happening."

Was the experience too much? You'd done five American tours by 1966.
"I think without realising it, we had road fever and were busted and exhausted by 1966."

Was that when drugs started making a serious contribution?
"That coincided with it. If you work almost every day of the year, you're already on adrenalin. It's an occupational hazard on the road and will be for time immemorial, I'm sure. You're a young guy in a dressing room with a load of other bands, some of which have been on the road for 20 odd years, and you're all sitting around waiting backstage, and you know you've got to drive 500 miles and do two gigs tomorrow, and you wonder how they do it, and someone goes, (puts on wheezy American accent) 'well, try one of *these!*' That's the way it is. It's part of the job and you have to deal with it one way or the other. It's not easy but that's basically you get introduced to drugs, with one guy helping out another. Truckdrivers do it all the time! But then we got fussy of course."

But you get written about in the newspapers.
"But that's got more to do with ambitious policemen than any really hard

news. OK, 'It's a fair cop'. . . I don't have a drug problem, only with the police."

Society's more to blame?
"Yeah, it is. At least, more than I am. Can we hold it here, I'm just going to fill this drink up (laughs)."

Do the early Rolling Stones recordings stand up as some of your best?
"Some of them. They're *good* records. It's always hard to tell. I think we've made a lot of consistently good records. Great? It's not for me to judge. I'm too close to them. I can listen to them now and again and some I like more than others."

Andrew Oldham had to lock you and Mick in a kitchen to force you to write your first song, which was 'As Tears Go By.' How come you came up with a ballad like 'As Tears Go By' (which went on to be a number one hit for Marianne Faithfull) rather than a Muddy Waters-inspired rocker?"
"I don't know, that was a very strange thing. It happens a lot when people start writing songs. There's no way you're going to attempt to write songs like . . . at the time, the idea of writing for The Stones was too big an order. It was just like, 'let's see if we can write a song.' We were trying to write 'Hoochie Coochie Man' and we came out with 'Greensleeves'! Funny that we'd write something totally opposite. But it gave us confidence to go on."

Did you think of writing something that would be a hit?
"No, we just wanted to get out of that kitchen! It was fairly easy to play because it's a fairly simple song, but maybe in retrospect, Andrew wanted a pop song. But we just wanted any song because he wasn't going to let us out until we'd got one. That was one of the hippest moves Andrew made, and he made a few. I had never thought of being a songwriter. To me, it was as different as a plumber was to a blacksmith. A different job entirely."

It must have been a bit of a shock to suddenly become a songwriter and write what people claimed were all-time classics.
"Sure, it was, but nevertheless I could live with it. I think that anyone who

can play an instrument can, if they want to, write a song, if they approach it in the right way. Whether they're great songs . . . . I've had plenty of time to hone down the technique of songwriting, under very high pressure. I had to come up with a number one hit every 12 weeks for about two years."

And that's where drugs come back again.
"Sure. You don't get much time working 350 gigs a year and having to write a hit song every 12 weeks. You'd take one to keep you awake to write the song and one to get some rest, to make the gig the next day. And maybe, in those days, you'd do two to three gigs a day, and in America, travel large distances in a station wagon."

What was the second song that you wrote?
"I think it was another hit that Gene Pitney had—'That Girl Belongs to Yesterday.' Some horrible song."

What was the first definable Rolling Stones song?
"The first one we felt happy with was 'The Last Time,' that we tried with the group. That was about six to nine months after 'As Tears Go By.' It was that long before we could find a style that would fit The Stones."

What kind of example do you think you can set to new groups?
"A pretty *bad* example! I've always ending up resenting people for thinking I've set a bad example. I can say, well, what can you learn from The Rolling Stones? To set a certain standard, depending on how serious you are on what you want to do. You shouldn't get too hung up on the flash end and the showbusiness end although you're going to get involved with it. Really, it's to try and keep as much control over what comes out from your efforts as much as possible."

Did you manage to?
"Probably more than most although it was never quite as much as I would have liked. Keep artistic control and don't let anyone try to tell you what to do. Don't be their vision of what you should be. You have to find yourself and know what it is. That's the name of the game."

13 |

STONE WINO RHYTHM GUITAR GOD KEITH RICHARDS CAN STILL RIP IT UP

IRA ROBBINS | 1992

Another of Keith Richards's interview mantras was once that he would never go on a stage without Charlie Watts. Touchingly loyal though that posturing was, he had to revise it when it looked during "World War III" as if he might never be given an opportunity to perform with Watts or any other Stone again. This interview feature sees a Richards who—having recently completed his second solo album—had now got used to the idea of working extensively with other sets of musicians after an entire adult lifetime in which there was no reason to do so.

Richards turned out to be wrong about Bill Wyman's retirement, a decision then unconfirmed. In referring to the death of the New York Dolls guitarist and Keef manqué Johnny Thunders, interviewer Ira Robbins touches on something disturbing about Richards's drug-drenched outlaw image: the fatal consequences of being in thrall to it.

Midnight at the oasis ...

Actually, it's 2 a.m. at the Hit Factory, but the mood is still calm as a desert breeze. Upstairs on West 54th Street, in studio A3, Keith Richards and his coproducers/X-Pensive Winos bandmates—guitarist Waddy Wachtel and drummer Steve Jordan, a pair Richards has dubbed "The Few"—are crossing the eyes and dotting the tease for his second solo album, *Main Offender*, due in record stores less than six weeks from this Labor Day weekend.

The night's work consists of nailing down the final mix of "Yap Yap," the only song of 10 not yet nailed down. In the control room, dressed in a tattered denim jacket, sporting the familiar accoutrements (Japanese headband, skull ring, handcuff bracelet), a Marlboro in one hand and a glass of his new preferred potion (Sunkist orange soda and Stoly: idolaters take note) gripped in the other, Richards chats amiably with a tipsy journalist. Wachtel and studio hound Niko Bolas, whose credits include Neil Young, Warren Zevon and Mary's Danish, are casually standing watch over a vast 48-track Neve board—a glowing computerized dashboard, complete with mouse, on which the look-ma-no-hands faders are moving up and back like keys on a player piano. The playback speakers vibrate loudly, carrying an unmistakable combination of true grit and hanging fire that could only be created by one man. Richards stands back from the action but dominates it nonetheless. He smiles fondly at his compadres putting the finishing touches on the track with diligent care. "They put it in the frame, and I sign it," he says.

Somewhere off in the night—California, perhaps, where Virgin Records America, now the berth of the Rolling Stones as well as its luminary guitar slinger, is HQed—some record company executive may be tearing out what's left of his hair, waiting with bated balance sheets for the album's 12th-hour completion. Back at the studio, however, you'd never know there was any deadline at all. "With harmony in the control room," says Richards, surveying his cheerful cockpit, "you stand a chance of making a good record."

Too old to be a brat, too bratty to be a snob and too rich to face mundane obstacles, Keith Richards can, and does, make his own rules. A charter subscriber to Bob Dylan's dictum that "To live outside the law you must be honest," he's as upfront and unabashed as they come. Asked about his forthrightness with the press, he replies, "How could I now possibly remember the lie I told somebody a month ago?" The impression Richards gives is of someone perfectly content to be who he is and do what he does with no evident regard for external judgments or objections. If there's anything he truly respects besides great music and great musicians—folks like Louis Armstrong, Muddy Waters, Chuck Berry, Otis Redding, Steve Jordan— it's nothing he makes an issue about.

"One of the most encouraging things about working in music is that you don't think about [people's] differences. What you play and the way you're playing it is the only thing that counts. It's very hard to comprehend that people have so much difficulty getting along out there, because with music it's always so easy." Referring to his triumvirate with Wachtel and Jordan, he says, "This is a funny lineup: the Jew, the black guy and the Anglo. We're a cross-section; it's a great three-way street. The way I think about it is that I'm working with New York guys. Charlie and Steve are from New York. Waddy's from Queens. Ivan [Neville] and I are the odd men out; he's from New Orleans. I'm an honorary New Yorker. I've lived here for so long, in all but passport and name I guess I'm just another immigrant."

So the clocks in Mr. Richards' neighborhood sometimes have to run backwards, keeping time in check while he works the graveyard shift all summer, making a record to his own standards at his own pace. Who's gonna pull rank on rock'n'roll's greatest living legend, now a charming, articulate family man nearing the half-century mark, and tell him to get the lead out just so some bureaucrat can put a tourniquet on his ulcer?

At least this wise elder is past the fatal attraction currently sweeping through the music world. "The flavor of the month is smack again. It's like déjà vu for me. I find it a weird dope to go into right now; I wouldn't do anything with needles these days." Regardless of what Keith Richards the man does, his past still casts a long iconic shadow. "It's the same thing Charlie Parker had to deal with—young kid horn players who thought they had to mainline in order to play. He'd say no, that's my thing, it's nothing to do with it. It's not gonna help. You ain't gonna inject talent into yourself."

I suggest to Richards that Johnny Thunders' death last year was like a child predeceasing a parent. "Guys that don't really know me," he says, "they're more likely to be the child of my image. That's something I have to think about, because I'm not exactly just like that. Chasing an image is a dangerous game."

The conventional wisdom on Keith Richards' solo career is that, since he's always been the heart and soul of the Stones anyway, the guitarist is perfectly capable of making respectably tradition-bound records without solo-stiff Mick Jagger as his boxing shadow. And if Richards' not much of a singer—the reviews of *Talk Is Cheap* (1988) and the short tour that followed it damn near exhausted whatever thesauri could offer to jokingly describe Alfalfa with a frog up his adenoids—his unflagging rock energy more than made up for it. As a solo artist the first time out, Richards was the sentimental favorite putting himself on the line with guts and glory. And in the rock'n'roll arena, those things count a whole lot more than pitch and vibrato.

This time, excuses and allowances don't enter into it. *Main Offender* puts *Talk Is Cheap* in perspective as a dry run, an experimental work in progress that hammered a bunch of sidemen—Wachtel, Jordan, bassist Charlie Drayton and keyboardist Ivan Neville—into something sturdy enough to reassemble four years later. "We already felt like a band just making the first record, but going on the road actually made us one. Playing live, we started to switch around a little on instruments. I kept that experience in the back of my mind while I was doing *Steel Wheels*; I dredged it up when Steve [Jordan] and I were talking about this album last year. We wanted to utilize more of the talents of the band. Ivan can do everything, which makes me sick. Charlie is basically a drummer, but he's also one of the best, most imaginative bass players I've ever played with.

"It only gets better when you start exploring the people you're working with. If you're working with people you only know vaguely you never really explore everybody's potential. What I like about making records is taking guys with different points of view and finding out if the focus ends up in the same place, if everybody's looking into that same spot. That's when it starts to happen."

What happened this time, in five studios on two coasts, was a focused, cohesive band album on which Richards' unceremonious growl is transmuted into a controllable musical instrument—not a smooth croon, mind you, but enough to satisfy the skeptics.

"My voice changed a lot from doing *Talk Is Cheap*, then going on the road with it, then doing *Steel Wheels* and taking that around. You keep singing all the time, and that makes a difference. With *Talk Is Cheap* I hadn't been singing for three or four years." The only tutors he will credit are the album's backup singers, Babi (pronounced Bobby) Floyd and Bernard Fowler (who also rolled with *Steel Wheels*). Beyond that remarkable development, *Main Offender*'s main achievement is to shake off the stylistic disorder, uncertain songwriting and calamity of studio guests that made *Talk Is Cheap* diffuse and patchy. "I didn't think we could do it all by ourselves; I felt I needed to utilize friends of mine. This time we felt more confident in what we wanted it to sound like, we had more focus. The first album was kind of a fishing expedition; we were just seeing what we could do. That's always difficult, because you can't create a style until you've got one."

Main Offender stumbles to its feet with the two weakest tracks sequenced right at the start, but the remainder is hard-hitting and hot: tight, tuneful nobody-but-Keith contenders topped off with one nifty reggae number and two tender soul ballads. Even when he's crooning softly, there's a tough center that keeps the edge sharp. "As long as the guts are there," says Richards, "that's the thing. You've got to get out there and play it—this stuff relies on muscle and sweat and the human touch. The music I play needs energy and power; I'm just trying to make it grow up a little within its parameters. I wanted to expand my interests and do some things that I had to put on the back burner because they won't work for the Stones." When it's suggested that no one else from his generation of British musicians has survived growing up with such unrepentant enthusiasm, Richards shrugs and laughs. "Maybe I'm retarded."

From pulsing evocations of *Exile on Main Street* (the amazing "Eileen," "Will but You Won't") to mellow Al Green romanticism ("Hate It When You Leave," a beautiful gift for Richards' missus) to sexy dance grooves ("Bodytalks," a duet with Sarah Dash), the album plays to the band's strengths, shifting the arrangements, the instrumental lineup and the drum sound to gear each song differently. On "Words of Wonder," Richards plays bass, Charlie Drayton handles drums and Steve Jordan grabs guitar. The well-realized goal was get the feel down and let details like lyrics—which tend intentionally toward the vague and evocative rather than anything explicitly rational—fend for themselves. Sometimes the simplest, most obvious ingredients cook up so sweet.

Five things you should know about Main Offender:

1) Its working title was Blame Hound. "I always seem to get blamed for everything," says Richards by way of explaining both options.

2) "Eileen" is named after his niece's roommate. "Steve and I were in my [N.Y.] apartment, writing. Because I don't live there very much, my son Marlon lives there and his girlfriend, and also my niece Marisa and her roommate Eileen. I kicked them all out when I came to town and I got them all settled down somewhere. I start playing the riff to the song on guitar and the phone rings. Steve picks it up. Hello? No, Eileen's not here. Bye.' This goes on every five or 10 minutes. By the seventh time I looked at Steve and said, 'You know what it's called, don't you?' A chick's name on a rock'n'roll riff—it's a classic."

3) The rattlesnake credit on "Wicked as It Seems" is for real. "We tried all kinds of shakers and rattles. We spent day trying rattling all kinds of different things that didn't work. I happen to have a walking stick from New Mexico which is a whole rattlesnake. The handle is its head; the tip of the stick is the rattle. And that was the thing that worked."

4) That's Babi Floyd making the horn noises with his mouth on "Words of Wonder." "Jamaican horn players don't play that stuff anymore: now they play in tune. That beautiful loose African dissonance—just slightly off—is gone. Babi laid down one line, and then went out and doubled it exactly. He knocked us out."

5) "I'm not an autobiographer. I write songs, I don't write a diary. I'm not baring my soul, I'm trying to distill things and feelings that I've had through my life and I know for damn sure that other people have had, and I try and evoke them. The only songs that interest me could mean anything to anybody. You can take what's happening to you and relate to it, and it will have a totally different meaning to you than it will to somebody else. I never think a song is finished being written just because you've recorded it and put it out. Now it can grow, because other people are going to hear it. That's when it takes on its real meaning."

When first and last heard from as solo artiste, Keith Richards was embroiled in an absurdly public pissing match with Mick Jagger. The singer had cast the first (ahem) stone with his solo debut, *She's the Boss*, in 1985. The group was making its own album, *Dirty Work*, around the same time and some of the band felt that Jagger was shirking his primary obligations. Tensions mounted after *Dirty Work*'s 1986 release, when Jagger nixed the notion of a Stones tour, a decision he stood by three years later in an interview with David Fricke: "The band was in no condition to tour. The album wasn't that good, the relationships inside the band were terrible, the health was diabolical." At the time, however, Richards, with typical candor, vented his feelings on the situation to the press. Jagger said a few choice words into tape recorders himself, and the fur really began to fly.

While the pair tore at each other with increasing vituperation, the rest of the Stones stood on the sidelines and waited for the dust to clear. Bill Wyman and Charlie Watts grumbled their own personal grumbles regarding the imbroglio and the protagonists, but seemed powerless or unwilling to do anything about it. And if Ronnie Wood—still the new kid, although he joined the band in 1975—ventured any opinion on the subject, it didn't make the nightly news. As Richards observed at the time, "The Stones are such a weirdo chemical mixture of people, such an unlikely bunch. Charlie's been totally embarrassed for 25 years."

With no plans to coalesce around, the Stones threatened to make their entropy permanent, to evaporate into the ether. Richards got sick of waiting around for something he couldn't control and made his move toward something he could. He signed a solo deal with Virgin.

In the fall of 1988, as Jagger was attempting a dubious tour of Australia and Japan to promote his second album, *Primitive Cool* (by then a year old and all-but-forgotten), Richards offered up *Talk Is Cheap*, which received a hero's welcome, while glamour boy Jagger was being brought down several humiliating pegs in the prima-donna stakes. But the final chapter had yet to be written, and a farfetched plot twist to be tried.

Richards wound up a short American tour with the X-Pensive Winos in mid-December, leaving behind the raw material for a live album and concert video, and headed to Eddy Grant's studio in Barbados for a songwriting summit with Jagger. If they could quit their fussin' and feudin', they would take a stab at turning the Stones' old engine over in the warm Caribbean sun before rolling the junker into the ocean. As he told every interviewer with a pen and pad, "I said to my old lady, 'I'll either see you in two weeks or in two days, because I'll know if it'll work the minute I get there." (Reports that the two reignited the band at the Rock & Roll Hall of Fame dinner in January were erroneous. "I don't think we'd have put that meeting on in public," Richards remarks.)

Of course, the pair of old cronies (one envisions the Glimmer Twins being played by Walter Matthau and George Burns in *The Sunshine Boys*, pushing each other's buttons with mirthless accuracy) managed to bury the hatchet—and not in each other. By February, word was out that the Stones would definitely be back.

Reviewing the whole imbroglio now, Richards says, "It was like the 25-year itch. Doing nothing is what led to friction. A lot of the shit that went down between Mick and I was basically us both boiling over about being locked in this Rolling Stones vacuum. You're either frantically doing something or you're doing nothing. That stop-starting is the worst thing."

He reckons *Talk Is Cheap* played a part in sorting out the band's problems, and cleared a plot for future construction. "It gave the Stones some continuity outside of the Stones, which made it easier for us to keep the Stones going in the long run. With a bit of luck, I think they"—Richards refers to the band in the third person—"have a couple of great records in them. The guys have still got the energy."

What's more, it readjusted the band's pivotal relationship. "I became able to talk to Mick and he became more reasonable. The Napoleonic bit went out the window: the delusions of grandeur were dashed."

Following the endless *Steel Wheels* tour of 1989 and 1990, a multi-legged trek which took the band to Eastern Europe, Japan and beyond (and yielded the obligatory live album and concert film), the Stones set themselves into several years' independent orbits, but gravitationally bound this time in a stable, friendly universe that ensures the band's return. Jagger's new solo record is due on Atlantic, former home of the Stones' own label, in November. Richards hasn't heard it yet, but doesn't seem optimistic. "I know he's cut it a few times with a load of different guys. I'm not sure if he really knows what he wants to do, or why he wants to do it."

Ron Wood published a book (*The Works*), released his fifth solo album (*Slide on This*) and is supposed to be on tour right about now. Charlie

Watts issued two tributes to Charlie Parker. Bill Wyman, who didn't make a record but did author an autobiography, remains the Stones' X factor. The group is scheduled to reconvene in February, with an album and possibly a tour before the end of 1993. Will Wyman, now 56, be on the iron horse when it pulls out of the station? "When it's time to work together I expect him to be there," says Richards. "I haven't seen Bill for while, I haven't spoken to him—but that's nothing unusual. One set of people around him say that he means it [that he's retiring], because he doesn't like flying anymore. But from other people who've known him longer, I get another drift: when it's all said and done he'll be there. I'm putting my bets—or at least my hopes—on those people."

What if Wyman does become a rock'n'roll retiree? "That wouldn't stop us," avers Richards. "I wouldn't want to change the lineup at this stage; it would be a wrench. But as long as you've got Charlie Watts and Mick and me and Ron . . ."

Back at the Richards ranch, however, February's a long way off, and the Rolling Stones will remain on the back burner till then. Meanwhile, there's plenty to keep Richards occupied. He's got this new album to sell, plans to finalize for another X-pensive Winos tour, a solid, stable family life, and lots of friends who like to play music. Over the past two years he's guested on records by John Lee Hooker, Bernie Worrell and former Chuck Berry pianist Johnnie Johnson. He performed with Dylan at a festival of the world's greatest guitarists in Spain. And now there's a third-rate biography of him in the shops. ("From all I can gather it's basically a rehash; going back through the files. I can't imagine why anyone would want to put it out.")

Richards renewed his occasional songwriting partnership with Tom Waits this year, leading to conjecture they were woodshedding for Richards' record. So far, the only thing to surface is "That Feel," on Waits' *Bone Machine*. "It wasn't *for* anything," says Richards. "We enjoy doing it, just kicking it around, having some fun. Maybe when we've got a few more songs we might think about doing it for something."

Waits was obviously paying attention during their creative bout, for his perceptions of Richards are downright poetic. "You can't drink with him, but you can write with him. He's totally mystified by music, like a kid. He finds great joy in it, and madness and abandon. He looks at the guitar, and his eyes get all big and he starts shakin' his head.

"He's made out of something that music likes to be around."

FILTHY, FILTHY, FILTHY! KEITH RICHARDS COMES CLEAN ON DISTORTION AND THE MEANING OF MUSIC

JAS OBRECHT | 1992

Keith Richards is one of the most esteemed guitarists in rock history. He's also one of the most unusual. Whereas axe gods are usually cut from a mellifluous, lightning-fingered cloth, Richards favors a stuttering and repetitive technique at which Jeff Beck or Yngwie Malmsteen might conceivably laugh but which not only somehow works but has produced some of the most memorable riffs of all time, "(I Can't Get No) Satisfaction," "Jumpin' Jack Flash," "Brown Sugar," and "Can't You Hear Me Knocking" among them. Almost as though just to prove he could stand his ground with the sort of aforementioned virtuoso, however, Richards is responsible for one of the most stunning guitar solos in the rock canon: Beck or Malmsteen would love to be able to claim credit for the scorching lines in the middle of "Sympathy for the Devil."

In this interview for *Guitar Player*, Richards talks with an experienced guitarist about his philosophy regarding his instrument. The technical stuff sometimes makes the exchange sound like a foreign language, but in the main it is highly intriguing. As a bonus, songwriting is also touched upon, including Richards's oft-aired theory that no songwriter "composes" as such but rather plucks melody from the ether via sensitive antennae.

Despite his skull ring and knuckles-in-your-face stance, rock and roll's ultimate outlaw proves to be a charming conversationalist, equal parts rogue, seer, cultural historian, and Peter O'Toole in *My Favorite Year*.

Keith Richards laces his answers with wheezy, rascally laughs and reckless cigarette jabs, and no subject seems taboo. Like his guitar playing with the Rolling Stones or X-Pensive Winos, Keith's thoughts are intuitive and funky, stripped down to the bare essentials.

We met in Manhattan a few days after he finished mixing *Main Offender*. Richards co-produced his new solo album with guitarist Waddy Wachtel and drummer Steve Jordan, who shared songwriting and production credits with Keith on 1988's *Talk Is Cheap* and *Keith Richards and the XPensive Winos Live at the Hollywood Palladium*. Although no other Stones appeared on it, *Guitar Player* called *Talk Is Cheap* the best Stones album in 17 years, and *Main Offender* mines the same vein. The grungy "999," which projects a looseness worthy of *Exile on Main Street*, and the hard-rocking "Eileen" are being considered for the album's first singles. "Words of Wonder" taps into Richards' love of heartbeat reggae, while "Yap Yap," "Hate It When You Leave," and "Demon" reveal his gentler passions. "Wicked As It Seems," "Runnin' Too Deep," and "Will But You Won't" provide prime examples of Richards' distinctive open-G-tuned 5-string guitar style.

During our two-and-a-half hours together. Keith covered more material than we could squeeze into this issue, so in future months look for his discussions of songwriting and blues heroes. On hand for our guitar lesson with Keith, music transcriber Jesse Gress contributed a few questions to this month's interview. Jesse and I were looking at the Gallery of Grunge photo spread in October's Distortion cover story when Keith sauntered into the room, a large tumbler in hand, and peeked over our shoulders.

Keith Richards: Ah, vintage fuzztones! Well, there's the first one [*points to the Colorsound*]. But where's that fucking "Satisfaction" one? They bunged me. I mean, it was a miracle. Whatever it was, it was the first one Gibson made. I was screaming for more distortion: "This riff's really gotta hang hard and long." We burnt the amps up and turned the shit up, and it still wasn't right. And then Ian Stewart went around the corner to Wallach's Music City or something and came around with a distortion box: "Try this." It was as offhand as that. It was just from nowhere. I never really got into the thing after that, either. It had a very limited use, but it was just right for that song. The riff was going to make that song or break it on the length that you could drag that [*sings fuzz line*]—*unless* you wanna get horns, which didn't work. We didn't have the time, and it wouldn't sound right. Yeah, it was one of those fortuitous things.

Distortion has become extremely popular again.
I suppose it's got something to do with the state of everybody's life. [*Laughs uproariously.*]

You've certainly been guilty of perpetrating some pretty filthy guitar tones.
Yeah, man. Still looking for 'em.

"999."
It's bad, huh? Yeah, I figured you might be talking about that. Believe it or not, that's through a Palmer simulator. A little box, no speakers. This is against all my principles, right? I plugged that mother in, and it's also through a Twin. But that sound basically comes out of the Palmer. Waddy and I are purists about amp sounds, but we couldn't deny that thing. At the right setting, it was, "Whoa! Hey! We can get this now, but it's taken a long time to find it."

Traditionally, how would you get distortion?
Traditionally, I'd set up that Fender Twin and maybe slave a little Champ. I've always found that a really good distortion needs to come from two different places. Obviously it's not true for "Satisfaction," where it's an obvious thing, but you want some distortion and some clarity at the same time where you need it, so I'd rather put it through two amps and over-load one of them.

Small amps?
Yeah. Champ or a little Silvertone, a Kay thing. I've got these little relics lying around, all of those weirdo amps. Bump that one up, use the other one for clear, and then you can mix the two in where you want them. It's very rare on a track that you want the same sort of distortion all the way through. I like to be able to play with it, put them on separate tracks so I

can juice the distortion where I want it after I've played it, because when you're playing it, you're not going to hear exactly what's going down on the tape. You've got the cans on.

Your Twin is serial number A00003.
Yeah. It's a bad amp, man! I wish I'd had it from day one! It takes a while to find those.

Your playing—especially in open G—is as idiosyncratic as John Lee Hooker's.
Oh, it is. I've been aiming for it. That's the best compliment I've had all day.

What was your passport into those types of open tunings?
In the '60s I knew some guys were obviously using other tunings, but we were just on the road so much, I had no time to experiment. Around 1967, I was starting to hang out with Taj Mahal and Gram Parsons, who are all students too. I mean, Taj, as beautiful as he is, is a student who basically approaches the blues from a white man's angle. He's got it all together, and always did have, but he's very academic about it. He showed me a couple of things. And then Ry Cooder popped in, who had the tunings down. He had the open G. By then I was working on open E and open D tunings. I was trying to figure out Fred McDowell shit, Blind Willie McTell stuff. So in that year I started to get into that, and the Nashville tuning the country boys use—the high stringing [the bottom four strings restrung and tuned an octave higher than usual]—and all the other things you can do. When I was locked into regular, I thought, "The guitar is capable of more than this—or is it? Let's find out."

Open C must have struck the resonant chord within you.
It did, man, it did. It's just that vibe. And I realized that one of the best rhythm guitars in the world ever is Don Everly who always used open tuning. Don is the killer rhythm man. He was the one that turned me on to [*windmill—waves his right hand*]—all of that. It's the weirdest thing, right, because it's country shit, basically. That was why the Everly Brothers stuff was so *hard*, because it was all on acoustic. So then I had to ask,

"Can I translate this 5-string thing onto electric, or will it just rumble and not make it?" By being electrified, you can overdo it. You've got to get a certain dryness of tone and distortion at the same time. So it's more working on the sound. Five strings, three notes, two fingers, and an asshole, and you've got it! You can play the damned thing. That's all it takes. What to do with it is another thing. After playing that concert tuning for years and years, it suddenly broke open the guitar again to me. It was like a new instrument almost, except I knew a few things so I could follow it through. It was like a rebirth. Suddenly I got enthusiastic about playing again, instead of thinking, "Oh, shit, I can't think of anything." Three of the strings were still the same [D, G, B], so you have the structure, so you say, "Well, what can you do? How do you make a minor? How can you do this and that?" So it was an exercise in a way, self-imposed. But it was fun to do, so I did it. When I first started with it, it was strictly blues stuff. The 5-string suggests new musical forms to you that you wouldn't do on 6-string. You'd say, "No way!" I'm still finding things on that 5-string, like the little [pedal-steel-type] break in "Eileen"—you wouldn't even attempt it on . . .

It sounds like a B-bender.
Yeah, there is a bender on there as well, but that's not the guitar that's playing that. I'm always aware of the weight I put with my thumb on the neck. Half the time if I'm playing a bender, the whole thing's gone out of tune because I've put some weight on there. So you have to learn to be pretty weightless on that thing to make it work. "Eileen" was my first attempt with it, but there's about eight guitars on there overall.

Before we started, I kind of decided to pick up on some of those experiments that I left off around "Street Fighting Man" time. I went into the heavy overlaying of guitars, all of them different open tunings, like "Street Fighting Man" and "Jumping Jack Flash," which is in open *E*, because there's a certain ring that you need there. And what's always fascinating about open stringing is you can get these other notes ringing sympathetically, almost like a sitar, in a way. Unexpected notes ring out, and you say, "Ah, there's a constant. That one can go all the way through this thing." And then it gets down to touch, like hitting the two bottom strings hard and leaving a little space for an open one to ring. You get into that. I thought I knew six strings, and I don't even know five. [*Laughs.*] Let's go to the ukulele, see what we don't know!

After all these years, *G* tuning is something I still look upon as a baby. There's so much in there, and you know that you're missing a lot of it half the time, because you're just sort of blocking in what it is you do know. It never stops to amaze me, that open 5-string. It's so easy to get a groove going with it, especially if you're not Chuck Berry and don't have hands with a six-feet spread!

Chuck was my man. He was the one that made me say as a teenager, "I want to play guitar, Jesus Christ!" And then suddenly I had a focal point, but not that I was naive enough, even at that age, to expect it to pan out. But at least I had something to go for, some way to channel the energies that you have at that age. And definitely with rock and roll, you have to start somewhere around then.

Right when your hormones are kicking in.
Yeah, yeah. Exactly. That's it. If you don't have the juice then, you never will. And then it's a matter of sustaining the juice.

Like Muddy Waters, you approach rhythm guitar with the primal energy of a sex drive.
Well, that's a compliment. Thank you.

Do you feel that way?
Yeah! He's my man. He's the guy I listened to. Maybe I just picked it up off of him. I recognized it. It was just the same as my drive. I felt immediate affinity when I heard Muddy go [*plays the opening lick from "Rollin' Stone"*]. You can't be harder than that, man. He said it all right there. So all I want to do is be able to do that.

Do you hear a correlation between Latin styles and early rock and roll? The Cuban clave rhythm figure is basically the Bo Diddley beat.
I have no problem with that, because basically any beat that you've got on this continent come from Africa. Really. The climate and the people

controlling your area—Spanish, French, or English—would determine from there which way it would go. But if you take a broad view of it, any music from the islands or Latin America is from Africa. It's the predominant tribal beat of that area. This is why I always found the islands like Jamaica and reggae so fascinating. To me it was just another manifestation of the movement of rhythm and harmony and melody over the face of the planet. That's what counts. Give me a tribe's music, and I'll tell you how they live, what they smell like, almost. That would give me more information than talking to them or looking at 'em.

There's no lying when you're playing music.
Exactly. This is why the Iron Curtain went down. It was jeans and rock and roll that took that wall down in the long run. It wasn't all those atomic weapons and that facing down and big bullshit. What finally crumbled it was the fuckin' music, man. You cannot stop it. It is the most subversive thing.

I was so surprised when we started getting busted. What have they got a hard-on against a rock and roll band for? And we're being perceived as some social threat to the world! Now I realize they were a little hipper than I was—where they got unhip was in their way of dealing with it—but they sussed it before I did: This shit could change the balance of the world. Meantime, I thought they were narrow-sighted. I mean, "Why hit on a rock and roll band? This is the British Empire! A 5-string fucking guitar and a couple of guys are gonna change that? And suddenly they're leaning on me?" And when all of this shit went down in Europe the last few years [*snaps fingers*], that's when I realized it. No wonder they were a little uptight, because they saw more of the potential than I did at the time.

Ry Cooder says that the truth of who you are is most evident when you play acoustic.
Probably because you've got nothing between you and the strings. Yeah, he's damn right. Every guitar player should play acoustic at home. No matter what else you do, if you don't keep up your acoustic work, you're never going to get the full potential out of an electric, because you lose that touch. You get sloppier. Electricity will give you some great effects

and some great tone, but if you don't control it, it can easily take you over the edge into some supersonic nowhere land. I don't play electric guitars at home. I play acoustic.

What's your favorite one?
Right now I've got that new replica of the L-1, *the* Gibson, which they gave to me and which I put on a lot of this record. They've done a lovely job on that. It's a great-sounding guitar, and I don't like new guitars, generally speaking. I like 10 or 20 years on 'em. This L-1 is the same one Robert Johnson played. I also have one that was made in 1934, but they do wear out. There's a possibility that in a couple of years this new one will sound just like the guitar that Johnson was playing—his guitar was probably four or five years old when he played it. They're not sturdily built; they won't last forever. But within four or five years, these replicas, being as well-made as they are, might have just the right amount of ring and bite on them.

Do other new guitars impress you?
Those new Music Mans I've been using impress the shit out of me. They made me a 5-string one and a 6-string bass. But just the basic guitar itself, to me, is the most impressive guitar since the Tele or the Strat. You can change that configuration of pickups in a few minutes. I've got a couple of them set up. I mean, I'm not one to go very much beyond the Teles. I have the odd Guild and Gibson and Gretsch shit that I use for extra color here and there, semi-acoustic shit. I love guitars. But the Music Man impresses me as an all-around working unit. Sometimes in the studio I can make the thing sound like a Strat or a Gibson.

Do you like high action?
It depends what tuning and what I'm going for. I've got no set thing for anything. I've got three or four 5-strings in there—one with high action, one with low, and one with medium. The combination of the guitar with the amp, to me, is more important than which guitar I play. No one guitar is going to sound great for everything, unless you're one of those guys that only has one sound [*laughs*], and if you don't deliver that, you're fucked. I

just keep shopping around. I say, "Well, there, he sounded good through that. Let's try him through the Bassman. Or the Bandmaster." I mean, you're talking electric guitar. What have you got? You got guitar, you've got your own asshole, and you've got an amplifier. Somehow these three things have to come to be where you want 'em all to be at once. "A Strat might sound good through that Bandmaster, but would the Telecaster sound better through that Champ?" It depends on what sound you're going for. Basically I'm talking recording here, because that's what I've been into for the last year.

For live work, I put the Twin up, and give me Teles and the odd Strat here and there. It's a different criteria. But when you're recording, you never know quite what you're gonna get. The great thing about music is its unpredictability. It never ceases to amaze me. I can be bored stiff—"Oh, man, I wish I had a night off"—and then a little problem will come up, and suddenly I'm in. I say, "How fascinating! Why should that . . . What's the difference between those sounds," and then you see faces light up in the control room. Suddenly you find the right combination, and you're on the track.

You've been described as being able to judge a room's sound just by the snap of your fingers.
Yeah, from echo.

What do you listen for?
The return off of the surface of the room. Where it ends and where it doesn't. You can't tell just by doing that [*snaps fingers*], but you walk around and say, "Well, this is where the drums should go, because we're going to play together in here." You get a bit of information from that, and you look at the size of it and the height. It's almost instinctive; it's not something that you can guide technically and say sure that this is going to work. But you can get a feel within five minutes of walking around a room: Is that a big enough space? Is the ceiling high enough? You give a couple slaps to hear where echo returns from and how quickly it returns. Ambience is one of my favourite things. All the stuff that I cut, whether it's with the Stones or the Winos, it's all room sounds. I've got 10 micro-

phones up in the sky—[*waves arms*] here, there, bring this one in, that one. The room is the important thing.

Has your method for recording acoustic guitar changed since "Satisfaction"?
No, not much. I started making records by saying, "Do I like it? Does this turn me on?" And I refuse to be budged from that criteria. Really. If I start to think about what do they want to hear, then I say I'm out of here. That's not the way I've ever done it. The only times people have liked my stuff is when I've done it because I like it. I'll reserve that for my criteria for anything I do. If I start trying to second-guess people, then I may as well be Liberace or Lawrence Welk. That means I *want* to be a star, instead of having to be forced to be one.

Why do you always play with another guitarist?
Because it's more fun. No one guitar player is that interesting. Not one—I don't care if it's Segovia, Hendrix, anybody. Robert Johnson is the most interesting idea of a solo guitar player to me, and he was looking to go for a band. I'm interested in what I can do with somebody else—how we can interact and play things back and forth and pick up a dropped beat and fling things against the ceiling to see if they stick—and if they don't and fall on your head, you still pick it up. To me, that's the fun of it. And at the same time, you're learning, because you're turning each other on. The solo guitar thing is a vacuum.

With the Rolling Stones, Woody could drop his pick and you'd intuitively cover his part. Do you have a similar relationship with Waddy Wachtel?
Yeah, yeah. I'd known Waddy since the middle '70s, and I've always liked his stuff. Waddy and I have always had that empathy, and he understands my music. I don't have to explain anything to Waddy. That's what you look for, that ESP doesn't come hard.

That's evident with Steve Jordan, who follows you to a T.
Yeah. I'll drop a beat, he'll pick it up and let it fly. We're playing with time, on this album particularly. But this is like life, right? What is life but playing with time? So on a musical level, that's what I'm doing. If you've got

the right guys with you, you can let it flow and get a little daring without being clever. You want to push the edges, and strict time becomes less and less important, since you can always find the one. That obvious structure just gets boring and unnecessary. You say, "Hey, this music can float a little more. I'm gonna use things I learned from Doc Pomus, from Leiber-Stoller, all of that Latin stuff and floating over the lines and leaving out lines and smacking the chorus in your teeth, and then pulling back." Just playing with it is more fun, and that will make it sound more interesting to other people. God knows what I'll do when I get back with the Stones and it's strict time again!

You've sometimes been criticized for turning the beat around.
See, this is what you get from musicians. You're always in this dangerous stall, especially when you've been in the game as long as I have: "What are you trying to do? Turn on the other musicians and give them a little jerk around? Ooh, that's clever." But that's not the name of the game. It's alright jerking around with the time, as long as it all falls in place for Joe Blow. I'm very conscious that a lot of musicians get in this cliquey little thing of turning each other on, and it's all little in-jokes, because you've got nothing better to do except get clever with each other. And it's almost an admission of failure to get into that. I'm very wary of trying to please other musicians.

Your music is not about precision.
No, it's not. It's about chaos. I suppose it reflects my life and probably everybody else's. Nothing happens quite when you think it's supposed to or when you want it to, but when it does, you've got to roll with it. You learn, and you get back up again and pick it up. It's very hard to explain, but I try to do the same thing with the lyrics that I do to the music—a juxtaposition that kind of slams you the wrong way here, and then suddenly it's in the right place. It's just like life.

The music is bigger than all of us. What are we? We're just players, no matter how good. If you're a Mozart or fucking Beethoven or Bach, all you are is just one of the best. If you're an Irving Berlin or Gershwin or Hoagy Carmichael—or if you're Herbie Hancock, God forbid—everybody's got their spot in this. I hate to see music being used as propaganda, which increasingly more it is. But then I think back and realize it always has been—national anthems and signaling [*imitates trumpet flourish*]. When it comes down to it, music evolved out of necessity, not out of pleasure. Somebody got lucky, whipped the other tribe's ass, and then they could use music for fun for a little while because there's no competition. So you get the rockin' down: [*sings*] "We won, we won." You know, so you start to get those songs coming in, apart from just the signaling. And after that, there's this progression.

Music's meaning to people is one of the great mysteries. Forget economics, forget democracy or dictatorships or monarchies. The most fascinating relationship is between people and music and how it can do what it does with no apparent sweat. Who knows what it can do? It's a beautifully subversive language because it can get through anything. I don't care if it's porous or bombproof or has a *Star Wars* shield over it—music will get through. That's my experience.

You've only got to look at the new *Billboard*—who's on the front? Fuckin' Beethoven and Mozart. You can't ask for better than that, boys. Imagine what they'd have done if they'd had a little DAT recorder, instead of all of that imagining it: "Well, that looks good; it might sound great." Those guys had to carry it all up there [*taps forehead*]. Imagine if Mozart and Beethoven had a fucking Walkman! You wouldn't have had 26 overtures, you'd have fifty-bleeding-nine. I mean, those guys would be *green* with envy, man. They would burn their wigs. "Off with it! Burn it! Give me that tape recorder!" [*Laughs.*] What they would have done! They'd have prostituted themselves for one of those things: "No problem! Yeah, give it to me up the ass! Just give me the tape recorder." Go to jail for that shit. And that's where we're lucky, and we can't abuse it.

Have you written any songs lately that seem better suited for the Rolling Stones?
That's a good question, because this leads me to my very point with Mick. In 1985 we started getting into solo shit, and I told him I didn't want to be put into that position after all these years, because I knew it would be

a conflict of interests. I fought him like a dog not to do that. I knew then that I'm gonna write songs and think, "That's mine. Stones can't have that. Oh, the Stones can have this." What do I do? Give 'em the best I got? The second-best? In retrospect now I was right to fear that, but at the same time, the Stones had been in that pressure cooker too long. If you're working with the Stones [*points to a world map dotted with dozens of locations of Stones shows*]—well, that's a year. And then it stops, and you do nothing. And that's what the Stones had to live with from the early '70s until the middle '80s: Constant work for a year and a half, and then nothing for two years. And that stopping and starting was fraying. That was the underlying force of what all of that shit was about. It could have been about women or solo records or quitting smoking or any other thing, but it had to happen. I'm now firmly on my other path as well, and I can see that it's better that I work, Mick works, Charlie, and everybody, so that when we do get together, there's none of this taking the thing off the block and lube jobs.

We'd been too long in that vacuum, in that bubble. You can't live in there forever. The Stones got too big, really, for what the Stones wanted to be. Suddenly you can't just go, "Hey, guys, let's go play down the bar," which is how the band started. It's a strange thing. I wish the Beatles were still around in a way, because they could have kept on doing what they always did first for us, which was open the doors and take the brunt. (*Laughs.*) Playing football stadiums, man, is not where it's at. It takes you into another realm where you don't really want to be. But if that amount of people want to be there, who's gonna say no? So you're, like, stiffed. Give me a 3,000–4,000 seater any time—with a roof on it, no wind, no rain. A good sound system in a controlled environment. Hey, we're rock and roll. What's it need? A basement, a garage. Start from there.

That's the other thing—fame. That can screw you. People come up and ask me about this and that, and I say, "You're talking to a madman." I mean, my view of the world is totally distorted. Since 18, I've had chicks throwing themselves at me, and by a miracle, I turned the little teenage dream into reality like that [*snaps fingers*], God knows how. And therefore my view is gonna be distorted, at the very least.

What's the most dangerous aspect of fame?

Believing it. Very, very dangerous. It's not very good for people around you, and even worse for yourself. That's my experience of it. It's one of the reasons I don't regret zooming into the dope thing for so long. It was an experiment that went on too long, but in a way that kept my feet on the street when I could have just become some brat-ass, rich rock and roll superstar bullshit, and done myself in in another way. I almost forced myself into that in order to counterbalance this superstar shit that was going on around us. I said, "No, I want to put my foot in a deep puddle, because I don't want to hang out up there in that stratosphere with the Maharishi and Mick and Paul McCartney." It was almost a deliberate attempt to get out of it. Like letting the broken tooth hang for five years— deliberate anti! I was doing an anti-gig, but it still stuck. In retrospect, it shouldn't have worked, but that's what I had to do. When I look at it now, that was one of my rationalizations for it. And the other is, hell, I was just sort of into De Quincey's *Opium Eater* a century too late. [*Laughs.*] I just saw myself as a laboratory: "Well, let's see what this does."

Which substances worked best for producing music?

Well, a speedball doesn't go down too bad! [*Laughs uproariously.*] Those were the days. Oh, fuck. You've got the answer there. [*In a loud voice*] A clear mind, a cold shower, and a 10-mile walk after breakfast—those are the ingredients that make good records, not dope.

Bill Wyman once claimed that the Rolling Stones are the only major rock band where everyone follows the rhythm guitarist.

Well, that's the best thing he's ever said about me! [*Laughs.*] He never told me that. Bill, bless your heart. I just hope he's there to follow me the next time around. Which leads us to that question, right? Whether or not he's in the band is up to him. As far as I'm concerned, there's no way I want to change that lineup, unless he's absolutely adamant. I have my spies out. I talk to his ex-old ladies, who can see him. Some people tell me he means it, and then I speak to some of his older friends who have a feeling he'll be there. So I'm getting these two messages. And Bill is not the guy . . . We don't talk on the phone, because he's too guarded and I'm too pointed. I have to see his eyes to know. It was a spin on my head when I discovered he just doesn't like flying anymore. Hell, you can't think of everything. There's all kinds of angles and possibilities on this thing with Bill, but I don't want to change this lineup unless I really got to. And he's the only one that can make me have to. Playing guitar is one thing, playing the other guys is another. I realize that more and more as I go ahead. Hey, I've become a psychologist over the years. I do it almost automatically.

Many people have mimicked your image and attitudes. What would you have musicians learn from you?
Forget about the clothes and the haircut and the moves, and then concentrate on the guitar playing. First, you've got to have that. I see a lot of guys out there—and it's like weird for me—and they've got it all down except the playing! [*Laughs.*] I mean, hell, they look more like me than me! It's like fashion. It's all got to do with video and shit. Once you start to get the eyes involved with music, music will take the back seat, and that's what the video thing is. Why can't video find its own niche in life and get off music's back? This is not going to endear me to VH-1 or MTV, but they know how I feel about it. It's a confliction of the senses. You're gonna judge a record by a TV screen and some images with some shitty little sound coming out of those boxy little speakers? The way they deliver a record is with some semi-nude chicks, which I have no problem with, but not to sell my music. The music becomes like elevator background music, relegated. And of course, then you've encouraged people to become poseurs and not composers. Andy Warhol's little dream's come true: Everybody's a star for 15 minutes.

Music, to me, is the joy, right? I love my kids most of the time, and I love my wife most of the time. Music I love all the time. It's the only constant thing in my life. It's the one thing you can count on.

15 |

STONES KEEP ROLLING

ROY TRAKIN | 2002

This being a book of Keith Richards interviews, Mick Jagger is usually mentioned only in passing. However, an exception has been made for this interview twinset, whose timing and content irresistibly provides a window onto how the two men have gone their separate philosophical ways over the years. Once so united in their defiance of convention that their joint imprisonment was perfectly symbolic, Mick and Keith have grown so much apart that in 2002 Jagger did something Richards would sooner die than contemplate: accept a knighthood. However, it's more than that. Richards seems now as warm and approachable as Jagger seems uninterested and uptight. To be fair, Jagger has to be admired for the way he has always refrained from succumbing to the temptation to be as publicly scathing about Richards's considerable failings as the latter has been about his. However, conducted only three months after the announcement of Jagger's acceptance of a knee-dip, these parallel conversations speak volumes about the now insuperable differences between the self-styled "Glimmer Twins."

In conversation, Rolling Stones founders Mick Jagger and Keith Richards couldn't be more different. Jagger is diplomatic, political, professional, making sure he doesn't offend a single potential Stones buyer, and filled with bonhomie, but chilled to the bone and easily bored. On the other hand, Richards is exactly how you see him, cigarette cocked between his lips, leaning up against Ronnie Wood, truly the salt of the earth, ready to say anything about anybody, listening and responding, giving you all the time you need, a real person.

A study in contrasts, Jagger and Richards are rock's greatest living duo—the heart and soul of the Rolling Stones for going on four decades now. They're celebrating the milestone with a number of high-profile projects, including the Oct. 1 release of their own greatest-hits answer to the Beatles' *1*, Virgin/EMI's *Forty Licks*. The set also features four new songs recorded with producer Don Was in Paris, including the first single, the aptly named "Don't Stop." In addition, Allen Klein's ABKCO has just re-released the band's entire pre–*Sticky Fingers* catalog—22 albums in all—in SuperAudio CD that have old fans raving at the meticulous re-mastering, which makes the discs sound like they were recorded yesterday.

Mick and Keith were in Toronto, where they recently played a warm-up gig at the Palais Royale prior to the launch of their massive Licks tour, which got underway this week (9/3) at Boston's Fleet Center. They were hoodwinked into spending some valuable phone time with *HITS'* stalker Roy *"Well You Heard About the Midnight Tummler"* Trakin.

PART 1: MICK JAGGER

The Toronto warm-up show sounded fantastic.
Mick Jagger: It was good fun. Some bits were better than others. [Laughs] It went really good.

The set list was pretty interesting. Is it close to what we can expect on the tour?
I don't know what we're going to do. It depends on the place we're playing, the town we're in.

So there'll be different sets depending on the size of the venue in each city.
That's the way I see it, really. In the cities where we're doing three venues, I see the theaters as much more the place to do songs that aren't perhaps so well-known.

For the real fans.
It's not so much that they're more real; they're no more real than anyone else. It's just easier in a small place to play what you like. You can hear

better. It's just more suited to experimentation. It's not so much of a show as a musical performance. The bigger it gets, the more of a spectacle it is. In an arena like the Garden, you have to strike a good balance between well-known material and something that's not quite as popular. And in a very, very big stadium, I think you have to veer towards the well-known. I think that's what works. You don't want to play too many mystery numbers in a stadium.

So you've been in Toronto this whole time?
Yup. Just playing, doing a whole bunch of songs. Last 10 days, we've been trying to narrow things down a bit. Getting the set lists together. [Laughs] It sounds good.

Is playing together like riding a bicycle for you guys at this point? Do you just jump back on and start peddling?
Some of it feels like that. But we had quite a lot of things to work out. If you're only going to do 22 songs, then it would be easy. But if you're trying to get a repertoire of, say, maybe 60–70 songs, that's quite a lot to remember. And there's a lot to go wrong.

Is it still as much fun for you as it's always been?
It was good to do the show the other night. It gives you a more realistic feel. Otherwise, you're stuck in a rehearsal room. Once it gets outside of there, it becomes much more real and more fun. You get feedback from an audience as to how they like one number over another. I mean, that's what you're doing. You're not doing it in isolation.

I noticed in the Toronto set list some chestnuts you really haven't played for awhile, like "Heart of Stone."
I can't remember when we played that one last. Years ago. Sounds a bit different now.

How did you go about putting together this greatest hits record?
First thing I wanted it to be was the most famous songs from the beginning to the present-day. Then I just threw in a few more favorites that

maybe weren't singles, but songs that have been played alot and people have always liked. And then, we wanted to put some new songs in, so we went to Paris to record. We ended up with four new songs and a whole lot more material we'll work on later.

Why did you decide to put out a best-of record at this point rather than a whole new album?

I thought it was good to put together this package, which had never been done. I'd hoped to put it together for a while, but I was ready to forget it, basically. But it seemed like a great time to get a whole overview of everything from early '60s to present-day.

You and Keith appear to be in mid-tour form with some of the exchanges going on between you about the solo album and your knighthood.

I don't do sniping.

When are you getting knighted?

I haven't heard anything about it since I got the first letter.

Keith said you shouldn't have settled for just a knighthood.

I don't do sniping. I told you that. So you can't get me to do it.

I was just curious about your take on being knighted.

It's a very nice thing to have. I mean, it's nice to be asked [laughs]. But it's something you should wear lightly. Understand what I mean? You shouldn't make a big deal about it. You shouldn't ram it down people's throats . . . or put on airs or graces. You should just accept it as a nice compliment.

Were you disappointed in the sales performance of your last solo album, *Goddess in the Doorway*?

Well, I think we did pretty well. We sold well over a million worldwide. We had a record company that was self-destructing in the United States. Which is still in the process of picking its pieces up. [Laughs] I know because I'm still on it. Outside the U.S., we did quite well. We did Top Five in Europe, which I think is good. In a lot of territories, we did as much as *Bridges to Babylon*. In America, two-thirds of the company was fired the day the record came out. [Laughs] It wasn't very good timing.

What's your take on the current disputes between artists and labels here in the States?
There's always been trouble, ever since year one. We used to have tremendous rows with our first record company [Decca], who were completely hopeless. They just didn't get it. One of the problems is, record companies cut costs. I'm not a great expert on this; I'm just kind of guessing. But as they cut costs, they employ fewer people that really have any rapport with artists at all. And people end up with lots of different jobs to do that they're not necessarily suited for, but are only too happy to do. I think that communication just gets completely broken down. Virgin was in a process of complete reorganization. They couldn't manage to sell the company, so what were they going to do next? And you get caught in the middle of that, even though it has nothing to do with you, to be perfectly honest. If you're caught in that, you can say they didn't promote the record properly. Trouble is, those people are more worried about keeping their jobs than promoting your record.

You may be one of the few bands with enough brand recognition to do break away from the major-label system.
I think that's definitely something to think about in the future. We all know the music business has shifted a lot. Music's evolving into lots of other formats. It's in a different place. I'm sure it's still exciting for some people, but putting out CDs doesn't seem to be quite the event it used to be . . . for various reasons. Wouldn't you agree? One has to reconsider the whole thing of recorded music and its distribution, but everybody is starting to.

So far, there hasn't been too much talk about this being the last Stones tour.
I think people have just gotten fed up asking. I mean, I have had that question. I always give the same boring answer, which is just sort of exis-

tential. Without even starting the tour, we could all get killed in a bus. You never know what's going to happen. You can't tell the future.

I just read your former manager Andrew Loog Oldham claims in his autobiography he once slept in the same bed with you.
I can't talk about my affairs from 50 years ago or something. This is a music magazine, isn't it?

What about your own autobiography? Haven't you been working on that for years?
That was 15 years ago. That's really old hat. I don't wanna go there. Are we almost finished now? Thank you very much. It was nice talking to you.

PART 2: KEITH RICHARDS

Have you been keeping track of the turmoil in the U.S. record industry these days?
Keith Richards: Of course. Things like EMI going, like, *doink* . . . I mean, we've worked with these people, off and on, all our lives. They're as true and blue as the British Empire and all of that. Changing times, man. They were living far too high and far too fat for far too long, ya know?

All the musician wants to do is play and record, but you guys seem to have taken care of business through the years.
We don't get involved to that extent. We make our deals and then we fulfill 'em. The difficult thing has been in the area of promotion. You have to argue how much they're going to put into this, and who's radio's favorite flavor of the month. And it kinda gets a little tacky. But it always has been. It's always been a pool of piranhas, and they always wore sharkskin suits.

I just read Andrew Loog Oldham's autobiography. It was a much different world back then, more innocent.
It was real. I remember our first record deal with Decca. We were in the boardroom with Sir Edward whatever-his-name-was, who was 80 years old and drooling. Actually, it was like a *Sopranos* thing. He was wearing

shades he didn't take off. And then he let us do what we wanted [laughs]. The first thing we did was lease tracks to them. We didn't sign a contract. Which was a famous deal. I'm glad we did it that way because that meant we had the all-important "artistic control."

I always know when you guys are getting warmed up for a new tour because the sniping in the press heats up.
Most of the energy has been very positive, real good. Usually, it takes a few weeks to knock off the rust. But I don't know . . . They've come in well-oiled, man. It's really sounding good. The only down side was the death of [longtime roadie Roydon] Chuch McGee. He's one of the pillars that kept the Stones up, though you never saw him. He had a heart attack a couple of weeks ago, which sobered everybody up.

What was your reaction to John Entwistle's death?
That was another surprise. Isn't it amazing, just before the first show of the tour . . . I didn't know him well. I don't know if anybody did, really. I'm sure he had a lot of close friends. I'd known him for so long. And he always sent me some nice notes. He was a very quiet man, ya know. When you get taken, man, you get taken. But it didn't stop Roger or Pete. I heard they got my old friend Pino [Palladino] on bass. And the tour must go on . . .

So no Bill Wyman again this time around?
No, no. I got a message from him just a couple of weeks ago. Now and again, we get in touch. Otherwise, he's too busy having babies. It's something he's good at. Since he left the Stones, he's had about three daughters. That's his favorite occupation.

Has he discovered Viagra?
Bill's always been like that. That's why he's so fuckin' skinny, man [laughs].

You recently put down Mick's solo record in the press.
I mean, where else could you put it? When they asked me about it, I said, "Oh, you mean *Dogshit in the Hallway*?" The quibble with that is Mick had told me months and months before he was not going to do any solo projects and we were going to concentrate on getting this thing together. And

then suddenly, his dogshit appears. And then I heard it, and I thought, "Yeah, it is dogshit."

And what about his whole knighthood thing?

I really flared up about that. I thought it was really stupid timing. Typical of Mick to break rank. I mean, right now, he could have done himself a lot better by turning it down.

You're anti-royalist?

Well, I'm not "anti." I just think people like Frankie Drake and Wally Riley deserve knighthood. I don't really see what pop singers have to do with it. But if they do, it's a bit of a paltry honor, innit? If Phil Collins is a knight, then you should hang out for the fuckin' peerage, man. Get a Lordship. They give knighthoods for covering a few Supremes songs.

So we're never going to have a Sir Keith Richards.

I very much doubt it. I'm too vocal. And also, I always thought Mick was, too. But I told him, "Now you've joined the brown-noses."

Have you heard any of the remastered titles?

Allen [Klein] sent me a copy of them. Very good mixes. Some very interesting work has been going on there.

It's like hearing these old songs for the first time.

To me, too. This new system of re-mastering and re-mixing them amazed me, too. [Laughs] I was hearing instruments I forgot I put on there. It's amazing what's on tape and what can be pulled out.

Have you watched *The Osbournes*?

No, I haven't. I wasn't in the country when it was on. It sounds like exactly what Ozzy needs. Ozzy's always going to pull something out of his hat every now and again. And that was a good one, I think. Ya know, it's kinda like *The Simpsons*, but live.

Have you ever considered a reality show yourself?
No way, man. Reality's enough without being virtual.

What do you think about this new garage-band punk movement? The Hives have a singer who looks like a young Mick Jagger.
[Mock sneer] What's so new about it? I'm not surprised because that's what they should be doing. Also, because last time we were on the road, five years ago, those 12-year-olds in the front row are now 17, 18 and they're rocking. A lot of these guys are my tribe, in one way or another. Even if they don't know it.

And now you're putting out a greatest hits album, like the Beatles' *1*.
The only difference between the Beatles and us is we're still going. So we thought it was necessary and important to at least put on some new tracks. Like a dot-dot-dot . . . To be continued, so to speak.

Keith, how long can this keep going?
[Incredulous] You're asking *me*? We've never said anything about it being the last time. It's always from the outside. Including now. I think they've just thrown up their hands in disgust and said, "We can't use the bit about it being the last tour anymore. It doesn't work. They keep coming back."

You always seem to have a good time.
Pursuit of happiness, man. It's in the Constitution. You don't have to be a rocket scientist to figure out that, if you're miserable, it's really miserable. The only other side of the coin is, enjoy it. Figure it out. It ain't that difficult. Some people just look for trouble and want it and other people just deal with it.

Do you go for medical check-ups regularly?
We have to do all of that to get insurance for the tour. The last report I got, I was 38 and didn't smoke. And I said, "I'll take that, doc." [Laughs]

So you haven't had one of these colonoscopies yet, where they put a camera up your butt?

What the fuck would people do that for?

When you're over 50, you're supposed to get one, to check for colon cancer.

Horse shit. They did all that crap. I have a very unexcited prostate, if you wanna know. And that's the way we like it.

You'll end up dancing on all our graves.

I dunno, man. That's not a pleasant thought. Where does that leave me, ya know? [Laughs]

16 |

KEEF

JAMES MCNAIR | 2005

The year 2005: another Stones world tour, another rehearsal period located in Canada for tax purposes, another round of publicity to drum up interest. Despite the familiar circumstances, James McNair found Richards an entertaining and revealing interviewee—even though it is immediately evident that it was by now impossible for "Keef" and any interviewer to have a conversation not layered with self-consciousness about the guitarist's über-hedonist image.

So the Grim Reaper is sitting at home watching TV when the doorbell rings. He opens up and Keith Richards is standing there in hooded black sackcloth, a sharp-looking scythe at his side. "Sorry," says the Rolling Stones' seemingly indestructible guitarist. "Your number's up."

Presented with the above vignette, Richards gets the joke. "Yeah, I'd like to see the Reaper off," he says with a gruff laugh, "but people shouldn't try and do what I've done with my body, because not everybody can." As though to underline that truth, he swigs at a large vodka and orangeade-based concoction called a Nuclear Fall-Out. Would I like to try one? No, I'll stick with beer, thanks.

Sixty-two in December, Richards is enjoying his tipple while chain-smoking full-strength Marlboros. Though it's only 5.30pm, his skulls-and-guitars-appointed dressing room is candle-lit. The air is heavy with incense, and a small, coffin-shaped box on the table lies open to reveal Keith's rolling papers. He's wearing lime-green work boots, and a black tracksuit top with the word "Jamaica" emblazoned in yellow on the back.

You take in his gnarly knuckled fingers, his swarthy, heavily latticed face. On his right hand is the familiar silver skull ring that he has long worn as a *memento mori*. Keith's eyes are so brown they are almost black, and juju trinkets dangle from his gloriously unkempt hair. An amiable rogue who has been described as "a grinning baboon" and "the human riff," the guitarist proves surprisingly well spoken. As the vodka kicks in and he starts to slur a little, he puts me in mind of Rowley Birkin, the genial, dipsomaniac QC from *The Fast Show*.

"I went to see my dentist the other day," Richards says, still on the topic of his rude good health. "Chipped tooth. Hadn't seen him in 20 years. He thought he'd put me out on anaesthetic, but he hadn't—I was just sitting there feeling pleasant with my eyes closed. First I hear him praising his own handiwork; then he starts rooting around with his dental tools. After a bit I hear, 'This guy's immune system is fucking unbelievable!' I chuckled to myself but didn't say anything."

Richards' dressing room is stationed within Greenwood College School. It is here, incongruously, in a quiet suburb of Toronto, Canada, that the Rolling Stones are once again rehearsing for an upcoming US tour. Richards' manager, Jane Rose, is on site, as is her tiny white Maltese, Ruby Tuesday, so named by Keith himself. On closer inspection the pooch is seen to be wearing a leopard-print scrunchy.

By Richards' account, rehearsals are going well: is contemplating the 43-date August-January tour like contemplating Everest?

"No, it's like downhill skiing! Nobody is dragging their ass to come on this one." Even Charlie Watts, traditionally the most touring-reticent Stone, can't wait to get going—and this despite the drummer's recent battle with throat cancer. "Charlie's fine now and he came back firing on all cylinders, maybe to prove a point," says Richards of his 63-year-old colleague. "If that's what chemo does for you, I'm going in for some."

Later, when I sit in on the Stones' rehearsal session, it's clear that Richards' claims about the camp's high morale are valid. It's fascinating to watch the group in something like private, Keith perusing the set-list through dainty pince-nez while he and 58-year-old Ronnie Wood's gritty guitars spar to glorious effect. Mick Jagger—62, black baseball boots *sans* laces, 28-inch waist still intact—looks almost boyish as he beams at backing vocalist Lisa Fischer during "Gimme Shelter." When he catches sight of me on the balcony he does a double take, however—the thought bubble above his head reading: "Who let *him* in?"

If the Stones' appetite for their upcoming jaunt is tangible, Richards, for one, was less enamoured with the notion of Live8, and actually vetoed the idea of the Stones playing the event. "I didn't understand why everybody who was trying to coax me in happened to be knighted," he says with a laugh. "I got hit on by Sir Bob and Sir Mick, but I said to Mick, 'We ain't doing it, pal. *You* can do it, but I ain't.'

"Decreasing debts?" the guitarist goes on. "It all seemed a bit nebulous to me. Plus I couldn't believe the amount of pressure, even from 10 Downing Street. I was like, 'We're finishing the new album and getting ready for the tour—sorry, but we can't spare the men.' I heartily applaud what they were trying to do, except that it was tied in with Government policy and I always try and separate politics and music. I mean, Bob's a nice bloke and all that, but ultimately he's the one who comes off best, isn't he?"

The new album Richards mentions is *A Bigger Bang*, due in September. It's the group's first studio outing since 1997's *Bridges to Babylon*, and as its title suggests, it sees the world's greatest extant rock band shirking complacency and roaring loud. Not every track is a classic, it's true, but "Laugh, I Nearly Died" is as agreeably raunchy as anything on *Sticky Fingers*, while "Rain Fall Down" is the band's funkiest moment since 1983's "Undercover of the Night."

Elsewhere, on the flagship single "Streets of Love," an uncharacteristically lovelorn Jagger delivers one of the most compelling performances of his career, his diction masterful and his ad-libs on the fade-out unmistakably heartfelt. Lyrically, it's one of several songs on the new record that have led some to posit that the work is partly Jagger's love-letter to his estranged wife, Jerry Hall. "The awful truth/Is really sad/I must admit/I was awful bad," sings the old philanderer at one point. It sounds awfully like he's acknowledging his costly dalliance with a 20-year-old Brazilian lingerie model by the name of Luciana Morad (in 1999, Morad bore Jagger a child; Hall filed for divorce shortly afterwards).

With Charlie recuperating and Ronnie Wood facing equally testing times (the guitarist was devastated when his first wife Krissy took her own life earlier this year) Richards says he and Jagger were forced to pull their fingers out on *A Bigger Bang*.

"We were short staffed," he quips, enjoying a quotidian phrase and deliberately sounding like himself as caricatured by John Sessions on *Stella Street*. "Mick and I got the news that Charlie was going in for treatment just as we started writing. There was a pregnant pause, and we thought, 'Should we put things on hold?' But then it was, 'No, let's forge ahead—it will be a good incentive for Charlie. Actually, this is probably the closest Mick and I have worked together since *Exile on Main Street*. Both of us took on tasks that normally wouldn't have occurred to us, playing bass or whatever.

"Mick playing great guitar helped," Richards continues. "I sleep downstairs and the studio is upstairs. One night I thought I was hearing this old Muddy Waters track I didn't know, but it turned out to be Mick working on a slide part for 'Back of my Hand.' He's always been a good, smooth acoustic player, but the electric seemed like an untamed beast for him until this year. When I heard him this time I thought, 'My God! The boy's finally got it.'"

This is how Richards goes on: holding court, spinning anecdotes, and generally leaving no buckle unswashed. No huge surprise, then, that he has reportedly been offered a part in *Pirates of the Caribbean III* (*Pirates II* is already in the can). While his pal Johnny Depp famously used Keith as a template when playing the roguish Jack Sparrow, Richards says he can neither "confirm nor deny" his own involvement in the trilogy.

"What I can tell you," he says, "is that when we were finishing the album in LA, Johnny came down to the studio to talk about the movie. Behind him was, like, the Disney wardrobe department or something, and we spent the rest of the afternoon hilariously dressing up in pirate clothes. I'm up for doing the film and so is Johnny, so hopefully we can schedule something in . . . I'd obviously bring my own cutlass, ha ha!"

Joking aside, this last is not a fact that anyone who knows Keith Richards would doubt. Ask director Julien Temple: before he worked on the 1983 video for "Undercover of the Night," Richards reportedly flicked open a switchblade, held it to Temple's throat and said, "You better not fuck up."

My host's liking for firearms has been well documented too, but he says that these days he leaves his handgun in the drawer at home. When he was scoring dope in the US in the late 1960s, however, he carried one around as a matter of course. "I'd read that Muddy Waters had one, and I suppose there was a bit of emulation going on there. America was a strange, lawless place back then. You'd be in some motel, and people would be shooting at each other, but unfortunately you'd be in the room in between. I used to keep my gun under my pillow [laughs], but then it becomes like your fetish, and you can't go to sleep unless it's there. Then you start wondering what you're worried about and if you'd actually use the gun anyway. I got pretty good at light bulbs and chandeliers, though. You had to check it was still working."

Asked what the biggest misconception about him is, Richards is stumped for a few moments. The public face of Keith Richards, he says, is a caricature with a large element of truth in it. "I've been cast in the role of the rascal and I accept the role gracefully," he laughs, "but everybody changes. The problem is that, when you've been famous for this long you drag all the key events and rumours of your life around with you like Jacob Marley's chain."

For Richards, these would include the night he wrote the riffs for "Satisfaction" and "Brown Sugar," the bloodbath that was the Rolling Stones at Altamont in 1969, the mysterious death of Brian Jones earlier that same year, and the persistent myth that a Swiss blood transfusion process akin to premature embalming was what enabled Keith to temporarily kick heroin prior to an important, 1973 tour of Europe. The mere mention of the latter proves enough to help Richards find an answer to my previous question. The biggest myth about him, he now posits, is probably that he was constantly endangering himself with drugs. "Actually, I would take drugs quite responsibly," he says. "A nice fix at breakfast, one for elevenses, and another one at teatime—it was like breaks at the cricket, or something.

"The times I fucked up was when I scored from people I didn't know and the stuff was laced with strychnine. I'm lying on the bed, and people are going, 'Well, he's still breathing . . .' It was a bit Edgar Allen Poe-ish; a bit like being buried alive. You could hear every word they were saying, but you couldn't say anything back because you were paralysed.

"John Lennon did that, too," Richards goes on. "He seemed to be in competition with me over drugs, and I never really understood that."

Was he a Rolling Stone in Beatles clothing?

"That's interesting—you might have something there. I think the Stones behaved like he'd like the Beatles to behave, and [because of that] he felt constricted."

Richards' main home is still in Weston, Connecticut, and he continues to share it with Patti Hansen, the Staten Island–born model whom he married in 1983. It was at home on the couch that Keith penned "This Place Is Empty" [without you], a fine country-style ballad from the new album that he croons raggedly à la Tom Waits. The guitarist concedes the song was partly written for Patti (one great line runs: "Come on, honey/ bear your breasts/and make me feel at home"), but the lyric's wider resonance may take in empty-nest syndrome.

"Our daughters, Theodora and Alexandria, have grown up and got their own apartment in the city," he says. "For a while we didn't know what to be doing, but then Patti said, 'Jesus Christ! We can do want we want! Let's be a couple again, darling!'"

There are also grandchildren to enjoy, these fathered by Keith's son, Marlon, who together with Angela, his other child by Anita Pallenberg, is now well into his thirties. "Marlon's got little Ella, bless her heart, and Orson, who's about five now," says proud granddad. "Thanks to Johnny [Depp], Orson actually thinks I'm a real pirate. He's coming up just nicely, learning all the right cuss words."

Clearly, Richards is in fine fettle. He's already had three Nuclear Fall-Outs, but this has merely whetted his appetite for the rehearsal session that will begin immediately after our chat. What, though, of absent friends and family? Richards has lost Brian Jones, and his own father, Bert. He has lost musical soulmates such as country star Gram Parsons, and the Rolling Stones' unofficial extra member and keyboard player, Ian Stewart.

As his own pension book looms closer, are there moments when Keith recalls these people? Does he dream of them, perhaps?

"They come and visit now and then, and not necessarily when I'm asleep. I'll be talking away to someone and Bert will come in and say, 'A fox never shits in his own hole, Keith!' Parsons sometimes comes to me in dreams, but that's more of a musical thing. Ian Stewart? Man, he just rings like a bell. Whenever one of us in the band tries to pull a number, somebody will drop a little Stu-ism like, 'Come along my little shower of shit.' These people resonate; you never forget them. I miss all those cats."

And Brian? Is it all just too long ago now?

"Brian could be the most frustratingly obnoxious, nasty person. Which he never was until the minute we had a hit record. It was a fame thing, maybe; something seemed to snap in him. It could be that he thought he was *numero uno* and Mick didn't like that. I wasn't thinking about hierarchy at the time—I was just trying to find [the chord of] E7.

"We were pretty mean to him. We started to pick on him just to let him know: either you're in or you're out. And then he got more and more stoned, and he'd check into a clinic in Chicago while we were touring the Mid-West. I'm standing on stage trying to cover two guitar parts—it doesn't endear you to the guy.

"Later, I made a real effort to hang with Brian. This would be '66–'67, when we finally got off the road for a year. Everybody's getting stoned out of their brains and there's acid flying about. We were having a good time, but unfortunately there was Anita [Pallenberg—Jones's girlfriend before Richards "rescued" her from him], and then we get into that. That was the final nail in the coffin."

At that, our time is up. One last question, though: does he have any kind of fitness regime prior to going on the road? "Yeah," he deadpans, "It's called 'Rehearsals.'

"Mick's your guy for a fitness regime and a schedule," he adds, "but then he has to cover a lot more stage than me.

"When I wake up in the morning I just say, Ahh! Jah wonderful! Let's see what the day brings! I'm happy to be here. I'm happy to be *anywhere*."

17 |

KEITH RICHARDS AND THE MAKING OF *EXILE ON MAIN ST.*

PIERRE PERRONE | 2010

When the Rolling Stones released their only double studio LP, *Exile on Main St.*, in 1972, it was greeted with reviews that mostly ranged from negative to lukewarm. By the time Richards was helping promote a deluxe remaster of the album thirty-eight years later, it had long been widely reassessed as a classic, even the band's magnum opus.

This interview with Pierre Perrone about *Exile*'s genesis is not just absorbing. It is a salutary reminder that though Richards is a candid interviewee and projects a devil-may-care attitude, he is also intelligent and business-savvy enough to know when to deploy discretion, for something else that had occurred in the thirty-eight-year interim was the settling of the Stones' legal disputes with their former manager Allen Klein, which meant that Richards was no longer obliged to stick to the story he and his colleagues had maintained for many years that the album's basic tracks were recorded exclusively in Richards' South of France basement.

Thirty-eight years on from its original release, *Exile on Main St* is the stuff of rock'n'roll legend, many people's favourite Stones album and the one Keith Richards is always happy to return to. So much so that the Glimmer Twins, who are notoriously loath to open up the vaults, have finally assembled a deluxe edition with 10 bonus tracks on top of the 18 first issued in 1972.

I've followed the Stones since I was a kid. I covered their songs in a garage band and failed exams because I travelled to see them in Nice the night before. I've seen them live over a dozen times, in France, in London, in the US. Three years ago, I wrote the liner notes for the re-release of the *Rolled Gold+* compilation. Over the years, I've interviewed Mick Jagger, Charlie Watts and Ronnie Wood, but never Keith Richards.

I'd resigned myself to his glaring absence from my lengthy list of interviewees until the expanded, remastered *Exile*, an ideal opportunity for a kid who spent half of 1971 dreaming of running away from Marseilles to join the Stones at Nellcôte, in Villefranche-sur-Mer.

Richards is tickled when I tell him this. He's at the Mercer Hotel, a luxury establishment in New York, the Big Apple's equivalent of LA's Chateau Marmont. No one bats an eyelid when he lights up. The old devil.

Fans are pretty excited at the prospect of the remastered, expanded *Exile on Main On St* coming out. What has it been like for you to listen back to the tracks?

A lot of déjà vu. There was a point where I was listening to it all and remembering where it was recorded, Villefranche-sur-Mer and old Nellcôte. I could almost smell the basement. I still like the album and often play bits of it. I've fond memories of making the record. It was a little crazy and, in a way, unique, because we'd never recorded outside of a studio before, so this was a bit of an experiment. But, once we started, it had to be finished.

Bands such as Traffic used to rent a cottage and get it together in the country, but you actually recorded in a basement in a villa on the French Riviera. What was the chain of events that led you to Nellcôte?

The full weight of the British establishment came down on us. First they thought they could get us with the dope busts and it did not work, so they put the financial screws on. To keep the band going, we had to leave England. France was convenient. At first, we figured that either in Cannes, Nice or Marseilles, maybe we could find a studio that we liked. But, when we got there, we realised it was out of the question. Then it was a matter of finding a house in the hills somewhere but, after that fell through, everyone suddenly looked at me (*laughs*). I thought: 'I know what they want, they want my basement.' That's how it ended up. I lived on top of the factory.

You already had The Rolling Stones Mobile Studio. You'd used it for live recordings and at Stargroves, Mick's place. The Who used it too. And Led Zeppelin later on.

Yeah. We'd had the truck for a couple of years. I can't remember quite how long. We'd never used it very much ourselves. We used it to cut a few demos. We used to rent it out to the BBC or somebody to do the race courses. But suddenly I realised, I think we all did, that we did have this mobile control room. Having that made it possible. The thing actually worked. We were amazed. It was a lovely machine, for its time. When we did put that truck together, we thought that it might come in useful. And sure enough it did.

There was quite a vibe in that basement, wasn't there?

Yes, you can call it a vibe, it was a thick one (*laughs*). It was a unique place to work. Upstairs, it was a fantastic place. The basement was another story. We had to sort of get around all kinds of problems, sound-wise and. . . But there was a certain determination in the band that, OK, we had to leave England. We can do what we do anywhere. There was a lot of determination in the band to step up to the plate and make an interesting record. It was obviously our first double album. We had to fight the record company about that. Record companies don't like double albums (*laughs*). We had to fight on that front and there were technical difficulties, but we overcame them.

The lead-off single from *Exile* was Tumbling Dice, which has got a great groove. You still play it live and it remains one of many people's favourite Stones tracks.

I love to play that one on stage. It's not so much the song . . . It's just a great thing to play.

Sometimes you come up with something and you think, "I could play this all night, all year." It's one of those. A lovely riff. It's got such a nice groove and a flow on it.

Are tracks such as Happy and Soul Survivor the ones where you get a real flavour of what was going on at Nellcôte?

Exactly. As I said, I can actually smell it. Because that basement hadn't been used for years. I don't think we really bothered to clean it up much. We just kind of moved in.

Happy is the quintessential *Exile* track and one of your signature songs.
Yes. To me, it was one of the benefits of actually living on top of the whole scene. Happy epitomized that. One afternoon, Jimmy Miller (producer) and Bobby Keys were there, but that was about it. The guys don't usually start work until after dark and I said: 'Look, I've got this idea. Can we just lay it down for later?' Jimmy was on drums and Bobby on baritone sax. By the time the rest of the band arrived, I'd done a few overdubs and we had finished the track. It was one of the benefits of living on top of the factory.

Was it a given that you would sing Happy? Over the years you seem to get a great kick out of doing that one live.
I think so. I'd 'stolen it' and captured it before anybody else knew it existed. So that was it. I play Happy quite a lot, more often than any of the others. I love playing it. It's not usually my genre. I'm not known for happy and joyful stuff. I'm probably more aligned to Lucifer and the dark side (*laughs*). But it was a damn good afternoon and I still love it.

Another track I love is Soul Survivor, which features loads of guitar tracks. And you've unearthed an alternate take for this release.
Yeah, that's a murky track (*laughs*). I'd have to really go back and count. There were endless overdubs. We would use a little bit from one. There's probably at least six guitars on there, in little pieces, not all the way through. But from the middle eight to the end, there's probably little bits of six overdubs going on, in and out.

Was some of the magic in the basement at Nellcôte the fact that you could tilt the amps and the sound would change as it would bounce off the walls?
Working at Nellcôte was strange because you never quite knew what you were capturing on the mobile. So inevitably, you'd do a few takes, and

then everybody would stamp up the stairs, get in the truck and have a listen. Sometimes, you had to do a bit of adjustment. It was a very interesting process. I realised slowly, as we were doing it, that this was a pretty unique way of making a record. There was something about the rhythm section sound down there—maybe it's the concrete, or maybe it's the dirt, but it had a certain sound that you couldn't replicate if you tried. Believe me, lots of people have tried.

Did you make friends with the locals while you were at Nellcôte?
Yes, a little, although we were very busy. We had a few local guys working with us. There was a chef who blew the kitchen up. There was a great explosion. Big Jacques I think his name was.

There was a lady caretaker as well, wasn't there?
She was great. How she put up with us all. . . The smile on her face all the time. I don't quite know what she was smiling at but she handled us all very correctly. I have fond memories of playing and working there. I mean there could be worse places to make a record.

There were stories that you stole power from the SNCF, the French railways. Can you admit to that after all these years?
I think we did, once or twice. Actually, it wasn't us that knew how to do it. It was a couple of local Villefrance boys (*laughs*). Yes, they did hook us to the railway line for a couple of nights when the power went.

You attracted the attention of the local police.
We had the usual amount of attention. You stand outside the front gate with the sergeant and the corporal. "Monsieur, excusez-moi." Usually things would settle down and you'd say: "Come in, have a cognac." It was like that. I can't quite remember going back that far. They were very reasonable, in their Mediterranean way. There were no big problems. Sometimes, they just wanted to come and have a look around. We did have a robbery and we got some of the guitars back. Justice prevailed. We'll leave it at that.

I know you're very fond of *Exile: The Making of Exile on Main St*, the coffee table book of the photographs Dominique Tarlé took at Nellcôte, and that you have given copies of it to friends and family. When you look at the book, does it prompt more memories?

Ah, Dominique, great guy, great photographer. We liked Dominique because he was about the most invisible photographer. You never knew he was there, he sort of melted in and became part of the band in a way. It's not often you really like to have pictures taken when you're working, but Dominique had a beautiful technique and I love the man. I was amazed by the book. I didn't know he'd taken that many pictures. A lot of people that you didn't intend to be there, like Gram Parsons for instance, ended up at Nellcôte, and stayed for a month.

There were some nice country touches on Exile. Was that because Gram had been staying with you?

We were swapping ideas. Gram taught me a lot of songs. We used to spend days singing George Jones and Merle Haggard, all the Everly Brothers harmonies. He is on *Exile* in spirit. The good die young.

You were also starting to explore a more gospel flavoured, soulful direction, something you continued doing throughout the 70s and beyond.

Yeah. Strangely enough, once we were down there, in the middle of France, we started to dig deep into American music. After all, basically, that's what we do. But we started to pull on different aspects of it, country music for instance, gospel. Maybe, because we weren't in America, we missed it. Quite honestly, down in the basement at Nellcôte, it felt like America. Especially with Bobby Keys around. It was a great room to work It was ugly, dark and damp, everything was like that . . . But, at the same time, I still have a great feeling for that basement down there. It was funky. I'll give you that (*laughs*).

Do you think, as a consequence of the fact that you were 'exiled,' that you weren't in England any more, that you thought about music differently?

Exactly. They'd kicked us out of England. That's why the album ended up being called *Exile*. We were very aware that we were suddenly out there, with our backs to the wall. We had to reinvent how to do things, make it up as we went along. In other words, there was no script, nobody had done it before. It was just a matter of necessity becoming the mother of invention.

Exile was started in England, at Olympic Studios in London, and at Stargroves. Then you continued in France. Why did you end up finishing the album at Sunset Sound in Los Angeles?
In order to mix it and to do certain overdubs and other stuff we wanted. We needed rather more sophisticated equipment than what we had in our truck. That was the reason we took it there: to polish it, give it a little touch of Hollywood.

Of course, in Los Angeles, you could call on people like Billy Preston and other musicians like Dr John and various backing singers.
Bill Plummer on upright bass on a couple tracks . . . The great thing about LA, especially in those days, you could make a phone call at three in the morning and say: 'We need a couple of voices.' Within half an hour, there'd be a couple of chicks ready to go, still wearing their nightdresses (*laughs*). It was like that. You'd have an idea and it would actually happen, which was kind of cool.

Was the idea to release a double album because you were finally free from the clutches of Allen Klein, who had been your manager after Andrew Loog Oldham?
Well, there was a feeling in the air that we'd reached a schism. We'd reached breaking point with certain things that we'd done before and with certain people, Allen Klein included. So we were kind of reinventing the Stones as we went along. It was a *miracle* it happened, quite honestly. The Stones had this streak of, what do you want to call it, luck, *bonne chance*.

Exile is now considered a masterpiece. It's many people's favourite Stones album, but it wasn't very well received at the time.

Maybe because it was a double album. We knew that there was going to be a sort of reaction to it in a way, just because it was very different. There were no hit singles. It was an album by itself. It shows our determination, the Stones point of view, that we insisted it was a double record, that you couldn't split it up in other words. That was what we did. We're the exiles and this is what we're doing. It was made with that kind of attitude.

The American tour that followed the release of *Exile* in 1972 was quite an eventful one. People tried to gatecrash the concerts, there were riots, you went on stage incredibly late in Boston . . .
Yeah, we've been late several times, Knebworth 1976 springs to mind. I've always been amazed at how patient some audiences have been for us. Usually, we're trying to get there. These days, obviously, we don't . . . show time is show time. But in the early days, the show started when the show started.

Because of what had happened in 1969, did you have increased security on the '72 tour? Was it different in that respect?
Well, a lot of things became different, especially about playing live around '69. I mean let alone Altamont . . . *Vive la différence* . . . Electronics and technology were starting to catch up. Suddenly, you could play with monitor speakers, you could actually hear yourself. Before that, quite honestly, you just went up there and hoped the wind was blowing the right way. Because, otherwise, you never knew what sounds were coming out or going to the audience. There was a whole lot of things going on, late 60s, early 70s. Things were changing a lot, and shows were getting bigger. Suddenly, there's football stadiums, enormous acres of people and stuff. You had to *learn* how to play these places.

Why do you think you succeeded in making that change and becoming the biggest rock'n'roll band in the world the early 70s? Do you feel there was a magic in the music that could translate to bigger crowds?
In a way, we were growing up along with the audience. If it was new to us, it was probably new to them, but it was a learning process. Quite honestly, I prefer to play in a nice little auditorium or theatre, ideally. But what are you going to do with the other 50,000 people who want to see you? So in

that respect, you just have to learn to go where the audience is and figure out how to play to them. You never know what's going to happen, that's one of the interesting things about the job—the excitement.

Over the years, you've often gone back to *Exile*. Many of the tracks work well in a live situation, like Shine a Light, which became the title of the Martin Scorsese film.

And Let It Loose and Loving Cup. We've found another take of Loving Cup for this . . . We do Rip This Joint quite often. That's one of the fastest songs in the world. That really keeps you on your toes. *Exile* is one of those records you can look at and say: 'Let's do something different.' Or Sweet Virginia, we've also done that live many, many times. And Sweet Black Angel. When you're in a little bit of doubt about what to play, or you want to play something different, basically you say: "Let's listen to *Exile* and we'll find something."

How did you decide what to add to this expanded version of *Exile*? Was it a difficult process? What did you do to the tapes? Did you go back and re-record anything?

There was talk of three, then four or five extra tracks. I'm not quite sure how we decided how many. We listened to them and we realised there were takes of Loving Cup, Soul Survivor and Tumbling Dice that would make interesting additions. And also songs that we really wanted on Exile when it was being made but we just didn't have any room for, otherwise it would have been a triple-album set. We had to draw the line somewhere and we decided that if we were going to repackage this thing and put *Exile* back out as a box set, then we should add some of the other stuff that we still had left over.

So there it is. It's kind of interesting. The tracks we found in the vaults are mostly as we left them 39 years ago. I didn't want to get in the way of what was there. I stroked an acoustic guitar here and there. Mick did new vocals for Plundered My Soul and Following the River.

Was it fun to listen back to all the out-takes and alternate takes?

Yeah, it was. Listening critically, I can hear stuff and go 'Oh my God, did

I actually play that?' Sometimes you just take off. And there's some real
. . . But, at the same time, the spirit of it and the feel of it, it's well worth
putting it out because it's the flavour of the era.

**Does the legend of *Exile*, the parties, the drugs, overshadow the reality
of what went on during those months at Nellcôte?**
We were making a record, we didn't have time! (*laughs*). Living on top
of the factory had its advantages. You went upstairs for a breath of fresh
air and a drink or two. Of course there were drugs, but it didn't affect the
work. We were out on a limb and it all came together.

**Some people were expecting live tracks from the 1972 tour as part
of the extras. There has always been talk of this great missing live
album in the Stones canon of live albums. The '72 tour is not officially
documented.**
No there's nothing live on there (*Exile* remastered). You might be right. I
might look into that. I know they put out *Get Yer Ya-Ya's Out* again. The
boxes, the all-important boxes (*laughs*).

**You had Stevie Wonder as support on the 1972 tour. You've often had
great support acts. Also The Meters in 1976.**
Ike & Tina Turner, and BB King in 1969. It was the days when shows
weren't just about one act. You had several other great bands warming up
and rocking. I kind of miss that format but *c'est la vie* . . . (*laughs*). I learnt
so much, in the early days, from playing and listening to bands that were
going on before us. Ike and Tina's band were so cool. As musicians, we'd
be checking these cats out every night and they'd be so tight. The way Ike
ran a band was phenomenal, unique.

You took a few tips from Ike?
Yeah, like that pistol-whipping piano players stuff (*laughs*).

**You've done some of your best work in France. *Exile* at Nellcôte. You've
recorded at the Pathé-Marconi studios in Paris as well, and obviously
A Bigger Bang was done at Mick's place in the Loire valley. Why do you
think it works for you in France?**

I don't know. It's strange, isn't it? Just thinking about it, I've only just realised that we've recorded in France at least as much as we have in America or England or anywhere else. Very good studios. The old Pathé-Marconi was great. It's a room you could get to know. You knew where everything was, where to put the drums. There's just something about Paris. If you've got to be somewhere for six months recording, there's nothing like a great restaurant around the corner, and a couple of crazy Frenchmen as friends.

After *Exile*, you went to Jamaica for *Goats Head Soup*. You must have liked recording in different places to get a different vibe.

We'd never recorded in Jamaica before. A lot of stuff on *Goats Head Soup* is obviously related to *Exile*. When you make records, these things sort of fold over . . . There's stuff from *Sticky Fingers* that went into *Exile* at one end and out of the other into *Goats Head Soup*. Nobody writes an album from track one to track twelve and says: 'that's it.' It's a continual process and hopefully it will continue.

I was wondering how your autobiography is coming along.

Oh! It's just about finished. I'm waiting for some proofs to come back and stuff. It's kind of weird reading about yourself, about your own life. Who'd be interested in that? (*laughs*). But then I realise there is a lot of interest so . . . It seems to be alright. I think there's some editing to do, but it's coming along. It should be out later this year.

Were there big gaps in your memory, or were you surprised how much you remembered?

I was, as much as to what I could remember, but also interviewing and talking to some of the people that were there and their version of events and trying to correlate it all. It was all very interesting, a kind of kaleidoscopic bunch of experiences. I'm hoping it will work out alright.

What memories do you have of your time in Switzerland in the 70s, after you left France?

Oh, Switzerland! First off, Switzerland was about the only country that would accept me at the time, so I'm always very grateful to the Swiss for that. Montreux, immediately, you have to mention Claude Nobs. He was a great help, since we were suddenly stuck there, finding us studios and just his constant encouragement. I actually learned to ski which was an *amazing* sight, believe me, to see Keith Richards ski (*laughs*).

You were working on Black & Blue when you were in Switzerland, weren't you?
Yeah. I would write it, work on it up in the Swiss mountains and then drive to Munich to lay it down. That was a German record.

We've had the extended Ya-Ya's and now Exile. What's on the horizon for the Stones? I gather there was talk of playing the whole of Exile, or a big chunk of it, to coincide with its release. You did that on the Licks tour, playing four or five tracks from Let It Bleed at Wembley Arena in 2003, as I recall. But the Exile live thing is not now happening.
Unfortunately. That's an idea that was thrown around. To me, it was interesting, I would have been quite willing to go along with it, the 'featured album' thing. I'd love to go up there and play just *Exile on Main Street*. Ideas come and go. We'll see if it bears fruit. Nobody's going to make a decision about what we're going to do until we get further into 2010. No doubt the guys are going to want to talk about whether we're going to record and go on the road in one form or another.

Maybe we're going to talk about how we do it, about doing it differently. There's going to be a lot of that. I would tell you if I knew. From my point of view, I'm finishing off a second record by the Wingless Angels, from Jamaica. A lot of stuff with Justin Hinds on it. The first one came out years ago, in the 90s. We did some more, we cut more stuff a couple of years later and we just kept it in the can. With Justin having died (in 2005), I want to put it out and give the money to his family.

You still love Jamaica and you go to your place there regularly, right?
I have very strong roots in Jamaica. I love the joint, I love the people, even though they're crazy. Takes one to know one.

18 |

KEITH'S *LIFE*

DYLAN JONES | 2011

In 2010, Keith Richards published his autobiography, *Life*. It was greeted rapturously and to some extent deserved its plaudits. However, Richards's likeability and his aura of incorrigibility led most reviewers to ignore such issues as this father of three daughters referring to women throughout as "bitches" as well as the fact that he failed to really address the matter of whether he had killed people by purveying heroin chic.

   The indulgence extended to Richards was rather demonstrated by Dylan Jones's interview, conducted in the summer of 2011 in connection with the guitarist's appearance at *GQ* magazine's Men of the Year Awards, at which *Life* had garnered Richards a Writer of the Year bauble. Though enjoyable, the dialogue is suffused with the sort of what-is-he-like! amusement that for so many people seems the only reaction possible in the presence of a man not only draped in cartoonishly decadent myth but also bemusedly playing up to it, both in his quotes and in an increasingly outlandish dress sense that is not too far removed from that of Captain Jack Sparrow, the movie pirate character for whom actor Johnny Depp employed Richards as a template.

Keith Richards has a face that conjures up many things. When he walks into his manager JANE ROSE's downtown Manhattan offices, it strikes me that he looks like a slightly ruined country house, with a leathery and runnelled face. As I shake his hand I'm thinking that this is probably what W. H. AUDEN would have looked like if he had worn leather trousers, or a cape. In different dress, Keith could also pass for an Afghan tribal leader, something that would probably please him.

   We are meeting today, in early June, to talk about Keith Richards winning this year's *GQ* Writer of the Year award for *Life*, the autobiography he crafted with the help of his friend JAMES FOX. *Life* is probably the best rock'n'roll memoir ever written, easily as good as BOB DYLAN's *Chronicles: Volume 1*, but six times longer. It is the result of painstaking research (one hundred and forty people are thanked in the book, many of whom Fox interviewed in order to fill in the hulking great gaps in Keith's memory), an eye and an ear for detail, and the sixty-seven-year-old's engaging way with an anecdote. Oh, and it is also one of the greatest rock'n'roll stories ever told, ever lived. Which is probably why the book has been so monumentally successful.

It's all here: sex, violence, drugs, myth-making, the character traits of some of the world's most famous people, and, of course, the truth about the ancient art of weaving. While it is written chronologically, it pinballs all over the place just when you least expect it, painting a believable, vividly colourful picture. There are some especially evocative passages about London after WWII, passages that go a long way to establishing why Keith ended up as "Keef."

The thing that struck me most when I first read it—and indeed, reviewed it at the time—was the refreshing way in which Keith discussed his monstrous drug-taking: not in a self-congratulatory way, but in extremely matter-of-fact terms. There are fascinating descriptions of what it's like to exist on heroin, extraordinary passages outlining his motivations for being under the influence, and wonderful accounts of Keef using drugs as though they were gears.

Keith and I chatted for two hours, in a suite of offices full of ROLLING STONES paraphernalia: a doll based on his character in *Pirates of the Caribbean: At World's End*; a poster advertising the MARTIN SCORSESE documentary *Shine a Light*; piles of tour T-shirts; acres of gold discs; a signed poster advertising their infamous 1972 tour; imprints of *Life*; a Diamond Award presented to JANE ROSE in recognition of *Hot Rocks 1964–1971*'s twelve million American sales; and a huge painting of the world's greatest rock'n'roll guitarist, memoirist and raconteur. As we talked, I was overwhelmed by a very odd sensation, one I rarely experience: this, I thought to myself, is a privilege.

As always.

Whenever critics start bleating about the Stones' lack of decent contemporary material, I'm reminded of what JOSEPH HELLER used to say when he was criticised for not writing another novel as good as his debut, *Catch 22*.

By all accounts he would nod sagaciously, look his accuser calmly in the eye, smile and then say, not without a soupcon of irony, "But who has?"

Dylan Jones: Keith, we share an agent, the man you've rechristened Ed "Fucking" Victor. Did you do a beauty parade of agents for the book?

Keith Richards: No. Ed was the person I wanted. Obviously, I drew up a shortlist, but it was always Ed Fucking Victor! And then he went to work on it, which was amazing. I wasn't involved in the business end of it, but Ed did everything and more than was asked of him. And I have to tip my hat constantly to James Fox for the way it was put together. They're my stories, but the way he crafted them, I couldn't have written it that way myself.

Up until *Life*, Bob Dylan's *Chronicles* had set a new bar for rock auto-biographies . . .

That was the other thing I couldn't go through, trying to outdo somebody else's. Everybody's got a different way of telling a story—and has different stories to tell. But *Chronicles* was fantastic. That was the benchmark. When we started, I told James a few school stories and said this is what I remember. But within a week, James had found the guy I was talking about, and got the confirmation that this story would hold up. After that, I started to get more confidence in my memory. I mean, it's been pretty fried.

Why did you decide to do the book?

The Stones had just finished the last tour, having been away for three years, and I knew there was going to be an inevitable gap where we would all be sitting around thinking about what's going to happen next. And the idea came up just at that moment, and it seemed the perfect thing to keep me occupied. It just seemed the right point in the story so far. And then other things fell into place and I knew that I had a couple of years to do it, basically.

What did you want to achieve with the book?

I just wanted to tell it from my point of view, and the incredible escapades we got involved in. It would be enough for most people's lifetimes if just one of those things happened to them. But I wasn't expecting the incredible reception that it's got. It's got me into a semiliterate area—people thought I was just a moron. I've actually got to like critics in the last year! It's like, "Wow, thanks pal, let me buy you a drink!" I thought they were going to drag me through the mud, as I'm used to that, but in actual fact it sort of elevated my opinion of myself. I don't want to get bigheaded here, as I always play myself down, but I've been pleased. To me, my biggest fear is getting a bighead, and that is when I get the hammer. Because it's very easy in this game to believe you're something special. Just look at BRIAN JONES—he died from it.

You've been fairly transparent about the partnership between you and James, and that's earned you a lot of credit.

I couldn't have told the story without him. In some uncanny way he captured the strength and breadth of the story. I've been friends with James for years, so he was used to my rhythm of speech. It helps that he's also a very good blues guitar player. So when I'd run out of ideas or taped the stories, we'd sit down and play some blues. But it's weird to drag through your whole life, because in the process you're actually living the damn thing twice. As we went on, I was shocked by thinking, "How did one guy go through all this?" And then I realised it was me! It put my past into a more coherent perspective. Before doing the book I'd look upon my life as incredible, disconnected episodes, and in the process of doing the book I managed to make sense of it. When I finished I felt more exhausted than after three years touring with the Stones. I felt a weight had been lifted off my shoulders.

What did you learn about yourself writing the book?

That I'm a much meaner bastard than I thought. But at the same time, I realised how much friendship had meant to me, and how much my friendship had meant to other people, which I hadn't thought about before. This is the rock'n'roll life, and you had to invent it as you went along. There was no textbook to say how you operate this machinery. You didn't know you were always walking on the edge of disasters, and there's nobody to turn to and say, "How did you feel?" because no one had been there before. It was very exciting. Still is, in a way. There are loads of things people wish I'd done, and some things I wish I'd done! You become a cartoon character, and I can play that to the hilt, and I know that people have come up with a great story and they go, "He didn't do it, but if he'd thought about it and he'd been there, he would have done it."

You were the rock'n'roll blueprint.
I hope so, and it's very nice of you to say so.

You're also very self-deprecating in the book . . .
I've slowly grown into that. When you're supported by millions all over the world, you can either go nuts, or try to feed off the goodwill. I always felt that it was my job to give back to them as much as possible. I want to make better records, better shows. So it's about reciprocation—there are millions of fans, and if you get that feedback, especially from an early age, it's indescribable. It's the same with the BEATLES, JOHN LENNON in particular. It's something you have to handle all the time. I've never taken it for granted. I just happened to be at the right place at the right time.

You spend a long time describing London after WWII.
Even though my memory of the war is pretty much nonexistent, as I was only eighteen months old, I still had a sense of sirens and collective fears. But as you're growing up in the Fifties, you're thinking this has got to change, it's too tight, the atmosphere, it's too restricted. The others running the joint want us to go back to the Thirties and we can't. And I guess as I was reaching the age of fifteen, sixteen, you've got the energy and you're bursting to escape. Plus, I fell in love with blues music, and that was where you found roots and a form of expression we didn't have in England. But as I was growing up, my mother was listening to a lot of BILLIE HOLIDAY and ELLA FITZGERALD . . . You hear things on the BBC, and then you start to bump into other guys who are into it, too; you realise it isn't just you sitting in a council flat. There are other guys out there listening to music, and somebody's got a new record from America and you're immediately at their house. You bring a bottle of beer—that was

your entrance fee—and you sit around and listen to records, which is nuts but it's beautiful. It was very innocent.

Were there parts you really didn't look forward to writing?
I really didn't want to go through and remember the death of my son. You spend a lot of time trying to bury that kind of shit, not bringing it up again. That was the hard one for me, to relive that. You don't forget shit like that.

In the book you describe using drugs as gears. What gear are you in these days?
I'm pretty much in neutral.

How many stories couldn't you include?
There were a lot for legal reasons. Especially concerning families who didn't even know that one of their relations was a drug dealer. A lot of my friends were very well brought-up boys, and I wouldn't want to upset the family just to name somebody. Everybody was experimenting and everybody was a pirate, especially in those days. In the club subculture, actually in every sort of culture, there are some very interesting people down there, but it's a great leveller where you find out who's one of your people or who's full of shit; who would stick by your side in a tough situation, and who would rat you out. It's not the most pleasant world to be in, but I do think it's kind of necessary to keep one foot in the gutter.

Why?
Because I never trusted the pavement.

Has this given you a taste for doing a bit more writing?
Yeah, there is talk about that, but basically I want to get the Stones back together and give it one more bash. I think they've got it in them. But it's about timing and an awful lot of very careful diplomacy.

Mick[Jagger] didn't love the book, did he?
Mick was obviously a bit peeved, but that was yesterday and this is today. We're two guys divided by life.

Did you read RONNIE WOOD's book?
Well, I think he tossed it off. Even Ronnie would admit that. Ronnie's got a much better story to tell than that book, that's all I can say. Charlie's book is the one I really want to read.

You haven't glamorised being on the road.
It actually wasn't a very glamorous life; it was a lot of hard slog, a lot of hard work. We were taking care of two hours on the stage and the rest of it; I wouldn't wish it on anybody.

How do you feel when you go back to Britain?
It's the only place in the world where I feel like a tourist, just because of the obvious changes. I always feel like a stranger, but I'm sure if I stayed there for a year that feeling would disappear. It's just that I'm not there a lot. But I do love the old country. Get me down to Sussex and you have to dig me out.

Six months before the book came out I bumped into DAVID REMNICK, the editor of the *New Yorker*, and all he could talk about was your book. He said that he was hoping you were going to explain the open G tuning. Which you did!
I'm amazed by that part of the book, and how much response I've got from the guitar players of this world. It's so difficult to put on to the page how you play an instrument, and I was amazed by the fact that I can, and I apparently made it fairly comprehensive. It's got a lot of tips in there, and that was the one difficulty for me and James—I didn't know how to put it into words. I know you have to do this and put this there, but on the page that will look dopey. But the translation worked.

And is there going to be a movie of the book?
Yeah, there are feelers out at the minute. I'm in no rush right at the moment. Also, how are they going to find me? The idea of a succession of Keith Richards coming down is horrifying. Maybe when I'm dead and gone they can make a movie of it.

CREDITS

"I'd Like to Forget about *Juke Box Jury* Says Keith Richard." First published in *Melody Maker*, July 18, 1964. © IPC Media Ltd. Reprinted by permission of the publisher.

"Keith Talks about Songwriting." First published in *The Rolling Stones Book*, August 10, 1964. © Beat Publications. Reprinted by permission of the publisher.

"Sue Mautner Takes You Round Keith's House." First published in *The Rolling Stones Book*, June 1966. © Beat Publications. Reprinted by permission of the publisher.

"The *Rolling Stone* Interview: Keith Richard." First published in *Rolling Stone*, August 19, 1971. © Robert Greenfield. Reprinted by permission of the author.

"And Sitteth at the Right Hand . . .". First published on jonh-ingham .blogspot.co.uk, February 2007. © Jonh Ingham. Reprinted by permission of the author.

"No One Shot KR: Keith Richards 1980." First published in *Zigzag*, November 1980. © Kris Needs. Reprinted by permission of the author.

"Keith Richards and the Making of *Exile on Main St.*" First published in *Record Collector*, June 2010. © Pierre Perrone. Reprinted by permission of the author.

"Keith's *Life.*" First published (in slightly different form) as He Is Keith Richards and You Aren't in *GQ* (UK edition), October 2011. © Dylan Jones. Reprinted by permission of the author.

Grateful thanks to the following for their assistance in compiling this book: Max Allen (for research and provision of scans), Michael Lynch (query answering and provision of scans), Michael Molenda (provision of scans), and John Stix (provision of scans).

INDEX

ALSO AVAILABLE IN THE
MUSICIANS IN THEIR OWN WORDS SERIES
FROM CHICAGO REVIEW PRESS

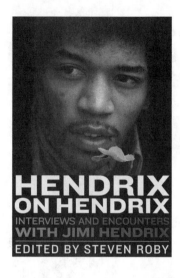

HENDRIX ON HENDRIX
Interviews and Encounters with Jimi Hendrix
by Steven Roby

"This beautifully edited and annotated collection provides abundant insights into the heart and mind of one of the 20th century's most influential artists. Jimi's story has been told ad nauseam, but often the hype overshadows the human, and the legend subsumes the man. Here we have Hendrix in his own words, with all of his confusion, contradiction, vulnerability, beauty, and brilliance intact." —*Guitar Player*

CLOTH, 384 PAGES • ISBN-13: 978-1-61374-322-5 • $24.95 (CAN $27.95)

COLTRANE ON COLTRANE
The John Coltrane Interviews
by Chris DeVito

"A fascinating and important compendium of the jazz icon's own words. . . . Through these gripping and revealing interviews, Coltrane comes alive. . . . Though many solid books have been written about Coltrane, this compilation of source materials provides an intimate view of the man and his music. Certainly one of the best music books of the year."—*Library Journal*

TRADE PAPER, 416 PAGES • ISBN-13: 978-1-55652-004-4 • $18.95 (CAN $20.95)

MILES ON MILES
Interviews and Encounters with Miles Davis
by Paul Maher, Jr.

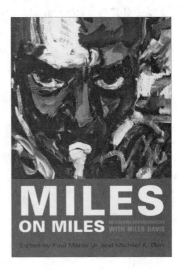

"Here is Miles Davis's less familiar voice, his speaking voice. . . . Maher and Dorr gather together Davis's greatest hits in Q & A, and they make compelling reading."
— Jack Chambers, author, *Milestones: The Music and Times of Miles Davis*

CLOTH, 352 PAGES • ISBN-13: 978-1-55652-706-7 • $24.95 (CAN $27.95)

THE TRUE ADVENTURES OF THE ROLLING STONES
by Stanley Booth

10 B/W Photos

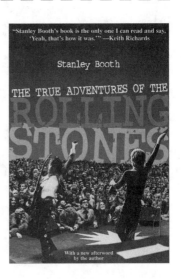

"Stanley Booth's book is the only one I can read and say, 'Yeah, that's how it was.'"
— Keith Richards

TRADE PAPER, 416 PAGES • ISBN-13: 978-1-55652-400-4 • $16.95 (CAN $18.95)

Available at your favorite bookstore,
(800) 888-4741, or
www.chicagoreviewpress.com

CHICAGO REVIEW PRESS